HOW TO BUY ANY BUSINESS

HOW TO DO IT, STEP BY STEP

Become a Millionaire In 365 Days

STERLING COOPER

Forest Manor
Purchased after the first "large" deal.

HOW TO BUY
ANY BUSINESS

HOW TO DO IT, STEP BY STEP

Become *a Millionaire In 365 Days*

STERLING COOPER

DEDICATED TO ALL THOSE BUSINESS OWNER
WANNABEES, WHO DREAM ABOUT OWNING
THEIR OWN BUSINESS OR AQUIRING THE
BUSINESS THEY WORK FOR NOW

THE SURE-FIRE GUARANTEED, CAN NOT MISS WAY TO BECOME A MILLIONAIRE/MULTI-MILLIONAIRE

Great sounding, to stimulate your interest title to get your interest to read further, but also a great description of what the book is really actually about; a step-by-step, easy-to-understand way of becoming wealthy, as a business owner, of your own multi-million dollar business, using the knowledge you already have, of the business you now work at, or have significant knowledge about how to run it, and really have a desire to significantly improve your financial position forever, especially if you are already smarter than your boss, and you know that you are anyway, so that is already a fact that you should take advantage of as soon as possible.

Becoming a millionaire in **365** days (if you are very busy doing whatever you are doing, then give yourself another week or two), is exactly what it says, a step-by-step guide to becoming **at least a millionaire, or multi-millionaire, emphasis added, during a one-year period!!!!!**

The details in this book do not, and will not, describe any real estate flipping program, buying foreclosed properties, making money on the internet by selling the junk out of your garage, mail order sales, making stuff at home and selling it for big money, multi-level selling programs where you sign up thousands of people to sell cleaners and detergents or my personal (just kidding) favorite, ads claiming that by stuffing 500 envelopes a day, you can make big money working from your kitchen table.

I can help describe for you the real estate get rich quick schemes, and they can work as simply as this: buy a house cheap, the worst shape in the best neighborhood possible, then spend as little money as possible fixing it up, and then sell it for as much as you can, hopefully for a profit. You can also do that in your spare time if you wish. That program, making $10,000 here and there after months of work, is not going to make you a millionaire fast.

Again you are the labor component, and you have to rely on so many forces beyond your control such as market value forces, costs of materials, labor (unless you are the labor) and of course you have to find a fool greater than you, who will buy the house you just bought, but at a price that will be a profit for you. Otherwise, you continue to own it, praying for a buyer. Also, do you think someone else may have the same idea? How many competitors will you have in your town or neighborhood?

Get real......those sound great but do you realize how much you have to sell your house, your products or your services for, to even make any money, after all your overhead expenses?

Get real, you will not become a multi-millionaire making a few extra thousand dollars every week. You need a plan that can realistically work for you, while you still hold your day job, and one that you can understand and execute within your own understanding, financial ability and of course, the approval of your spouse.

As we all know, spouse's approval is very important. So make sure that the spouse realizes that you, as a millionaire, suddenly get additional important attributes such as higher credit card limits applicable to the spouse's card, possible staff to do the laundry, and of course, a personal shopper when needed. I am certain that you can come up with additional great reasons to become more attractive to your spouse as a result of your new millionaire status.

Also, as we all know, if it is "hard" to make real money, the kind that really improves your lifestyle, the kind that we all see depicted on television, and the kind that you are certainly capable of if you have the right information, and the right guidance.

I cannot think of any of the well-known multi-millionaires in the news, who were not just regular people with a regular job, and making regular money before they took the steps needed to make it to the millionaire level.

There is absolutely nothing that stands in your way of attaining that status, except YOU. You are holding yourself back by not taking the needed next step, or you can.

Making "real" money, unless you inherited a $10 million or a $100 million trust fund, will never involve you working out of your spare room, or your garage or just fiddling with internet sales. It will and does involve having/owning a "real" business, with real employees and revenues. It will involve having others work for you, and not just you working 24/7.

After all, there are only so many hours in a day, and working out of your home, when the kids want to play with you, the dog wants to bring you toys to toss, and your spouse wants to know if you can run out and pick up some milk at the convenience store and get a car wash too, is not the secret of your future business success. I should add to that list the many items that get added to that list every day such as cleaning out the garage, painting the deck, black-topping the driveway, etc.

The simplicity detailed here is just that; it is simpler than you think and that is a SECRET most non-millionaires do not understand.

Becoming a millionaire is actually easier than you may think, and if you already consider yourself one, then this book will add some more to your already substantial net worth, and you will definitely learn a few more ways to become even wealthier, maybe substantially more wealthy than you are at present.

It is true that the more money you already have, the easier it is to make more, because you already have the most important ingredient to making money; working capital, or free available cash. This simple fact is the most important ingredient to making money in all cultures in any country in the world.

The quest to becoming a millionaire is going to be a short one, because we all are an impatient lot and want to see results FAST......fast food, fast weight loss, fast, fast...speed attracts us all. If it is not fast, we lose interest, after all if we can not become a millionaire in 365 days, we may lose interest in becoming one at all, NOT......

YOU WILL BECOME A MILLIONAIRE IN 365 DAYS, REPEAT......I WILL BECOME A MILLIONAIRE IN 365 DAYS......REPEAT......UNTIL YOU COMMIT YOURSELF TO THIS CONCEPT. DO NOT CONTINUE READING THIS BOOK IF YOU CANNOT COMMIT TO THIS STATEMENT.

Also, you will be able to use my personal web site to get one-on-one help with your quest and receive personal coaching along the way to your goal achievement! In fact, my web site will coach you through each and every day of the 365 day quest, if you choose that option, along with helpful hints, as well as ranting when you do not make progress toward the 365 day goal.

You will not be alone, you will be able to get all the help to get there, in 365 days!!!!

There is even a daily diary to work on to make sure that you are actually doing something on each day to show your progress.

Relax, the above does not have to require consecutive days, just 365 days in total.

Now I need to share an even bigger secret, using the guidelines in this book: it will NOT take 365 days to accomplish that goal......it will most likely take you less days!

TABLE OF CONTENTS

APPENDIX LIST

INTRODUCTION

THE BIG PLAN FOR THE MOST IMPORTANT ACCOMPLISHMENT OF YOUR LIFE: BECOMING A MILLIONAIRE AND GETTING THERE QUICKLY.

"MILLIONAIRE IN 365 DAYS"

THE SURE-FIRE GUARANTEED, CANNOT MISS WAY TO BECOME A MILLIONAIRE/MULTI-MILLIONAIRE

(Great sounding, to stimulate your interest title to get your interest to read further, but also a great description of what the book is really actually about; a step-by-step, easy-to-understand way of becoming wealthy, as a business owner, of your own multimillion dollar business, using the knowledge you already have, of the business you now work at, or have significant knowledge about how to run it, and really have a desire to significantly improve your financial position forever, especially if you are already smarter than your boss, and you know that you are anyway, so that is already a fact that you should take advantage of as soon as possible.)

A great benefit of becoming a millionaire, will be that you will also, magically transform overnight, to become better looking to your spouse, your kids and neighbors. If your spouse got you the book as a present, take the hint...become a millionaire.

Becoming a millionaire in 365 days (if you are very busy doing whatever you are doing, then give yourself another week or two), is exactly what it says, a step-by-step guide to becoming at least a millionaire, or multi-millionaire, emphasis added, during a 365 day period!!!!!

The details in this book do not, and will not, describe any real estate flipping program, buying foreclosed properties, making money on the internet by selling the junk out of your garage, mail order sales, making stuff at home and selling it for big money, multi-level selling programs where you sign up thousands of people to sell cleaners and detergents or my personal (just kidding) favorite; ads claiming that by stuffing 500 envelopes a day, you can make big money working from your kitchen table.

I remember as a kid, reading the back classified ad pages of magazines, that contained enticing advertisements asking for $5, and a return self-addressed envelope, and they would send back the magical formula on how to make riches at home instantly......those ads are STILL THERE!!!

The real estate get rich quick schemes, and they can work out for you, are simply this; buy a house cheap, the worst shape in the best neighborhood possible, then spend as little money as possible fixing it up, and then sell it for as much as you can, hopefully for a profit. You can also do that in your spare time if you wish. That program, making $10,000 here and there after months of work is not going to make you a millionaire fast. These programs, many times touted by well-known individuals who succeeded in making money with real estate are often well meaning, but impossible to carry out due to the fact that it is YOU who have to do all the work.

No matter what you heard about "THE DONALD", it was his father who kicked off the real estate projects, he just followed in his footsteps and had that important "kick start" to his real estate career.

In every real estate scheme, in every envelope-stuffing scheme, in every internet resale scheme, you are the labor component, and you have to rely on so many forces beyond your control such as market value forces, costs of materials, labor (unless you are the labor) and of course you have to find a fool greater than you, who will buy the house you just bought, or to purchase the trinket you just bought for re-sale but at a price that will be a profit for you. Otherwise, you continue to own it (house or trinket), praying for a buyer.

Also, do you think someone else may have the same idea? How many competitors will you have in your town or neighborhood?

I actually was involved in these schemes at an early age.

I purchased really inexpensive mobile homes to rent out to tenants. I could not afford "real homes", and my plan was a very sound one. In

19

fact my plan was better, with a greater return than those promoted in the various get rich quick schemes. I purchased the "homes" for $1,500 to $2,500 each, and rented them out at $400-$500 a month!!!!! That was a great return on my investment...better than any promoted real estate scheme where you were to buy a $100,000 to $200,000 home and rent it out for $750 or more.

I got my entire investment back in as little as 3 months...an annual investment return of a whopping 400%, sometimes more, when I rented the mobile homes "furnished".

I never saw the stock market do that for me, or anybody else. This is with mobile homes......this is still possible, however as I checked the market, today the prices are likely to be $2,500 to $6,000 for such a deal. Still not a bad deal at all, since today you can rent out such "homes" for $400 to $600 monthly maybe more, if you get 10 migrant workers to rent them out, you could get $100 each as your rental. This actually works very well in those areas where migrant farm labor is needed and the rentals may involve even more "renters" per home (I am not joking, really).

This still involves a whopping return on your potential investment, that will usually beat the market averages each year. But, there is always a "but" when you own property, especially property in which YOU are the manager, and YOU always are the manager of the property...believe me, YOU will be the manager, no matter what you may think.

Here is what happened to me in my great "real estate" investments.

My "tenants", and I use that term very kindly to describe them, would more accurately be described as people who apparently never lived in an actual enclosed abode. Many also did not realize that they were supposed to use the toilet, not the sink, and they did not know that stuffing dirty diapers down the toilet or the sink was not the proper disposal method for diapers.

They also routinely had interesting lifestyles, and many were quite enterprising and actually apparently ran successful "home based businesses" out of the rental homes such as: dog kennels, firewood storage and sales, gun and ammo sales, car repair and oil change facilities, rooming houses for vagrants, safe houses for dope dealers, pet motels, storage facilities for questionable merchandise, day care facilities and elderly care facilities for what appeared to be mental patients, among others.

As the successful landlord and property investor, you are the one that gets the calls at night to repair something like the ceiling fixture that "fell" off the ceiling (after the tenant's kids apparently used it as a play swing) and to fix the propane tank, only to discover that it is missing.

I actually had the tenants move out and take all the furniture and the wall fixtures and appliances out of furnished homes with them, leaving holes in the walls, making new holes on the walls to provide for what appeared to be "pet" doors. Often, tenants would "customize" the homes for their use by adding indoor fireplaces, with vents through the ceilings and walls made with the aid of what had to be hatchets and machetes, and using the wall paneling and wood furniture for firewood.

I actually had a tenant who "took" the home with him when he moved. He was a great tenant, he pre-paid his rent each month and actually pre-paid for two months at one point so that I did not have to come and see him for two months, thus apparently giving him time to "move" far away and plenty of time to do so.

Ah, the fantastic return one can make from rental homes is so tempting, yet it is true, you can make these returns! I did it and can share this "secret" of making money in real estate with you.

Get real......those sound great but do you realize how much you have to sell your house, your products or your services to even make any money, after all your overhead expenses, such as repairing the homes between tenants? Even on the property that may be commercial rentals, just drive around your neighborhood and look at the FOR RENT signs. What happens to your tenants when a newer building in a better location pops up, how will you keep up with the mortgage payments when you do not have a tenant for a month or two?

I am not slamming real estate investments, I wanted to share my story with you on my great success in that business, since I had such high investment returns. If you want to make 400% in real estate rentals, just use my technique, it is simple and described above in all the detail you may need to run your home rental business.

Get real, you will not become a multi-millionaire making a few extra thousand dollars every week or month, you need a plan that can realistically work for you, while you still hold your day job, and one that you can understand and execute within your own understanding, financial ability and of course, the approval of your spouse.

As we all know, spouse's approval is very important. So make sure that the spouse realizes that you, as a millionaire, suddenly get additional important attributes such as higher credit card limits applicable to the spouse's card, possible staff to do the laundry, and of course, a personal shopper when needed. I am certain that you can come up with additional great reasons to become more attractive to your spouse as a result of your new millionaire status.

Also, as we all know, if it is "hard" to make real money, the kind that really improves your lifestyle, the kind that we all see depicted on television, and the kind that you are certainly capable of if you have the right information, and the right guidance. I cannot think of any of the well-known multi-millionaires in the news, who were not just regular people with a regular job, and making regular money before they took the steps needed to make it to the millionaire level.

There is absolutely nothing that stands in your way of attaining that status, except YOU. You are holding yourself back by not taking the needed next step, or you can take that step now.

Making "real" money, unless you inherited a $10 million or a $100 million trust fund, will never involve you working out of your spare room, or your garage or just fiddling with internet sales. It will and does involve having/owning a "real" business, with real employees and revenues. It will involve having others work for you, and not just you working 24/7.

After all, there are only so many hours in a day, and working out of your home, when the kids want to play with you, the dog wants to bring you toys to toss, and your spouse wants to know if you can run out and pick up some milk at the convenience store and get a car wash too, is not the secret of your future business success. I should add to that list the many items that get added to that list every day such as cleaning out the garage, painting the deck, black-topping the driveway, etc.

The simple steps detailed here step by step, are just that, it is simpler than you think and that is a SECRET most non-millionaires to not understand.

Becoming a millionaire is actually easier than you may think, and if you already consider yourself one, then this book will add some more to your already substantial net worth, and you will definitely learn a few more ways to become ever wealthier, maybe substantially more wealthy than you are at present.

It is true that the more money you already have, the easier it is to make more, because you already have the most important ingredient to making money; working capital, or free available cash. This simple fact is the most important ingredient to making money in all cultures in any country in the world.

Also, when you achieve that status, you will be able to do it over and over again.

The quest to becoming a millionaire is going to be a short one, because we all are an impatient lot and want to see results FAST......fast food, fast weight loss, fast, fast...speed attracts us all. If it is not fast, we lose interest, after all if we can not become a millionaire in 365 days, we may lose interest in becoming one at all.

YOU WILL BECOME A MILLIONAIRE IN 365 DAYS, REPEAT......I WILL BECOME A MILLIONAIRE IN 365 DAYS......REPEAT......UNTIL YOU COMMIT YOURSELF TO THIS CONCEPT.

Also, you will be able to use my personal web site to get one-on-one help with your quest and receive personal coaching along the way to your goal achievement!

In fact, my web site will coach you though each and every day of the 365 day quest, if you choose that option, along with helpful hints, as well as ranting when you do not make progress toward the 365 day goal.

You will not be alone, you will be able to get all the help to get there, in 365 days!!!!

There is even a daily diary to work on to make sure that you are actually doing something on each day to show your progress.

As a memento of your success, you may also order a diary for your own documentation of your progress toward millionaire status. Just go to my web site.

Relax, the above does not have to require consecutive days, just 365 days in total.

Now I need to share an even bigger secret, using the guidelines in this book, it will NOT take 365 days to accomplish that goal......it will most likely take less days!

CHAPTER 1

GETTING THE NECESSARY CAPITAL TO GET STARTED.....

If you thought that becoming a millionaire was going to be hard, you are wrong......it is not hard at all, it simply takes knowing how to do it, not working hard, but working smart, and having a plan that is easy to follow and understand.

My book will NOT contain complicated formulas, or complicated and impossible to follow instructions. It is simple, and ready to follow. I did it and you can too.

The first and most important ingredient to becoming wealthy is to have some money available to start working with...that is a fact that you must understand and that you must get some or have some become available...this is a fact.

This book is not a magical way to suddenly become wealthy, overnight, but you will become so in 365 days! Additionally you will be able to get online help along the way.

All over the world, micro grants and loans are providing the basis to start small businesses that allow small business to succeed in even the poorest countries. Loans of $100-$300 are starting small enterprises and raising people out of endemic poverty. These loans allow the purchase of simple equipment such as sewing machines, bicycles, tools and the like to allow a simple business to get started. This is the seed capital, the working capital to start a business in those regions, and such small amounts are sufficient.

The 2006 NOBEL PRIZE was won by a person who started a bank which made $50-$300 loans to enterprising poor people all over the third world and he created an economic miracle for over 6,000,000 people worldwide, allowing them to own their own business though such micro loans.

In the United States and most developed countries, it will also take relatively little seed capital to get started as well, this little known fact is usually obscured by the erroneous thinking that it takes massive amounts to be a business owner.

Think about it; many business owners, even the most successful ones, started with very little capital, or even just an idea, and no cash yet committed; Bill Gates (now the richest man in the world!!!)-started in his now famous kitchen/garage, and Fred Smith was a student when he wrote his now famous theory about overnight delivery service, Federal Express.

I remember how Federal Express first got started and their salesmen came to my office asking if I would commit to sending one package a day for approximately $25 so that they could stay in business to pay for a few clunky jets they were leasing, since their scheme was still untried and in a start-up mode.

I started my first business at age 14 with an investment of $50 in stationery and created my first impressive looking accounting service, headquartered out of a post office box. Then as I learned about business operations by doing the necessary accounting for small businesses, I learned about a variety of different businesses.

I decided that my business would be to buy the businesses of my clients who were NOT SUCCESSFUL, since I would make them an "offer they would not want to refuse", that of taking over their troubled business and thus allowing them to walk away from their troubled business. I was fearless, since as an outsider, I was not jaded by the pre-conceived notions of that business and how to succeed.

I did not need much working capital to take over their businesses such as hair salons, paint stores, hardware stores, wallpaper stores, retail stores, paint contractors, building contractors, accounting services, wholesale distributors and a variety of similar small businesses, and even larger businesses. The creditors of these businesses were more than willing to work with me to get the bills paid of the failed business, and allowed me to take over after meeting with me and hearing my plans to continue the business.

Many of these businesses were long established, and had significant goodwill built up to allow me an instant recognition in their marketplace. One of my favorites, which I purchased (at age 19) at a trustee mandated auction sale, free and clear of all debts for $3,500 (while there was a blinding snowstorm where only I and another bidder were present), allowed me to take over $300,000 in assets, and claim an established retail and wholesale business established since 1948!!!!

In this purchase I even inherited the "former owner" an elderly wonderful woman, who built up the business with her husband the prior 30 years and established a great reputation and helped me run the business!!!! She felt relieved to have someone else help her...I got a going business whose purchase price I recovered during its first day of operation!!!! (I borrowed the $3,500 from my uncle and repaid him the following week).

This story points out a very crucial fact that must be dealt with at this stage...you must have cash to acquire or start a business! There are no shortcuts, but there are ways to accomplish this for everyone, even for those of you that may have the proverbial "bad credit" or no credit or little money or even no money to start with.

However, there is no possibility, short of winning the lotto, to start or acquire a business with no money, so let's consider the ways to get the money to start or acquire your own business.

First, do not stop here, or give up here. You will have the funds needed to launch, or acquire your own multi-million dollar business!!! Notice I use a lot of exclamation points; that is because I think of ideas with exclamation points at the end! You have to have exclamation points at the end of every big and small idea!!!! START THINKING WITH EXCLAMATION POINTS AT THE END OF YOUR IDEAS!!!!

What are your means that you can consider to get some working capital????

Working capital is simply the term describing the funds you will have available for you to buy or start your business. Those funds will be required and necessary to be available to you before you go any further in your 365 days to become a millionaire.

You will get this working capital......you will, and you will become a millionaire in 365 days!!!! (Notice the exclamation marks!!!!!)

The capital you will require will be directly linked to the type of business you will start or acquire, so the next step will be for you to determine exactly that.

WHAT DO YOU LOVE TO DO, WHAT JOB ARE YOU GOOD AT, WHAT BUSINESS CAN YOU OPERATE AS THE OWNER??????

Fill in the blank.........maybe fill in a couple of blanks. Have several choices, but make them choices of something you truly love to do, are currently employed in a related business or are passionate about. Nothing is out, remember this book will in 365 days have you owning your own multi-million dollar business. This is a step-by-step plan that YOU will execute, with my help if you wish.

Oh, I forgot to add that another possibility will be for you to own the business you now work for!!!!!! (Notice the exclamation marks again here.) What better business to acquire than the one that you are most familiar with, now work for, and YOU could/will be the new owner!!!!!

Have you thought that you, and maybe your other employees, or just select employees could own the business you now work for????? Yes, you can...........maybe it slipped your mind before, but not anymore.

In fact, now that I have planted that idea in your mind, that is all you will be thinking about every day at work...every day you will start to want to buy the business you are now working for.

Does this thought now allow you to better understand that the prospect of your ownership of a multi-million dollar business is right in front of you? Do you know how close you are to the prospect of business ownership? Hello, you are now working there, you know how to run that business.

This book will show you how to buy out your boss, or how to buy the business if it is now owned by a parent company, of which it is a subsidiary, division or business unit. I will even help you with the structure of the acquisition and getting it financed, if you wish. Thus you may not have to go far to find the ideal business to own!!!!!

In addition to your current employer, you should consider acquiring a competitor of that employer, etc...a business that is similar enough for you and/or your other employees (also known as your potential partners/investors) to run.

Also, consider what you truly love —it would be nice to own that marina, yacht brokerage, aircraft rental service, exotic vacation island rental, bed & breakfast, specialty boutique, repair shop for muscle cars and custom built motorcycle shop, custom home builder, transportation company, real estate brokerage, consulting business, restaurant, night club or whatever you truly love.

On the other hand, if the business you acquire is large enough, your management will be running it, not you, except in your capacity as "owner" you will reap the benefits.

Now to that most important working capital part…how to get it and where to get the seed money to start your business and/or buy your own multi-million dollar business. You will be surprised to learn that today, each of us has so many ways to raise capital that was not available in the past.

Let's make a list, add to it as much as you can since every one of us has other ways to raise some working capital, more ways than I can possibly cover in the book. Start by assessing your own resources without having to resort to relatives and potential partners by making a short list of ways to tap into home equity lines, lines of credit, unsecured credit lines, loans that may be had by other assets pledged as collateral such as valuable artwork, jewelry, investments in brokerage accounts that can be used as collateral, excess value of any assets and properties.

Based on these available means alone, how much can you raise??? Make the list.

Surprise…is it more or less than you thought????

Is it enough to get started…how much is it????

Add up your list, and put down that dollar total…all of it. If you want coaching help further, make me your partner in the acquisition, and I will help out too. See the website.

Now add to that list as follows:

How much can you raise by borrowing from your relatives, friends, business associates????

Remember, loans have to be repaid, but making these people your "partners" may provide working capital you need without having to repay them. The downside is that they will be your partners and they will want to participate in their share of profits, or as stockholders they will have other rights as well according to the laws of your state of incorporation. In addition, as partners in your unincorporated business, your rights and theirs need to be clearly spelled out.

One of my first partners in an incorporated business provided the $10,000 that was necessary to maintain a minimum capital requirement as required by the licensing authority, but he controlled the account it was in. He took the funds out without my knowledge, and left me to fend for myself. A better agreement would have avoided that problem. He made a bad error in judgement, as that business grew into a multi-million dollar business and he would have been well rewarded for his seed capital.

This particular business was started based on my knowledge of a particular business and then through an opportunistic purchase of another business in that same industry, my business grew empirically, while making the profits necessary to comply with the increasing capital needs.

It only took $10,000 in seed capital to start this business and grow it to a multi-million dollar enterprise.

Can you convince people you know, relatives and friends that they should invest in your business or to provide you a loan???? If so then start adding up what amount of seed capital you may be able to obtain this way. Don't be shy, make it an exciting presentation.

What is the total so far???? How much can you raise? Have you presented your ideas well?

At this point I will not cover the implications of the legalities of the business arrangements, that will be covered in Appendix 8. For now, this is your hypothetical capital raising program to determine your seed capital possibilities.

Another crucial consideration will be what equity (ownership) will you be willing to give up in your business in return for your partners' capital contribution? My suggestion is to never give up more than 49% to any partner, unless you and the partner are such good friends, or get along so well that you can make joint decisions about everything, or agree to do so on a 50/50 basis.

I have always had partners of some type. They either contributed capital, time, expertise consulting or actually worked in the business performing specific tasks that we agreed that each of us were to perform in our partnership. The pay was also generally related to the ownership interest in the business, so if we each owned 50%, then we were equally paid or distributed the share of profits equally.

Please note here that great thought should be made as to the choice of partners, since they will be the ones that everything in your business will/may depend on. If you like to get to the office at 5 am, maybe your partner is a late worker and starts at 10 am? Agree to the basics, if he will be working with you.

Partners can make your life easier...having someone to talk to about problem solving (two heads better than one), and backing each other up. Otherwise in an important matter, what if you are sick or traveling, who will make the needed decision and how will it be executed? Have you ever noticed how in a well-run restaurant business, "Nick" and "Gus" are always around...if one is gone the other is always there???

Having a trusted employee may not always be what you expect. When I owned an airline in the Caribbean, before I was married, I was doing what I truly liked...flying to all the exotic Caribbean islands for instance.

I went on a Caribbean vacation and liked the islands so much I made an Offer to purchase the airline! That sounds like that commercial we all heard about the guy who liked the shaver so much, he bought the company......

Anyway, I was thrilled to be there. I also had my private pilot's license, so any excuse to fly was a great one...I could fly as a co-pilot everywhere. I was headquartered on St. Thomas, in the US Virgin Islands, and my competitor was to my great surprise, none other than my favorite/greatest actress of her screen era, Maureen O'Hara. I could not believe that she of all people was also the President of the competing airline, Antilles Air Boats.

Her story was more interesting than mine as to how she got to be the airline president. She married the owner of the airline, and he died in his own plane crash, thus she inherited the president's position and there she was, just like me in St. Thomas. Stranger still was that Al Marshall (founder of the discount store chain) also was an airline president headquartered in St. Thomas, Marshall Air.

For a minute there, I was daydreaming of meeting John Wayne, Humphrey Bogart and Ingrid Bergman and Lauren Bacall as airline presidents too.

I was the sole owner, but due to the operations of the airline on many islands, I had to rely at times on "trusted" employees. One such employee who was in charge of the maintenance of the aircraft, was regularly given a blank pre-signed check to pay parts vendors on the island of Puerto Rico which was our main supply for items needed to maintain the aircraft.

That worked until the day when he did not return from his parts buying trip, and cashed my pre-signed check for a substantial amount, literally cleaning out my company bank account. I had very little to say to the authorities or the bank, since his position was that this was me, approving and signing a check for his termination bonus! So much for trusted employees and lack of partners.

Partners can be silent partners (not active in the business) providing working capital for the business, or active who provide the added manpower. Which ones you choose may be dependent on the type of business you are in. For instance if your business provides 24 hour service calls as part of its service, you may need an active partner rather than a silent one who will not be available to help out when necessary.

Well here we are, you have chosen a business to start or buy. You are also thinking that you may be able to buy the business you are now working in, and that you may be able to raise a fair amount or the needed amount to do so through loans, friends and partners as described above.

At this point you have a plan, ready to execute, but it is also at this point that FEAR sets in.

Fear of the unknown, fear of "what if ", fear of telling your spouse about the crazy idea you got from this book, and that your family's life savings and even worse, your borrowing capacity and all the rainy day money may be put at risk due to YOUR crazy idea. Notice that I said YOUR crazy idea, not mine.

If you got this book as a gift from your spouse, take that as approval for your crazy idea.

Worse still, wait till your spouse hears that you have also involved your friends and relatives in your crazy business ownership scheme (to potentially lose all their money too!!!!). This will be your toughest obstacle to overcome; the fear of your spouse about the prospects of your crazy idea and its potential for failure. Don't get scared, you want to be a millionaire!!

At this point, some of you will now stop reading the book...you were never meant to become millionaires......anyway, since you need the suspension of fear, and an abundance of confidence in yourself. After all, why are you not afraid to go to your job...you know how to do your job, would you forget how to perform your job if you were the owner, the boss?

The next fear you have to overcome is the fear of failure. John D. Rockefeller went bust many times drilling for oil, but he did not give up. Does Standard Oil (AMOCO) bring back memories of failure or success? Remember the shoe string budget of a teenager named Michael Dell who realized that you can build a computer for about $100 in your spare room??? What risk was he taking, that he would lose $100??? You are not a loser, so quit thinking like one!!! (Notice my exclamation marks again.) DO NOT LET YOUR SPOUSE MAKE YOU A LOSER, MAKE HIM/HER YOUR FIRST AND MOST SUPPORTIVE PARTNER!!!!

I do not want to create the impression that you are to quit your job during the 365 days of your climb to millionaire/multi-millionaire status. Quite to the contrary, you will accomplish this without ever leaving your job, or the security that it offers, for you at this time.

You will accomplish this all, while still working at your regular position, keeping your health benefits, pensions, etc. You will do this all during the spare time you now waste watching TV reruns, and maybe using up all your vacation time and "sick" days allowed.

Rule one, suspend the fear and do not quit your present employment until your success is assured through the plan outlined in the book, and you buy the target business.

Now, is your fear gone???? You are NOT, I repeat NOT going to scare your spouse, and your friends and relatives with your crazy scheme... you will appear during the next 365 days to be normal, except for your plans to become a millionaire/multi-millionaire.

The above is not to be confused with loans that may be used to buy a business you will be targeting, The working capital is YOUR cash that will be at risk, YOUR money and that of your friends, partners and associates. This is referred to as your "skin in the business", what you have at risk. Lenders want to make sure that they are not your partners in a business, and that your money is at risk too, not just theirs.

You can go to my web site and get help with all this, so relax, you are in good hands.

I will cover in another chapter how to leverage your business acquisition through loans used to acquire it directly through bank loans, SBA guarantees, seller notes and seller investment in the business as your partner, and other financing techniques which will make your becoming a millionaire strategy successful. You can get guidance all along the way, with me as your coach and business consultant, thanks to the wonder of the internet.

CHAPTER 2

CHOOSING THE BUSINESS TO BUY (HINT: BEST CHOICE-ACQUIRE THE COMPANY YOU NOW WORK FOR) DAH........

The hardest decision to make will be your final choice of the business you will enter into or buy. Remember, you want it to be a million dollar business, or it will become one soon due to the forecast of its financial success. Make a list of the type of businesses you may want to start, and add your favorite to that list and work on YOUR favorite. You should simply reference the SIC CODES (Standard Industrial Classification) by getting a print out from an internet search, used by the government to classify every business category.

I MUST STRESS THAT THIS IS NOT A GUIDE TO STARTING A BUSINESS, BUT RATHER ON ACQUIRING AN EXISTING MULTI-MILLION DOLLAR BUSINESS. STARTING A NEW BUSINESS IS TOTALLY DIFFERENT FROM WHAT I WILL BE ADVOCATING IN THIS BOOK.

Also, believe me, starting a business from scratch is really hard...you do not want to work that hard when your alternate is to acquire a successful established business instead.

You must make this determination NOW. Do not pass GO, do not read further until this is decided NOW, or soon you may also choose a broad category such as MANUFACTURING or simply RETAILING, for example and/or go through the SIC codes to determine a more focused category. The many services that provide you with specific SIC classified businesses can help you to identify those that are close to home or in locations that you would like to be.

Write...think... enter your druthers here ... Does this involve buying your boss out due to his retirement, or the purchase of the subsidiary or a division of your "parent" company which owns the company/business you now work for? If so, then depending on the size of the business, you may/will need partners (hint-maybe your co-workers and managers) due to the larger size of the business.

Do not lose your focus...the best way to proceed, in my opinion is to buy the business you now work for since you know it, you know how to run it too and it is "comfortable" for you to be involved in its running and ownership (maybe with your co-workers as partners).

Another great choice is to buy another business that you are passionate about, or know already like that marina you spend a lot of money with and your love of boating or yachting, or another business you may already do business with or know intimately, such as one that may be owned by a friend, relative or long-time business associate.

All the choices should involve businesses that have revenues of at least $2-$25 million or more. In fact, the bigger the business revenues the better and easier will it be for you to finance such a purchase. Did you know that? I can help with the financing too!!

Surprise (little-known secret)—instead of buying that pet store or paint and wallpaper palace, it will be possible for you to buy a much larger business with less hassle, and most importantly such a business will provide you with greater profits and earnings.

Fear not, you are on your way toward millionaire, or multimillionaire status or better.

Start thinking like a successful millionaire, look like a successful millionaire, start having your spouse notice that you are now even better looking since you are on your way to becoming a multi-millionaire. Think bigger things, bigger thoughts. Go look at million dollar homes, better cars, plan better vacations, mingle with "better" people, attend political events like a millionaire. Notice I did NOT say buy...just look and start thinking......planning to get these. Visualize yourself and your family in that spectacular home. There are mortgage plans that will provide payments which would be under $3,600 a month for a million dollar home, for instance.

Did you read that, the monthly mortgage payment for a million dollar home may be as low as $3,600 or less with the many mortgage options available today. Start living large, and thinking large, it costs less than you think and it will change your life.

I am amazed every day as I discuss with business associates their financial plans. They have mortgages that cost double what they could be paying and cars that are improperly financed, all costing them more than they could be spending and then living large on the same funds they are now living on.

Your psyche has to get psyched!!!!!

I remember looking at mansion homes, and thinking which one I would buy "when" my acquisition would be complete. I moved from a $60,000 home I purchased from my parents allowing them to retire, to the home shown inside the front pages of this book. It really psyched me to think big, and to daydream with a plan to become wealthy.

Take a look at the mansion, I bought that after just the first larger deal.

The home was used in a movie by "Arnold..." the new California governor, the former actor. You may have seen it as the home where the leader of the crime family was supposed to live, the movie *Raw Deal*. It was in fact a true story. It was formerly owned by Tony "big tuna", the reputed boss of the Chicago mob, and reportedly the former driver for Al Capone.

I bought it since it was a bargain due to its "history", and its ownership inspired me to bigger things. I used to watch the weekly television series "Dynasty", and I would compare the room scenes in that show with my home and compare which was better.

It was a great feeling. You may see the home in my available video. If you did not buy it with this book, it is available on my web site.

Bankers, business associates and investors were impressed, and I loved the living large part as well. It was truly inspirational, all its 25,000 square feet, indoor gold leaf swimming pool, the two lane automatic bowling alley, it was great to live there, inspirational. See it in the video.

As you choose your business to acquire, you will have to start thinking like a successful future multi-millionaire. Life is short, better to live like a millionaire, don't you think?

By the way it does make sense that during this process, for you to invest $1 weekly and play the best and biggest weekly lotto game, just in case you get lucky.

A high school acquaintance of mine, did just that, invested his $1 weekly and won a $3 million lotto collecting a nice stipend of $150,000 annually for 20 years and used the funds to start a variety of businesses with this handy "working capital". What have you got to lose to cover this simple possibility?

So, are you committed to this (YOUR) 365 day plan????

If not, if you have not chosen your target yet...quit now, read no further, if on the other hand you are forging ahead......keep reading, you are on your way to millionaire/multi-millionaire status in 365 days or less!!

Additionally, I hope that by now you have come to realize that the best consideration to consider is the acquisition of a going business, and not starting one from scratch. There are possible businesses that can successfully be started from scratch, but all involve a lot of work and the chance of failure is high. Therefore my strong recommendation is to BUY AN EXISTING BUSINESS.

Due to the world wide internet, it is now easier than ever to locate a business to acquire, unless you plan to buy the one you work for now, which is my strongest suggestion. Have you heard of a management buyout, or an employee buyout?

Try a search for businesses for sale, business brokers, investment bankers and the easiest of all, your local newspaper for stories, and the business for sale classified ads (these ads tend to typically list smaller revenue companies) but often, especially in the weekend or Sunday editions, they tend to have more listings and bigger companies for sale. Many businesses can be "inferred" to be for sale even though they are not officially "listed" as such or announced to be for sale in a press release or news story.

These acquisition opportunities may be some of the best possibilities for your consideration since they tend to be companies that have some real or perceived "problems" such as losing money - taking in less revenues than they are spending, or making a product whose future prospects are looking glum. How would you like to be working at such a company, knowing that your continued job prospects may be looking glum, making a product that can, or is being made in a low labor cost country and will drive the company out of business, or just a company whose management/ownership has lost focus and the company needs a new business plan.

There is a danger as well as an opportunity here. Remember all those news stories about how large steel companies started to experience financial problems, and their parent companies or owners announced the closing or planned closing of these companies? The announcements also included the doom and gloom prediction of hundreds or thousands of workers losing their jobs, remember those stories? There are always those stories every month.

Well, contrary to the predictions of their demise, many of these companies managed to survive and prosper through employee buyouts, others survived a few more years thus extending the employment of the doomed employees by a few years, thus benefitting them.

Sometimes, even the seemingly doomed company survives through aggressive management actions and decisions by the employees to fight for its financial survival and by becoming owners directly, they make the decisions that are needed, while the ownership by a large international corporation was incapable of making the decisions, or the correct decisions.

Think about the survivors who you may recall; Union Carbide survived, after their India plant experienced a chemical disaster killing thousands of people; the famous (by his own determined promotion and financial resuscitation actions), Donald Trump, who at one time was $900 million poorer than all of us (having liabilities $900 million greater than his assets); Worthington Steel, whose employee buyout was one of the many which saved thousands of workers their jobs and was the model for many subsequent similar employee buyouts; and of course Chrysler Motors, who survived twice—once with the aggressive pursuit (the first and only successful action of its type) of a $1.5 billion loan guarantee by the government, and the second time by being acquired by the German auto giant Daimler Benz.

Plenty of others did not survive, in a variety of industries. They took no action, or the wrong action, and just slid into oblivion such as:

DeLorean Motors; Tucker Motors; Studebaker; New York Central Railroad-the largest rail enterprise in the country; Consolidated Freightways—the first all 50 state trucking firm, which was at one time the largest trucker in the world—I tried to acquire it but it filed for bankruptcy two days before I was to make my Offer announcement; giant truckers McLean Transportation (which I wanted to acquire quickly before they went under, but their investment banker was calling me on a phone line I just reported out of order, and they filed for liquidation not hearing back from me); Trans Con, Lee Way Freight; TWA-Trans World Airlines: Pan American Airlines-the world famous international airline, and the first certificated as such (which I and my business partner tried to buy in their last days), we planned its financial turnaround through a simple strategy of becoming the first low cost international carrier with a simpler route system (they only had international routes and really grumpy/and anti-customer/anti-management employees who in my opinion were the single most destructive factor in its demise).

Other big known names include Arthur Andersen the mega-billion international accounting firm; Gimbels, the famed department store chain made famous in the popular holiday movie, *Miracle on 34th Street* (which we also tried to purchase, however its fate was sealed since its real estate holdings were worth significantly more than its retail business would ever bring), thus its sale for the value of its real estate holdings was inevitable.

When we formulated our bid for Gimbels, we actually put together a business plan forming a joint venture with a condominium development group, who was planning on developing the 34th street, entire square block landmark property, by retaining the famed store on two of the lower floors, and adding a 50 story condominium addition on the Madison Avenue side.

Our plans were thwarted by an influential preservation group of New Yorkers, including Jackie Kennedy Onassis, who opposed the changing of that tired store, and we dropped our bid, since there was no way to take the risk of being stuck with a costly white elephant (which it remained when it was closed).

The chain was sold to others and promptly liquidated, as were many other landmark stores Alexanders; Zayre Stores; Robert Hall (their advertising touted-"where the models buy their clothes"); the first discount store chain who invented the discount store category-Goldblatt Bros.; Venture Stores; Bond's Stores the largest men's store chain; Bonwit Teller, the upscale boutique; Montgomery Wards (which we tried to acquire as well, by offering $3.5 billion for it), however it was acquired by its management instead, and countless other businesses who stumbled such as the now famous Enron corporate energy giant.

Although these companies stumbled and did not recover, thousands did, and there were plenty of acquisition opportunities possible to complete and succeed with a recovery plan put together by its management or a buyout group.

I believe that the purchase of opportunistically priced businesses (bargain priced), is not for everyone. However, it may be the best or only plan for a management or employee group who is facing closure or business failure, and that may be their best option for survival, even if it only delays an eventual filing for bankruptcy reorganization.

Many businesses reorganize through the Chapter 11 process, and then continue in business. At one point literally every rail company in America was in a bankruptcy reorganization, and today one of the most profitable enterprises are railroads.

Buying a "bargain" involves a lot more close scrutiny and deeper questions to determine if it is a project you want to undertake, or if you want to (or could afford to) lose all your money in the process.

I know of a group of gutsy managers/investors who ONLY acquire deeply financially troubled and problem plagued businesses. They however have become so good at their business, they actually get paid to "acquire" really troubled companies. This process is sometimes very attractive to larger companies who may own a troubled subsidiary and they do not want to suffer the negative publicity related to its closure—they sell the business to this group, who has had a very successful track record of turning around these types of businesses. This group then sells the business for a very significant profit, usually within 2 years!

I once solicited a seller of a business to come and see us in our offices since he had some operational problems with his company (an $8 million business) and was in a panic, and indicated that he was looking to sell his business immediately.

He came to our offices with a suitcase full of information to be able to give us the entire picture of his business, its operational problems and plenty of great plans that he could not execute alone.

We just happened to be interested in his industry and listened intently the entire afternoon to his presentation. After he presented his "dog and pony" description, he said to us in closing, "and where else can you buy such a business for only $1 million dollars?"

We chuckled (but only on the inside), and left the conference room to discuss the possible interest in the purchase of his "bargain" priced business. He said it was only priced at $1 million dollars, a seeming bargain price in his opinion. However, we did not see it as any type of bargain, and used the pricing formula illustrated in this book.

We came up with a purchase consideration of $100, YES ONLY $100.

Normally, such a challenging purchase possibility would simply be a rejection; we do not want such a challenge.

The possible purchase presented a challenge that was quite a challenge in our opinion, but we had plans to place a very diligent and experienced person in this type of business, who just became available for such a challenge by just giving him a 20% ownership interest in the troubled enterprise, so we made an Offer to acquire 80% of the company, right then and there…for $100.

In this acquisition we would have two partners, the former owner who would now own 20% and our new 20% owner who would be the hard working stockholder, with us owning 60%, still a controlling interest, nonetheless, and at $100 total cost!!.

Then it got better, or funnier.

We had our secretary (those were the days when we had secretaries) print out a copy of our form letter, "standard" acquisition LOI (Letter Of Intent), which spelled out our proposal to acquire the business for $100, but that is was only valid for the next 30 minutes.

The seller, responded immediately, not waiting 30 minutes, and we expected a counter offer which we were simply prepared not to accept...unless of course it was for $200 or $300.

We were prepared to accept that counter offer and I had my wallet ready.

Instead, the seller agreed to our $100 price, without a counter proposal or argument!

We accepted immediately, and I took out my wallet to turn over the agreed upon cash payment as was agreed to in the LOI to seal the deal.

I discovered that I did not have $100 in cash......so I suggested that the seller simply make the acknowledgment, in writing, that he received the $100 payment (receipt is hereby acknowledged) since it was just a token anyway...he agreed and we "purchased" 80% of an $8 million revenues business for the total price of $100!

As the week after our purchase progressed, my business partner and our new working turnaround expert went to visit the offices of the company we purchased, and I was waiting for their report.

On Thursday nights, it was my regular plan to leave for my weekend lake home (of course purchased as a bargain that needed "some work" and was a former turn of the century rooming house on a great resort area lake, with 10 bedrooms after remodeling) with the family-three kids, the dogs, the housekeeper, and the newly popular conversion van complete with the newly invented kid pacifier system called a VCR player, into which the kids were glued watching their favorite movies all they way to the destination.

I waited for my report from my associates, to hear about our latest acquisition.

On Friday morning I got the call I was waiting for.

My long time business partner, Gil, to whom this book is dedicated, who has a very steady and a straight man type of humor, called with the long awaited report.

I quickly asked with great anticipation in my voice, "...so????". He immediately responded, "I think we overpaid, and he hung up."

That was his way, short and to the point and hilariously funny, in his way.

I called him back of course, and he outlined the many challenges that we faced, but the good news was that our new 20% partner involved in the turnaround, and the former owner were getting along well and that there was positive improvement even in that short time frame.

"Ok," I thought, "our investment was safe".

CHAPTER 3

DUE DILIGENCE, YOUR FACT FINDING RELATING TO THE BUSINESS

The due diligence process will allow you the opportunity to learn about all aspects of the acquired business.

You will need to make sure that you cover all aspects of the business that you may need to know about and use the due diligence form in Appendix 2.

You will most likely be asked by the seller to execute a Confidentiality Agreement of some type, or you may use the simple form in Appendix 3.

It is common to sign a confidentiality agreement of some type since the seller usually does not want any disclosure that discussions are taking place, in order not to "scare" employees into thinking that their jobs may be on the line.

Employees of smaller businesses may be especially prone to suffer from fear, but I have seen larger businesses have entire departments quit out of fear of the unknown new owner's plans.

It is best to pretend to be the new client, the new insurance guy, etc., when visiting the business with the owner.

Have the owner complete the due diligence form and then you study carefully the answers and discuss with the seller all elements that may be red flags (problems).

This same due diligence form may then be used to share with the banks that will be considering the financing of your acquisition.

If you have significant knowledge of the business being acquired, you may add any additional items that you may want to cover/find out.

After review of the due diligence answers, in conversations with the seller, you will be ready to proceed to the next step...making an Offer to buy the business.

If the business is being marketed or represented by a business broker or intermediary of some type, you will receive an initial

Offering Memorandum or descriptive brochure that may detail all aspects of the company and then an indication of interest and price range will be solicited for the business.

Investment bankers usually will have a professional book of information prepared, while business brokers may have nothing other than a faxed copy of some financial statements.

Due diligence will then proceed for those potential buyers who may be offering the best price or terms.

Do not be put off by the form. There is nothing complicated there, it allows you to have a snapshot of the business for your evaluation.

Anybody who can read can evaluate what it reports, you can too.

This form and others are available in the appendix.

CHAPTER 4

PRICING YOUR ACQUISITION

The most important part of the acquisition process is…to be able to acquire the business you are seeking!!!!!!

The only way to acquire the business is to be the best Offer, best price or just the best overall deal for the seller. Each of these elements has different reasons to be potentially the most attractive Offer, and you have to become good at figuring that out, and you will.

Contrary to what you may have heard or read, there is no magical formula to determine a "price" for a particular business.

Each business must be evaluated separately, based on its individual characteristics, financial condition and earnings that it generates for the owner. You can and will do it, it is NOT necessary to be a rocket scientist. In fact, if you are a rocket scientist, it may be harder to figure all this out. My 13-year-old step-son is currently doing pricing analysis.

There have been developed a number of pricing models, formulas that are computer based and generated, but the most effective in my opinion will be the one that YOU generate yourself based on common sense financial interpretation of the businesses ability to support the loans taken out to acquire it.

That's it…that is all there is to the pricing formula!!! COMMON SENSE…you got some???

Now you know as much as the most sophisticated buyers and takeover firms and their sophisticated computerized pricing models.

The buyout firms, however, often have no such formulas to consider. They may be working with huge sums of money, other people's money for which they demand (settle for) smaller returns and thus can pay ridiculous prices, planning their exit to be something you can not do, such as an initial public offering (IPO) to get cash out of their investment.

Often these firms are more interested in acquiring well-known names, at any price to support their high profiles, and maintain their status as buyout kings, rather than getting returns beyond the minimum you and I will settle for. Fees are also a big consideration, since it is not unusual to pay themselves a consulting fee that may be in the hundreds of millions of dollars.

In the now famous acquisition of RJR NABISCO, the firm KKR reportedly got a consulting fee of over $650 million for advising itself in that acquisition!! That made the several partners very rich very fast. If you read the book about that acquisition, you would discover that what they actually did, and how they did it, you can actually understand the process.

You will be doing the same thing, but on a smaller scale.

In the traditional acquisition you will be making, you will not receive this type of fee, but the business may be able to pay you significant compensation, perks and dividends, and much sooner than later. This compensation may be significant and may provide you with a million dollars over a relatively short period of time, or its ownership may provide you with a market value of the business to be several millions of dollars.

The common sense approach to any acquisition FOR YOU is the same as you would consider in applying for your home mortgage…can you make the payments on the debt that was used to acquire the business, from the free cash (cash that is not needed for operations and generated by profits of the business, see Appendix 4 for the form and calculator) generated by the business??

If the answer is yes, then the business debt can support the purchase price offered. If not, your Offer is too high and nobody will finance it, since you cannot pay back the debt and it makes no sense to buy such a company at a price that does not allow the payment to support the debt repayment.

Most importantly, will the business first pay you a salary and benefits that are sufficient to maintain your present lifestyle and MORE, and then still have sufficient funds to pay off the debt on reasonable terms satisfactory to the banks?? How does this work, how do you price the business in making the Offer?

In analyzing the profitability of a business, especially a privately owned one, like the one you are likely to acquire, it is vital that you receive the correct profit information, minus the hype.

Privately owned businesses tend to under-report, shave earnings and stretch or overstate revenues through a variety of legal and other possibly "grey/shady" methods. You need to make sure that you clearly understand the methods, if any, that your seller is using if he is in fact using questionable reporting methods.

The reason to accurately understand this is related not only to getting an accurate financial picture of the true earnings of the company, but also to avoid any future tax liabilities that you (your business) may inherit if the company is audited by the IRS and they discover previous financial shenanigans. The liability attributed to the company you now own will follow it, and you and or your company may be stuck with this liability.

Throughout my years of working with sellers of privately owned businesses, especially those that do not have an independent third party accounting firm auditing their financial results (issuing an audit opinion), I have seen every means and methods utilized to minimize earnings by sellers.

The easiest means are by manipulating and under-reporting the true inventory at the fiscal year end. This is the typical and easiest to manipulate each year. This under-reporting creates the impression financially that the company made less money, since the cost of the goods it sold was higher than the actual cost.

This method utilized by sellers, regularly provides a lower earnings statement for tax purposes, and it is virtually impossible to audit or correct. You need to make sure that you can feel comfortable with the actual adjusted earnings and the taxes that may be due as a result of under-reporting. You may want to conduct your own actual inventory prior to the purchase.

I just turned down the opportunity to make an Offer on a very successful retailer who has understated his inventory by $8 million dollars, thus creating a hidden tax problem for the new buyer, since the seller wanted the new buyer to report the shortage and pay taxes that would be due on that chronic under-reporting.

The seller tried to convince me that he made $8 million dollars as profit, while I explained to him that he had understated his income by $8 million dollars, instead, and at some point the taxes on that will be due to be paid by him or the new buyer.

Additional add backs (items that the owner gets) in a private business may be numerous. These are additional compensation items in fact that would accrue to the new owner, and needs to be considered as part of the "profits" anticipated to accrue to you, the new owner.

This may include a long list of perks and benefits such as dues to clubs, charities, autos, condos owned by the company and used for business entertainment of clients, hunting lodges, boats, airplanes, race horses, gardeners and maids on the payroll, relatives that do no work, and payments for a variety of personal expenses ranging from subscriptions to travel payments.

As a business owner, you have lots of advantages that may accrue to you as the new owner. You want to make sure that you understand that these payments will now either no longer exist when you buy the business, thus giving you a bigger profit, or you can continue them for your benefit.

Let's get real, when a business owner tells you that he had revenues of $25 million last year, but the net profit of the business was only $25,000 as reported to the IRS, do not expect that you can buy that business for $100,000, since there may be a lot of perks and his salary may be $500,000 as well.

Calculate the ADD BACKS, and determine how real they are. Sometimes the add backs are overstated as the seller shows off and overstates what he takes out.

In using your Due Diligence form from Appendix 3, you will be able to compare the IRS reported earnings to the "hype" the seller explains as his version of the "true" earnings. Common sense will allow you to determine the truth, and you can discuss this with the seller's accountant to see if he agrees with the calculation.

At this point you may wish to tell the accountant that you intend on keeping him after the acquisition due to his long experience in dealing with the company. This may help you significantly with getting the REAL financial results.

Additionally you can use the accountant to help you interpret the assets and liabilities that pertain to the business you want to acquire. This is especially helpful if you are new to reading and interpreting financial statements (balance sheets and income statements).

You do not have to be an expert, a financial genius or an accounting major to understand financial statements. Just look at the Balance Sheet of the business and …read each line under the ASSETS section. There will be absolutely no line item listed that you will NOT understand. These are the ASSETS of the business you are looking to buy.

That was not hard, was it? My 13-year-old "apprentice" has learned this.

If all else fails, use some common sense or ask for the seller or accountant to explain in more detail any entries that may not be clear. Do not be afraid to ask until you understand all the assets that the business owns.

Now that you have understood the ASSETS, look at the LIABILITIES……

Do the same for the individual line items listed in the LIABILITIES section, read each line item and make sure you understand each described item. A further explanation in greater detail of each material item will be contained in the NOTES TO FINANCIAL STATEMENT section. There you have it, those are the assets and the liabilities of the business you are acquiring.

It was not necessary to get an accounting degree to understand that, was it???

Now, you have to go back to what you learned in math class and calculate the company's NET WORTH, by taking the TOTAL ASSETS listed and subtracting from that number the TOTAL LIABILITIES listed.

The amount you get by subtracting is called the NET WORTH. This may also be described on the company's Balance Sheet as "Stockholder's Equity (same thing as NET WORTH, just another synonym).

NET WORTH is the difference between the assets of the business and the liabilities, as calculated mathematically. The term, NET

WORTH is not the REAL WORTH of the business; it is just an accounting term.

YOU AS THE BUYER WILL CALCULATE THE REAL NET WORTH (WHAT YOU WILL BE WILLING OR ABLE TO PAY) OF THE BUSINESS IN FORMULATING YOUR OFFER FOR THE BUSINESS.

Calculating the price you will pay for the business (the Offer price) will involve a simple calculation of what the business will be expected to earn as a profit based on previous years...that's all you need to do. You will need some common sense again...look at the profits that the business earned/reported during each of the last three years and calculate the add-backs to the profit as described previously for each year.

Add all the totals and simply divide by three...this answer is the average yearly earnings of the business.

In theory, this is the amount you may reasonably expect to make if you are the owner of this business, and your only additional estimate is to determine if the business will be expected to also earn a similar amount this year. This may be determined based again on common sense...for instance if it is the middle of the fiscal year, has the business earned about half of the average amount of the last three years previously? If so, it may be forecasted to hit the average number again...Maybe??? Is the trend of earnings heading higher, or lower????

Asking questions like "Have you lost customers?" and "What new business have you closed or expected to close soon?" will help you calculate and forecast in very simplistic terms if the business will be likely to again reach it historic profit or not, or maybe it will be more profitable this year.

Write down here the amount of profit you expect for this year for the business:$_____.

Use your common sense...there is nothing to fear here. These are the most simple concepts of understanding financial statements, and they apply to every business, yours or EXXON. Anyone can calculate this, and you have to since you will be the future owner, and must be able to understand these simple concepts!!

You must learn these simple concepts if you are to become a millionaire/multi-millionaire.

You can, and you will. Repeat; "these are simple concepts, and I will know them……these are simple concepts, and I will know them"…repeat again and again.

Now start believing…you are on your way to owning your business……and pricing it to buy it and to be able to finance its purchase.

Ok, we know and understand the NET WORTH of the company as reported on its Balance Sheet and calculated by your subtraction (it should be the same figure). We know the estimated profit of the business for the forecasted year and the average of the last three years.

Now you must calculate what the business can be purchased for and that you can afford to buy it, and finance it.

By making these simple calculations, your buyout calculations are equal to the most sophisticated business acquisition models used by the largest buyout firms, yet your calculations and forecasts are just as good if not better and more accurate.

Be proud of your new analytical skills, and let's now use them to calculate the purchase price you will offer for the business.

The most accurate and fool-proof way to calculate what you can borrow using traditional lenders (ABL Lenders-Asset Based Lenders) is to simply go back to the company's Balance Sheet and do the following calculation:

List the assets and their value as listed in that Balance Sheet as follows:

Percent of Value Amount on the Considered Amount of
Balance Sheet by Lender Likely Loan

Cash	$_____	100%	$_____
Accounts receivable:	$_____	85%	$_____

Inventory:	$_____	50%	$_____
Real Estate (Net):$_____		75%	$_____
Equipment (Net): $_____		50%	$_____

Other assets are
NOT likely to have
any loan value

TOTAL	$_____		$_____

SUBTRACT FROM THE ABOVE AMOUNT ALL EXISTING LOANS LISTED IN THE LIABILITIES SECTION OF THE BALANCE SHEET, AND ENTER BELOW:

TOTAL EXISTING LOANS ($_____)

TOTAL NET AMOUNT OF LENDABLE ASSETS AVAILABLE TO BUY THE BUSINESS
$_____

YOU SUBTRACTED THE LOANS OUTSTANDING, FROM THE AVAILABLE LOAN VALUES. YOU HAVE JUST CALCULATED WHAT THIS BUSINESS MAY HAVE AS AVAILABLE COLLATERAL FOR THE LENDER TO CONSIDER IN POSSIBLY lending to acquire this business, AND THE MAXIMUM NET AMOUNT THAT YOU CAN OFFER FOR THE ACQUISITION OF THE COMPANY.

Was that very complicated?

The existing liabilities owed to the bank/s (but not its general business creditors such as suppliers, utilities, employees) will be (must be paid) so as to provide unencumbered assets for the new lender to use as collateral for the acquisition loan.

The balance remaining will be the amount of possible NET funds you will have available to acquire the business, when using only the assets of the business, to make and calculate the acquisition value, but......there is slightly more to an acquisition.

The business you are acquiring will not be able to operate on a daily basis without sufficient working capital that must be calculated as well. These are the daily operating funds needed for at least 60 days of operating the business going forward.

Working capital is necessary to meet the ongoing obligations as they come up for payment when due, and needs to be considered as an integral part of any acquisition. Lenders will also require that you invest your own funds into the new acquisition to have a financial commitment to the business and "some skin in the game". The lenders do not want to share your ownership risk alone, but want you to be on the line financially and committed to the success of the enterprise you are acquiring.

There are two ways to meet this need; subtract the amount needed from the Offer for the acquisition, or calculate it as being available from the funds that you will be investing into the business that you initially planned to collect from your own resources, friends, investors and relatives.

Calculating accurately this amount is best by working with the seller and the accountant involved in the acquisition (yours or the seller's) to make sure that it is sufficient.

I have used as an illustration the most understood and financeable means of calculating the possible purchase value and its possible financing method, using Asset Based Lenders. These lenders utilize established formulas as presented in calculating values that represent reasonable lendable amounts.

If you have access to significant investment funds, have raised sizable capital to start your acquisition program, it will also involve the same calculations, but will provide your new business with stronger working capital availability and greater comfort for the prospective lenders.

DO YOU WANT SOME HELP IN PRICING THE BUSINESS, CONSIDER THAT OPTION ON MY WEB SITE, AND YOU WILL GET PERSONAL HELP TO PRICE YOUR ACQUISITION AND EVEN STRUCTURE THE ACQUISITION IF DESIRED.

Yes, I can also help with finding the lender as well; relax, you are in good hands.

Now that you have determined the possible Offer price for the business, you have to make sure that the business can afford to pay back the loan you have calculated to acquire the business.

Calculating this ability is called the DEBT SERVICE RATIO. Lenders use this ratio to calculate the ability of the business to pay the debt owed. Lenders vary as to their acceptable RATIO but this ratio should be in excess of 1.2 and probably give the greatest comfort to be at least 1.3 to 1.4.

This means that if the payment required by the lender on the debt is $1, then the business should generate cash of $1.20 to $1.40 to provide comfort to the lender. This ratio may be lower if the working capital you will provide personally is sufficient to provide the lender with the feeling that the business is on sound financial footing, and thus the ratio becomes less of a critical factor.

Thus, if your calculations show the business being able to borrow $2,000,000, but it has to pay $500,000 annually to the bank (interest and principal), with the required minimum ratio of 1.2, it must earn $600,000 in order to meet the required bank ratio ($500,000 times 1.2 equals $600,000).

Under this illustration, this business must earn at least $600,000 annually in order to be able to meet the bank's lending ratio earnings requirement. If this is the case, go ahead and make an Offer at $2,000,000, if this ratio is not met, adjust your Offer price until it does. You would have to adjust your proposed Offer price downwards in order to meet the ratio as established by the lender, otherwise you will not have a lender that will be capable of lending the amount needed to support your Offer.

Another possibility is to ask the seller to accept a Note, a deferred payment, for a portion of his asking price to make up the difference in what he wants to get and what you can reasonably finance. This is called seller financing or a Seller Note. It is a normal and reasonable request especially if you want to have the seller committed to your future success.

This Note can be related to the company's future profits, or some other factors such as achieving certain pre-determined goals such as getting a certain customer, reaching revenue goals or customer retention.

This may be most reasonable if you are dealing with a seller who knows you, such as your current employer, and has greater faith in your abilities than if you were dealing with a total stranger. Also, there may even be a better way to make the acquisition by acting together (a group of employees) and pooling your funds together, which is my strong suggestion.

You should note that the lender will likely have the final say as to you being able to make any future payments to the seller, and the seller will more than likely have to subordinate his Note to the rights of the lender as a creditor. The lender always wants to be first in line to get paid.

There will be times that in calculating the amount that the business assets may be able to support, there is no net loan amount possible…and that business is one that you will not be able to acquire, nor should you acquire one that can not pay its acquisition loan.

That is all to it…that is how it is done. Nothing magical, just a few calculations.

I want to add here that you should attempt to find and acquire as large a business as possible, since the calculations are all the same!!!! Practice on your employer first, if you do not buy the business you now work for, you may establish yourself as a smarter and possibly better looking employee suitable for that upcoming promotion.

Do you want to own a 50 employee business or one with 500 or 5,000 employees?

Which one do you think will pay you a bigger salary?

My personal experience is one that you may find interesting in this regard.

I was doing fine and making a nice living acquiring small businesses, retail stores, service businesses, small manufacturers, etc……until I met my long time business partner who was a veteran of acquisitions in the 1960s and 1970s.

His advice for me was, "it takes the same effort to acquire a large business as a small one, but the financial rewards are bigger, so why do you want to screw around with the small stuff?!" I took him to heart and started a lifelong partnership that lasts till this day.

The first business we acquired together, using the philosophy of identifying and buying a larger business was our purchase of a long established department store chain that was a publicly traded company listed on the New York Stock Exchange involving approximately $100,000,000 in required financing!!

The revenues of the acquired business were over $160,000,000 annually, and it employed approximately 4,500 employees. Thus we went from 3 employees to 4,503 overnight. In addition we acquired a well-known trade name and established impressive offices on the 10th floor of our own 800,000 square foot headquarters building that was part of the acquired company's assets!!

We approached over 75 different lenders with our acquisition financing needs, we were turned down as many times, before we convinced three of them to fund the deal (it still took less than 365 days to accomplish it all).

Each lender required a full presentation, a "dog and pony show"; visits to the company, the stores, and warehouse. In addition various lenders had their own additional questions and forecasts that we had to prepare. At closing, at the eleventh hour, we had to agree to pay for one of the lender's lawyers fees of some $125,000, or they would not agree to have the lender fund the deal (which came from the closing funds and not out of our pocket).

After this transaction, we followed up shortly thereafter with the acquisition of a 12,500 employee transportation company which had almost $900,000,000 in revenues, this time taking only a few days to close, using one of the lenders who participated in the department store chain's acquisition!!

Did you learn something about using the lender that know you from a prior acquisition? Within a month we had a $1.1 billion revenue business group, and 17,000 employees.

Our acquisition formula was the same as described in this book, with one exception: we paid substantially less than the amount we calculated as being able to borrow (as calculated in this book) for each of these businesses, thus we were able to use the excess funding for working capital.

You may also be surprised to find that from time to time you will run across a business to acquire that has very few assets to leverage (get a loan against), but very substantial earnings. This type of business is typically one that is great to own, but difficult or impossible to acquire without substantial personal capital, rather than using bank loans.

I personally do not like that type of business, a business with few assets that may be dependent upon personalities or patents, or other special and unique qualities. Most of these types of businesses tend to be service based such as consulting services, accounting, law or engineering firms, non-stocking retail and catalog businesses, restaurants, contractors, print and design firms, etc.

It is hard for me to consider buying a business that has $500,000 in assets, but makes $1 million a year in profit, and has an asking price of $4 or $5 million. I personally also would advise you to not consider it, unless you are crazy and have your own $4 or $5 million to personally invest in the acquisition. In that case, if you would be willing to buy such a business, I have a bridge for you in Brooklyn...to buy.

Now you have become a pricing maven, and will be able to determine the Offer price to make for any business you may be wishing to acquire. But, will you be able to acquire it?

What if the seller says, "are you nuts, Offering me $2 million for the business I have spent my entire life building up?" Your reply may be, "but Mr. Seller, I read this book on how to price a business, and that is it, I can not otherwise acquire it if it is more than $2 million."

Perhaps you feel your dream of becoming a millionaire or multi-millionaire slipping away?

Hello, NOT.

Would you accept the first Offer you got from some crazy guy that read my book to sell your long established business? You have got to get real. You have got to start thinking of the acquisition strategy, not just the price. The process may take longer than you think, but remember there are other companies that you will be bidding on as well, and you may buy them all!!!!

After locating a great business for sale, I made an Offer to acquire it. It was a 30-year-old established outdoor sports, hunting and fishing and clothing retailer being sold by its founder who wanted to retire. It was similar to a Dick's Sporting Goods store, but on a smaller scale.

The seller was very detail oriented and he wanted to make sure that the new owner would commit to keep the employees and the unique character of the store, which was famous in its three-state trade area. In fact, shoppers would come in just to look at the merchandise displays because they were so unique.

The company had been consistently profitable, and appeared to present itself like a great deal to acquire. The Offer was made, on the formula just like described in this book, and the seller rejected it. He thought that is was worth more (no surprise there, is there?).

The seller proposed a counter-offer and we (my business partner and I) had to analyze if it was possible to finance such an Offer. After analysis, discussion with lenders, we simply could not increase our Offer by much, but we structured it differently than an all cash Offer.

We proposed that the seller receive cash plus additional payments in the future, but the seller wanted to get all the cash right away, and also wanted to rent the building to the company in the future as well, as part of the sales proposal that he would accept.

Since the company was only an hour and a half drive from our office, we kept visiting with the seller and stayed in touch with him, had lunch with him regularly, all the time telling him that we were interested in the acquisition but that we could not finance the purchase due to his asking price. He never received a higher price or better terms and we acquired the business for our Offer price years later. Staying on good terms with private sellers can pay off.

Personally, I set a time limit on the acquisition strategy such as 2 to 3 months, to have the seller and I talk, visit, get to know each other, counter the Offer discuss financing with lenders, etc. My partner hates to give up on any deal, so he is willing to keep discussing it until they die, or sell, whichever comes first. He told me the story of his early acquisition days when he made an Offer to acquire the stake in Disney from Walt Disney's grieving family right after he passed, claiming to be an old friend. Only then he discovered that he was not the first, others have already beaten him to the Offer table claiming to be old friends too.

Never give up, never stop making proposals, counter proposals and cultivating a friendship with the seller/s. You may win by default as other potential buyers fall off, lose interest or are just figments of the seller's imagination.

I am currently dealing with a seller who is 80 years old and his children all work in his manufacturing business. They now also own a minority stake in the business and are interested in having the father sell out. The business has revenues of $16 million and profits of $1.8 million, and manufactures a basic plastic commodity product, one that all of us own, and it was either manufactured by his company or a competitor of his. Nice company, an easy plastic product we all have and need.

The man is firm on a price that has no relation to reality or in the ability of being financed, and is holding out for this price. The business broker that represents the seller is useless, since he has not been successful in educating the seller about the possible value of the business. I have asked the family members to talk with him about the sale, since they were offered an opportunity to own 20% of the business after it is sold, and after they all get a few million in cash from the sale. They will get nothing if "dad" keeps holding out for a ridiculous price.

The "dad" just told me that he got an Offer of $16 million all cash for his business, and gave me the opportunity to "beat that Offer", but he forgot that he told me that he had an Offer of $18 million last month! His kids or the broker do not know about such an Offer, so it is probably just a negotiating tactic.

Sometimes you get such a seller, so just try your best, keep up the conversations and hope that he sees the light as other Offers, even the imaginary other Offers disappear and you become the REAL buyer.

We had many strange experiences including a seller who in his sales agreement with us was able to keep the "excess funds of the company" at the closing. He then went to the bank the next day, asked the banker how much was in the account and simply transferred the money to himself, while all our outstanding checks simply bounced. He did not realize that the outstanding checks were written before the business was sold.

One of the strangest things that happened to us was where a seller asked if he could buy his company back within two months of a sale, since he was so bored and could not figure out what to do with himself, not going to the office and being in charge. Now that I think of it, this happened twice!!!!!

CHAPTER 5

ACQUISITION FINANCING SOURCES AND STRUCTURE OF THE FINANCING

Did you know that there are thousands and thousands of lenders who are waiting to finance your possible acquisition? Make that tens of thousands!

Banks, finance companies of every type, and ABLs (ASSET BASED LENDERS), have business development officers whose entire job is to try and find YOU and support your crazy scheme of trying to acquire the business you have made an Offer on!

There are commercial banks, commercial banks with ABL lending divisions, business finance companies, ABL only lenders, factoring companies, specialty lenders, high risk lenders to weak companies, LBO (leveraged buyout) lenders, small business lenders, etc., etc., etc......the list is almost endless.

I AM ALSO ABLE TO ASSIST YOU DIRECTLY THROUGH DIRECT LENDER INTRODUCTION. Just go to my web site for help.

Whatever they refer to themselves as, they want to lend you money if you want to buy a business. Yes, that is a fact, like the well-known ad says, lenders are out there "competing for your business".

In addition, the government is also willing to help you buy the business by providing your lender with a guarantee of YOUR loan! Finally you discovered that the government can actually REALLY help you get rich!

Thanks to the internet, you can research this yourself by going to the web site for the Small Business Administration and learn about the SBA Guaranteed loans. In addition your bankers will be willing to "help" you get the SBA Guaranteed loan since your loan is...guaranteed!!!

Not all lenders participate in the Guaranteed programs, since as expected, there is a lot of paperwork, but this paperwork is worth getting a guarantee. The larger banks in many cases are preferred lenders, and will have personnel who will explain the available programs for you.

Do not pass up the opportunity to get your money's worth from the SBA.

There are so many sources of possible financing, that you should first do a little research.

Check out as a starting point in Appendix 5 to get you started. Call the lenders and find out what they can do for you.

Some will like certain types of businesses, and will not consider others for financing. Some will have minimum sizes such as $1 million or $5 million, or geographic limitations. If you are buying something close to home, check out lenders close to home but do not overlook that most ABL lenders work nationally or regionally and will love giving you a proposal.

Be prepared to shop around before committing to a lender, and make sure that you are getting enough to close the deal. If you have a good relationship with your banker, talk with him too. He will want to help you.

Remember how in Chapter 3, you performed "due diligence" on the business you wanted to acquire? Well, the lender will want to perform its own due diligence to assure itself of the factual and financial issues and not just trust your fact finding. If you had the seller complete the form in Appendix 2, you may have most of the work completed.

You will be able to show the lender your information that was gathered and be able to explain any items that they may need further explanation about, such as a loss of a key customer, or declining profits. Feel free to involve your seller in helping the lender in this process. After all he will be the beneficiary of the deal closing!!!

The lender will provide you with a FINANCING PROPOSAL to consider, providing an outline of the terms and conditions he is willing to operate under in providing your acquisition loan. This proposal will also contain a due diligence clause for the lender, and require you to sign it and provide for a fee to conduct the due diligence and audit of the company at your expense.

You may reimburse yourself for these costs at closing and they will typically run about $1,000 per day per person with some type of minimum or maximum for this service. Expect to pay $5,000 for a smaller deal to $15,000- $25,000 for a larger one. This will exclude legal and documentation costs which will be billed typically at the closing and will approximate $25,000 to $50,000 or more, depending on the deal complexity and size.

These costs and fees are somewhat negotiable, as are the conditions presented, so use your negotiating powers at this time. After all, it is your money, and the lender knows that once you pay his fee you are not likely to go to several lenders.

See Appendix 6 for a sample of a Financing Proposal.

CHAPTER 6

PREPARING THE FINANCING PROPOSAL
FOR YOUR LENDER

Can you believe it, you are now about to buy a business!!! Your own multi-million dollar business!!!!

This assumes of course that you have an accepted Offer from a seller on terms that you believe will be able to be financed on reasonable terms as described in previous chapters.

You may have had to review a number of businesses and made many Offers and carried on negotiations to get to this point, but you will be there sooner than you think, and the business you will buy will be larger than you expected. This is due to the fact that you will be able to finance a bigger business faster and on better terms than a "mom and pop" business...nice......going...

I learned long ago that a fancy presentation looks nice, but who is going to read it with all those charts and figures and boring numbers? The answer is...nobody......

Also, such a presentation is not only boring to read, it is boring to make up, and why waste your time preparing something nobody will read anyway?

YOU CAN HAVE MY ASSISTANCE IN PREPARING THE PROPOSAL, JUST GO TO MY WEB SITE.

To start with, make the presentation very simple and easy to understand, not more than six or eight pages maximum!!

The first two pages will describe the business you want to buy, in the most descriptive and glorified terms, yet short and easy to understand. Stress the positives like its steady predictable earnings, well-established client base and future prospects. You can add any significant positive future plans or a short business plan if you wish. At this state keep it short, it can always be added to later.

Limit the above to two pages!!

Next you need to make up a page that looks exactly like the page of calculations described in Chapter 4, make it word for word, and title it: ASSETS AVAILABLE FOR FINANCING.

That page will be by itself, ONE PAGE.

Next and most important will be the page that describes what your transaction is looking to accomplish, describing the acquisition price and terms, and special conditions as well as the capital you will be investing into the proposed acquisition.

This will also be ONE PAGE.

Next will be a page describing the proposed ongoing management team and its experience in the business and any reference to the ownership that any of them may have in the new company with you. Stress their accomplishments if any, such as got the biggest account ever for the company or achieved his sales goal ahead of schedule, etc. Stress your experience in the business as well.

This will be ONE PAGE.

The next page will be an entire page describing you and your investor group if any, listing your experience in similar businesses or accomplishments and highlights. Do not start this page with your high school accomplishments!

This will be the last page of your write up. The total so far, six pages.

Next, after these six pages include the actual financial statements (balance sheets and income statements, and the accounting notes) from the last three years of the business you want to acquire, and add any company brochures, photos and information that may look impressive.

The final page, will be making up your title and cover page to be inserted as the front page which should simply state:

FINANCING PROPOSAL

Acquisition of (name of business) $ Amount of financing required

Insert Photo of Business Exterior Here

Principal Buyer and Contact
Your Name Here
Your Contact Address and Phone/ Fax
E-mail Address

The above should be prepared both in electronic form and available as an E-mail attachment, and a hard copy as well, neatly bound which will be able to be sent to lenders if necessary.

Your cover letter or E-mail should read, RE: Financing /Acquisition $insert amount

The copy of the E-mail or letter should be short such as:

Attached please find my financing proposal for the acquisition of (name of company).

I look forward to your response relating to the possible interest in financing my proposed acquisition of this fine company.

Please contact me directly at:

and sign the letter.

There is no need to have more information to be presented to get the interest or initial rejection from a lender. Additional information about the business you may share with interested lenders by making a copy of the due diligence information you obtained from the business previously and used in your initial decision.

That's it. You are on your way to becoming business owner, of a multi-million dollar business.

CHAPTER 7

ACQUIRING STOCK OR ASSETS AS YOUR ACQUISITION STRUCTURE

When you make your Offer to acquire the business from the seller, you will also need to determine if you want to be acquiring just the outstanding shares of the business (assuming it is a corporation), or its assets and liabilities.

Based on my years in the business, I firmly believe that your best way to proceed is to acquire the stock, and not the individual assets and liabilities. I will not go into a long explanation here, there are plenty of other smarter people that can explain all this in 200 pages of exhaustive analysis, and yet the same conclusion. I just saved you a lot of reading, and buying lots of expensive books.

Just take my advice here and Offer to buy the stock. The seller gets capital gains treatment and low tax on his profit from the sale and you get what you want, the business in its corporate form.

The purchase of assets and liabilities has a number of negative implications (unless you are buying it through the bankruptcy court and have a court order that states what your limited liabilities will be) that outweigh its positives.

If the business is a limited partnership, buy its partnership interests. End of advice.

Since you will hire an attorney and probably use your accountant as well to assist you in the acquisition, they can explain to you the reasons for the type of acquisition structure I am proposing.

Also, you can access additional information on my web site.

CHAPTER 8

SETTING YOUR COMPENSATION

Well, you are going to be the boss, the big cheese, the big guy (or big girl? that does not sound right).

You determine what your compensation should be after the acquisition.

A starting guideline would be to review the compensation that the previous person in your position received. Was it fair for the work done or was it the result of the perks of being the owner, the big cheese?

If the work you will be performing will be similar to the work performed by the former owner and he received a salary of $300,000 plus a $50,000 year-end bonus, then that should be your compensation.

If you have business partners, their pay should also be set relating to either the work they will perform and agree upon to do or a set monthly advisory fee for being on the Board of Directors or the Board of Advisors.

Also, you need to make sure that you did not include the figure in the payments to the lender that you calculated as being available for the lender to pay his scheduled debt repayments.

Additionally, the lender may review your proposed pay schedule if it appears that you are going to receive excessive compensation and possibly not make the scheduled debt repayments.

The IRS wants you to be well compensated, and will actually consider that you may be paying yourself too little and penalize your Corporation for NOT paying you enough. Talk this over with your attorney or accountant. It is interesting how the government cares for us all, especially when as the corporate big cheese we pay ourselves too little for their liking.

On the other hand if we get over $1 million in salary compensation, it has other penalties!! Go figure.

I bid on a well-established trucking/delivery business that had revenues of $35 million, but as a corporation, regularly showed puny, but consistent profits of only about $50,000-$75,000 annually. This company specialized in making the timely deliveries to grocery stores and warehouses and was an integral part of the infrastructure and delivery/distribution systems for food store chains.

The principal stockholder and president of this enterprise would regularly meet with his customers and show them his accountant certified, audited financial statements with these puny profits. He would then over lunch with the client, literally cry about how little he was making in his business, and he would beg the customers to allow him to raise his prices by just 2%-5% so that he could "make a living".

They usually agreed to let him raise his price, and the following year, he would show them again the same puny profits, and go through the same sad story to which they reacted by allowing him to raise prices again.

As I met with the seller, I told him that this was a very effective way of holding on to a customer and with them allowing the price increase since they felt sorry for him they felt an obligation to stay. I was going to use this technique in the future myself.

What I did not tell you, is that the seller in this case was paying himself a salary of $5 million dollars! Every time his business made more money due to the price increases, he increased his salary accordingly so that at the end of the year, only this puny amount would be shown as the corporation's profit!

So, your compensation should be reasonable, but what is reasonable may be very subjective. As the corporate big wig, you also may consider employing your spouse, kids that can do some work, and those relatives looking for part time work as well. Your entire family can benefit from your position.

CHAPTER 9

MANAGEMENT OF CORPORATE AND FINANCIAL OPERATIONS

Your business should reflect a professional corporate structure with clear responsibilities for all the management personnel, and a job description for each person in the organization.

See Appendix 8, for a sampling of various forms that you may customize to your needs. In addition, you may go to my web site and incorporate in any state for fees as low as $99 plus the state fees.

As part of the incorporation package, you may order a complete set of documents needed for the basic operation of your company, a complete corporate Minute Book, recording the meetings of the Board of Directors, etc…

This is your opportunity to reward key employees, and/or your relatives by making them corporate officers, etc., with fancy cards and titles.

There are many companies and office supply catalog companies that provide ready-to-use employee forms, performance review forms and the like, so feel free to use them. In addition, the company you are acquiring probably already has them anyway, so use theirs.

Managing and motivating your managers is important, but even more important is your management of the corporate checkbook.

We as absentee owners, have had to develop a variety of simple and effective cash management techniques to allow us to know the company's daily/monthly cash position, as well to assure ourselves that in the event of a planned turnaround, the financial position of the company was actually improving, and improving as planned and quickly.

After much experimenting with complicated systems and procedures that needed training for managers, endless budget meetings, and taking up significant time for us and the management, we developed the most simplistic, and easy-to-understand system.

The system is called: THE CHECKBOOK SYSTEM.

The checkbook is just that, a checkbook. It works like a checkbook, it acts like a checkbook, it is understood by everyone who has a checkbook. That is it; you know how it works.

If you do not have a checkbook, or know how a checkbook works, do not read this book any further, or in the alternative, ask someone, anyone...they will explain the process in one minute or less.

Maybe someone should explain this to our politicians; they are the only ones I know of that do not know how to work with a checkbook. In fact, you may recall our esteemed members of Congress had personal checkbooks at the Capital Bank, and if the balance was ever insufficient, none of their checks would ever bounce.

The best thing about the Checkbook System, is that everyone in the company will instantly understand the program, and they can all then understand what you are trying to accomplish.

You need this Checkbook System to manage a successful company or a company in a turnaround mode.

Basically, you already understand the basics, those of how a checkbook works.

You have a certain amount of money in your checkbook, and you can only spend what is in the checkbook, and no more. Only our government can afford otherwise...for the rest of us, it is considered a crime to knowingly write a check that is returned due to insufficient funds.

Thus, the checkbook system works just like a checking account. Your company management cannot spend more than the amount of money that is in the checkbook.

It is simple to understand, and with this simple concept, you have also accomplished an indirect budgeting process that can be tied into the entire process by giving a checkbook to each department manager, etc., for his own department to spend as their checkbook.

Thus, if the payroll department checkbook has $100,000 in it for the week, you cannot spend any more, or you will be "overdrawn", and that is not possible.

Understand how it works?

The same for the insurance department checkbook, the purchasing department checkbook, the transportation cost department checkbook, the managements' salary department checkbook, the advertising department checkbook, the office expense checkbook, etc...Done, you understand how it works.

Using this program, the Checkbook System, a company which is operating at break even (matching its revenues and expenses, but creating no excess cash or profits), will require that you deposit some amount smaller than its current expenses in its checkbook.

For example, if last month's total company expenses were $550,000, and it was a financially break even, then this month you will "deposit" $530,000 into the company's checkbook, thus theoretically creating a possible "profit" of $20,000 the following month.

Think about it...you can reduce power costs by turning off lights and computers that are not needed or when not in use, you can meet with your insurance carrier or broker to reduce rates, ask your transportation providers for discounts, cut out a lot of unnecessary expenses. Some credit card companies even give you 5% rebates (your company just saved 5% of your purchases) if you make all your purchases using their card.

Since 5% of your revenues as a net profit would be a major step in the right direction toward improving profitability, or creating it, these programs could be very beneficial to your business and your checkbook.

This System is strictly to regulate the expenses, since controlling them is usually the most important means of generating a profit, and it works. Your manager may take some time to get it right, but it will work by making it possible to make small adjustments yet bring the needed financial rewards.

I can assure you that every company in existence today can find savings of 5% OF ITS COSTS OTHER THAN SALARY EXPENSES JUST BY LOOKING AND ASKING FOR THEM FROM SUPPLIERS/VENDORS AND OTHER "FIXED" OPERATING COSTS.

Just think what it can save if every manager had a checkbook and you told them that they had 10% LESS TO SPEND NEXT MONTH.

If you master the Checkbook System, you are well on your way toward having a successful and profitable business, and will be especially effective in managing a business in turnaround mode as well.

Best of all, you do not have complicated decisions and software to manage either.

CHAPTER 10

RETAINING THE BEST PERSONNEL

The library and your favorite bookstores will have hundreds of books advising you on how to hire, who to hire, the tests you can give to your employees and tests to test who is suited for what job.

However, having just acquired a business, you just inherited, by default, all the employees who were there before you were the owner. So, forget all the advisory books and get to know every employee.

The simple interview, one by one of all the employees, or a group interview, with each person talking about themselves, their job and their personal interests will get you to befriend each of them and provide them an opportunity to get to know you.

Remember, first rule of being the boss, is…you should remain clearly the boss. There is no need for you to share your personal life in every detail, but rather this is your opportunity to establish your vision for the future of the company, and enlist the employees in that quest, through new incentive programs, etc. You will clearly be the most popular boss, ever.

Set specific goals and have your management stick to them by consistent and constant updating and monitoring.

Build your company by having the management and employees do the work while you set the goals and visions of the business. Do not micro manage—they are the management, use their skills.

I should mention a possible caution…be careful about the employees that you retain and make sure that they are on YOUR side and not working for themselves.

Remote construction sites and offices that have company equipment without a well-tracked inventory, or company trucks and trailers present tempting targets to employees who do not think you have a tight ship.

We had a situation develop where the president of the company, who we recruited, who received an ownership interest in the business, and who had full discretion as to business decisions, actually had started his own competing business, and used our own company's trailers to haul his company's freight. We found out that we were renting them at our cost while he benefitted personally by using them at no cost to his company, and paid us nothing for it.

In another instance, the top management of a $25 million revenue company we acquired from a large conglomerate, secretly used the funds they were paid to remain with the sold business as our top management, to start their own competing business. They solicited the top accounts to switch to their business. Make sure that you avoid this potential problem by covering that in your proposed Purchase and Sale agreement.

When you are the business owner, you have to carefully spot check all operations, do some walking around daily, and definitely understand where the company's "original funds" are being spent.

One of the original inventors of the "boot strapping" of a business (prelude to leveraged buyouts), buyout "kings", and one of the most feared takeover artists, Victor Posner, at one time controlled businesses with billions in revenues. He would actually, personally, review each check that was written, and ask the management specifically what it was for, if it was a really needed expense, and then he required HIS signature to be as the second signature on all checks, or in the alternative, it could only be his signature on ALL the checks.

I learned a lot from his simple system of making the management accountable, and it ties in very nicely with our CHECKBOOK SYSTEM, giving you a great deal of financial accountability and control.

On one of our acquisitions, the remaining management was resentful that we, instead of them were the successful buyers.

Since it was an acquisition from a large corporate parent company, the sales agreement required us to change the company's name and that it was to be done over a certain period of time, so there would be a cost on this name change on the buildings, equipment, stationery, etc.

This company was huge, it had over 900 people in its corporate headquarters office, and the management chart looked like an octopus with many more tentacles. It reminded me of the scene in the movie Wall Street, where the character played by Michael Douglas quipped at a stockholders' meeting, "...they have 75 vice presidents," which this company did ......

The company described above, paid an average of $10-$15 million in weekly bills and payroll; they did not think that we would be reviewing each and every check written and then ask questions before they were sent out. Thank goodness we did! In the very first few days of our new ownership, there was a check for approximately $3.5 million that was about to be sent to a company that we never heard of, and its address was at a post office box.

If we did not review the checks being sent out it would have been sent, since its disbursement carried the approval and signature of the top management, as well as the Chief Financial Officer (CFO), so the disbursement department, would not have any authority to question such a check. It would have been sent out and paid without any questions.

By the way, there are three movies that should be, no make that MUST BE, your required viewing: WALL STREET, OTHER PEOPLES' MONEY and just for fun, PRETTY WOMAN.

All of the above movies typify the acquisition process, and the movie OTHER PEOPLES' MONEY, is especially helpful in having you understand how acquisitions of the type we are describing are done!

Well, I asked the Controller (chief disbursing officer) to explain what it was for, and he had no idea, other than knowing that since it had the required signatures of the top officers of the company, it would be approved and paid without any questions—that was the extent of the checks and balances at this company!!

I was shocked, and asked to review the purchase order that was the basis of this check disbursement, as well as the underlying supporting invoices. There was an invoice, invoice #1 (can you believe it), an invoice with that suspicious number, attached to the purchase order, stating that this was a pre-payment for all the necessary signs that the company would be ordering in compliance with its required change of the corporate name, and the company that was supposed to be performing this task headquartered at a post office box, but a phone number was listed as well.

The Controller and I smiled at each other one of those smiles that indicated we had "smelled a rat".

A check for $3.5 million, was about to go out to a company located in a post office box, and this apparently was its first invoice issued, ever!

I decided to call the company. The Controller was holding back his laughter as I dialed the company's phone number, and inquired as to the exact nature of the $3.5 million invoice. To our shock it was the home phone number of one of the company's corporate officers. His wife answered not with the company name, but with a, "hello?"

We now got the idea...I asked about the reason for the invoice and if the services of the sign painting were completed yet. She answered, no, they were going to be done in the future but that this company needed to first buy the raw materials. I then asked her why then were we being billed for the entire price of the project right now? She did not know but verified that it was indeed invoice number 1 that was sent out and that the company was just formed, and that it never did any sign painting and that this was its one and only account!

Wow, what a story. We were about to send $3.5 million to a company owned by select corporate officers, with no competing bids or even a specific price quote for what we were supposedly paying for or getting.

With our simple financial review, we saved $3.5 million on just one check payment. Now back to the real work.

With the retained management, instead of trying to motivate them to improve revenues and earnings, consider growing the business, the easy way......do you know how to grow your revenues 50% or 100% each year????? Answer: by making another acquisition, just like the one you just made!!

Growing revenues the hard way, through increasing your sales quotas for salesmen, working hard at developing new accounts (which means that you have to take them away from your competitors, and then they take away your accounts, etc...) is pointless.

Buy out your competitor instead!! Have you not learned anything yet?? Put to use what you learned so far and increase your revenues substantially, through an add-on acquisition using the techniques you learned.

Keep doing it, use your existing management to become partners with you in your next acquisition. They will all want to be a multi-millionaire like you. Now go to the next chapter......

CHAPTER 11

INCREASING REVENUES 50%, 100% EACH YEAR...THE EASY WAY

The most important and crucial part of a business is maintaining sales momentum and increasing the company's revenues and profitability consistently.

This is a constant and daily struggle for every business, large and small. You probably noticed that public companies are under constant pressure to deliver increases in earnings and revenues each quarter to maintain their popularity with investors, and to maintain their stock price.

You will have your own version of this pressure each quarter from your lenders who will be constantly watching your financial performance to make sure that their loans are repaid.

It is just so hard to constantly be operating under pressure to increase revenues and profits. What if your sales manager quits and joins your biggest competitor, and tells them all your company "secrets"?

What if your best and most popular product is upstaged by a new and improved version introduced by a competitor, from China, at half your product's price?

Most businesses, would find it hard to survive such events, and they do happen to the best of companies with the best of managements. "Nobody expects the Spanish Inquisition". Remember that quote in business.

Protect your business and keep it growing without all the hard work...acquire another complimentary business!!

Making an acquisition of a business whose revenues equal that of your present business, will DOUBLE your company's revenues in one year!! That will be a lot easier than growing it through new accounts.

Additionally, you should not just plan to acquire a complimentary business, you should acquire your competitor!!

Owning a business (your current business) to start with, may allow you to propose a "merger" with the competitor thus not having to expend any cash, yet creating a bigger and more profitable business composed of the two enterprises.

The issues to consider will all relate to how well you get along with the other owner/s, and how well your employees relate to the different management cultures at each company.

The bottom line is that your growth plans must include a way to increase you revenues and profits through growth, and the easiest growth is accomplished through acquisitions, not internal growth, which is the hardest to maintain. Also remember that as you get a "new account", your competitor just lost one, so what do you think may be the natural progression here?

Think of the auto industry as a great example of this concept. As the "other" company cuts their price, on a particular car, the competitors cut theirs to compete...only one will get the sale, the others lose, and yet they all have not found ways to compete other than on lowering and lowering their prices, and thus likewise lowering their profits (what profits?).

Can you imagine it, the U.S. auto industry has revenues of some $700 BILLION, and its executives are being paid MILLIONS in salary and BONUSES, yet they lose millions for their stockholders. Imagine, your company revenues at $700 BILLION, would you find a way to make a few million in this enterprise???

If I was in charge there, the first action would be the instant termination of the seemingly incompetent and worthless management that is NOT generating any profit on such enormous revenues. Would you pay millions in compensation to a management team that made you no profits at all?

Finally, did you notice that literally ALL the major auto companies are considering merging with each other as the panacea for their ills? At least they can grow their revenues, but profits may still prove to be a challenge.

Bottom line, grow the business the easy way......acquire another similar business or your competitor and plan for 50% to 100% growth each year!! Think about it, with my help, after you get your business growing, I can help you acquire a much larger business, perhaps one with revenues of $25-$100 million or more......will that increase your financial status???

CHAPTER 12

SELLING OUT FOR MILLIONS!!!!!

"What," you may ask? "Selling out, but I just bought the company, I am just starting to have some fun?".

Yes, you are having fun, and it is time to make sure that you will continue to have fun, by making sure that you have a million dollars (or more, maybe lots more) in the bank first! Does that make you feel better now, about selling out?

I also want to point out that by selling out, I do not necessarily mean selling your entire interest in the business, let's just say 80%, while you retain 20%. In this way you will continue to benefit from the future good fortune of the new owners-your employees, managers or ESOP (Employee Stock Ownership Plan).

You will also more likely still be the largest single stockholder in the company, thus you want to make sure that you are a member of the Board of Directors as well, and maybe its Chairman as well.

In my opinion it would be the best for you to sell to your best possible new owners-your employees or managers. A sale structured as a sale of stock to an ESOP (in which all your employees and managers will be participants) will have additional significant tax benefits to you (deferred tax on your capital gain from the sale), and even advantages to the bank financing the transaction as well. Discuss this with your attorney or accountant skilled in ESOP related transactions. I can help you set all this up as well.

You may also check my web site for the ESOP information. It may be tempting to continue to be the owner, the big cheese, and have all the "status" of being the President of your business. But what is wrong with being the Chairman, and having big bucks in the bank?? Get my point??

Don't fight it, just do it. Sell out to your employees, take the money, tax deferred, and park it in the bank for now, invest it later in a nice new mansion, yacht or your own private island…now enjoy your life, really enjoy.

Live the millionaire's life you always wanted.

Quit the daily office stuff, and have fun with your family while being the Chairman and advisor to the company. Make sure to ask for a reasonable salary (have it right in the sales contract) so that you have steady income from the business on an ongoing basis.

If you are really interested in still being more active, consider doing what you just learned, all over again, and again, and again......have a 20% interest in several companies that you sold out an 80% interest.

Also, you will have the working capital and investment capital to invest in the additional businesses at any time you wish.

Remember, this is a 365 day program, how many consecutive years to do want to do this over and over again?? You decide, one year, two or?? You will quickly discover that you can do this over and over, and best of all, it will get to be easier and easier since you will have a greater confidence in your abilities to do this over and over, if you want to.

The idea of selling out provides you with the comfort of knowing that you have made it, you cashed out and you have the financial stability and comfort you deserve.

You know what to do to make it all over again and again......take my advice enjoy your life. Buy that lake house, the vacation condo, and travel to exotic places with your family.

Maybe try this idea, do this all on your new weekly schedule, working Monday thru Thursday, and getting that new European work week started.

CHAPTER 13

PLANNING THE 365 DAYS!!
REALLY!! DO YOU HAVE
WHAT IT TAKES?

Most people, and I mean 99% of people, never reach the status of becoming millionaires, because they do not try at all to do so. Is that the strangest fact, they do not even try, try in the smallest slightest way.

The best way to become a millionaire is to be a business owner.

Can you believe it, there was nothing in the book too complicated for you to understand. The plan was simple, the execution was your doing. You did it, not me, you, YOU did it. Did you really do it, or did you just read up to this section. Will you go back and do/take the simple steps, or will it be too hard for you??

I will help guide you, and monitor your daily activity for each of the 365 days, if you so choose, by going to my web site and choosing the option that will allow you to work with me and record your daily log of activity.

Every item described in the book is simple, described for your comprehension and instant use. You will be able to do it since you had the guidance of a simple, easy to understand step by step guide to guide you through what would normally be intricate details, explained in charts and books that are too complicated to follow, and certainly do not advocate this simple workable approach.

I have followed these simple principles developed on over 3,100 acquisitions that I was personally involved with pricing, acquiring, structuring the acquisition, structuring and soliciting the financing, presenting an Offer to acquire, auction bidding at bankruptcy sales, corporate divestitures and the like.

I have seen the get rich quick programs that get really complicated, have many forms and complicated schemes and require you to really work so hard at impossible goals.

I have looked at many of these programs since I am always willing to learn some new and better way of making money. Each program appeared so complicated and long, that I would lose interest pretty quickly in actually following through to a successful proposed transaction that was described.

What is so difficult to understand about buying out the company you work for, when you understand the process? There is not much to it, once you understand the process. You are already thinking that YOU could probably run the business you work for much better than it is being run now, right???

I have placed this particular chapter as the last chapter in the book, because I know that you will read the book though first, to   this chapter. Most people will; the book is short and to the point. Most people will only get this far, maybe they will go to the web site too. But that will be the end of their quest to become millionaires, they read the book they give up because they just do not see themselves as millionaires.

To these people, even the simple steps will seem hard to follow, the quest will end, even though it would otherwise only take 365 days to reach the level of the highest earning people in the world.

Did you know that the top 1% of income earning people, are people who earn only $75,000 annually. This amazing fact is not noticed by most people. It would seem that the politicians like to demonize the "top one percent" the "wealthy" the bad evil top one percent. By the way, all of them are in this category.

That is all that it takes to be in the top 1% in the United States. If you calculated that for the world, it would be significantly lower.

Nobody ever made a fortune just sitting around. My favorite quote, I do not know where I first heard it is, "You will have to wait a very long time to have a fried chicken fly into your mouth."

Think about it, travel, improved lifestyle, great   home, vacation/lake home, yacht, etc… Is this what you want for the future, for you and your family? What is holding you back then   from reaching the lifestyle, how about this: YOU……??

If you are your worst enemy, if YOU are holding yourself back from the life you could have, you also have the will (power) to move forward toward the top income group, and millionaire status.

Do you think that your boss, or your millionaire neighbor just won the lotto? No, he just had a plan, his plan that he executed in his way, and he made it. Now you can "make it" too. The plan is in the book, step by step, all you have to do is follow it.

Go to my web site for encouragement, for support. You will have your life changed in 365 days...ok if it takes a few more days and weeks, so what, you will get there.

You will feel your life changing all along the way as you identify the business to buy, go through the negotiating process and then hear that simple little statement from the seller, "We have a deal!."

Picture yourself in the picture you need to paint, with you, and your family in it.

Now, here is the plan, for every day of the next 365 days......if you start now; THE DAILY RECORD OF MILESTONES AND PROGRESS REPORT.

To motivate you further, order the nice hard copy DIARY of your progress, and share the contents with me as your coach.

If you start, you must follow it, with all the fervor you can muster, do it every day, even if it is just for an hour here, and an hour there, do it every day, keep your daily diary, to keep yourself on the target date and the completion of each of your needed milestones.

The progress chart as shown in Appendix 9, will be your daily diary of milestones reached each day, and a daily reminder of the progress or lack of it to motivate you to go on toward success. Keep the chart as your mantra to succeed, your daily progress chart of your success.

I might even send you helpful hints and guidance to motivate you along.

At the same time, if you are failing to provide a daily progress report, expect that I will scold you and keep pressing you toward the timely completion of all milestones. We will be partners in this venture if you like me to do that for you, just check my web site for more information.

You will be able to share your experiences online and get helpful hints and help when you need it. Can I help you any more? You bet. I can also be your partner in the purchase if you need me. See the web site for more information and details. I will not let you do this alone, I will help all the way, if you need me.

THE 365 DAY PLANNING CALENDAR FOR YOUR DAILY ACTIVITY, YOU MUST WRITE DOWN YOUR ACTIVITY AND TRACK IT DAILY IN ORDER TO SUCCEED. WE HAVE A SPECIAL HARD BOUND DIARY JUST FOR YOU ON THE WEBSITE...

On each day you MUST make a diary entry. The days do not have to be consecutive, as long as there are 365 days of work to be documented. Specifically write down what you did, be specific, accomplish some specific task every day!

Of course you can take off for a weekend get-away, but there is nothing stopping you from E-mail access for a few minutes or clipping a news article, etc. Caution, if you do one day a month as your entry, it will take you 365 months, and if you do one day entry per year, it will take you 365 years!

The pleasant surprise that I want to tell you is that if you follow the process, you should accomplish the task in a lot fewer days, probably under 100 days! The more time you spend each day, the faster you will accomplish the task of actually owning your own multi-million dollar revenue business.

Every day must have an entry of your specific work specifically listed and names of people or specific companies/sources contacted. If you are spending less than a couple hours a day on the tasks assigned, you are spending too little time.

The next day is the follow up of each prior day's work, and if not finished, then it is the continuation of work that was started and not finished. The "day" is NOT finished if the daily listed items are not completed. Until the work is completed, the day is NOT finished and you cannot go to another day.

You may also sign up online on my web site and keep the diary there, you will get hints and suggestions, and you can get a personal reply, at your option to specific questions and problems you may encounter, as well as hints to help guide you.

MAKE IT A DAILY DIARY AND DATE ENTRY TO CARRY ON WITH YOUR DISCIPLINED PROGRAM OF ACCOMPLISH-

ING THE ASSIGNED TASKS. Make a copy of the daily diary pages as presented herein and use a 3 hole puncher to make a binder to keep the diary pages and refer to them often.

If you sign up for my web site consultation, the diary and the video are sent to you at no cost.

Start toward your goal today......

Day 1- Date:

Determine the preferred business you will want to try to acquire, or choose a broad category and also choose an alternative and the ways you will be working to identify it AND start the search process. Watch the movie, OTHER PEOPLE'S MONEY.

Day 2-Date:

Make a list of sources of possible capital you will raise. List all possible ways and the amount from each: Bank lines of credit, savings, sale of stock and investments, friends, relatives and co-workers.

List the total you will be able to provide:

$_____

Day 3-Date:

Same as Day 2 until you tap all the sources of everyone you know.

Day 4-Date:

Work on all the items in day 2 and day 3.

Day 5-Date:

Finish getting responses from all the people in the last 5 days and adjust your capital proposed to be raised total that you guessed at on day 2 above.

Day 6-Date:

If you are considering acquiring your present employer, list the steps and plans for that presentation and identify the persons that are to be contacted. If the acquisition will not be your present employer, what are your search plans?

Day 7-Date:
Develop the needed information from day 6.

Day 8-Date:
Consider recruiting your co-employees if the acquired target is your present employer, and if not, consider recruiting your co-employees for the other target company. Do not forget to include possible targets who are your competitors currently, since you may be most familiar already with their management or owner.

Day 9-Date:
List other possible targets from all sources and identify third party sources such as business brokers and the like to help you identify targets. Read news articles and business publications to identify possible sales and divestitures. If you are working on your employer as the possible target, finish up a rough draft of your "pitch" for your owner or the "parent company".

Day 10-Date:
Finish up the work from day 9, and allow another day if needed.

Day 11-Date:
Definitely be finished with your initial pitch for your employer, and if third party sources, solidify who they will be and get them started searching for you.

Day 12-Date:
Plan a meeting with your employer, or parent company to discuss your thoughts about the purchase. List the time and date and prepare the questions you may have and your "pitch" about wanting to buy the company. If you are not acquiring your employer, then make daily follow-up with the finders or brokers you engaged. DO THIS DAILY.

Day 13-Date:
Continue to search, even if you plan on acquiring the employer since you may be turned down. The search process is daily, continuous and constant.

Day 14-Date:
Follow up on any open or undecided potential partner/investors that have still not made up their minds, and get a yes/no answer from each.

Day 15-Date:
Run an ad in the paper, classified and display to say that you are looking for a business to acquire. Potential ad copy "Selling your business, or looking to retire? I will buy your business for cash quickly and run it." Call......or write your own longer copy. Place the ad for the daily and weekend edition. Repeat three times each month. Follow up on the calls.

Day 16-Date:
Follow up on all loose ends from all days and watch the Movie-OTHER PEOPLE'S MONEY again, and the movie WALL STREET.

Day 17-Date:
Write down your problems to date, and a suggested solution for each one.

Day 18-Date:
Solve the problems listed in Day 17 diary.

Day 19-Date:
Have the meeting and the presentation with your employer/parent company and make the "pitch". Do not forget to bring the Due Diligence Questionnaire to obtain information in order to make your Offer.

Day 20-Date:

If you get or are getting business to acquire proposals from brokers, your ad, etc., follow up and get the information on the questionnaire or review the information that they present and do the acquisition value calculations as shown in the book to determine price for your Offer.

Day 21-Date: Complete day 20 follow-up.

Day 22-Date:

Repeat and follow up for each open item from days 1 through 22. List all open items and planned solutions.

Day 23-Date:

Repeat day 22 open items, work on each open item with a solution proposed and a time-line.

Day 24-Date:

You must be finished with any open items relating to raising the basic funds, identifying who will be your partners, if any, and determining the final total amount you will have as your capital. What is the total now and how does it compare to your previous estimate?

Day 25-Date:

Discuss your progress with the family and realize that you are moving at a great pace. Do not go further if you are still not sure of the target company or until you have a target company to acquire through making Offers or identifying the target otherwise.

Day 25 again-Date:

Take a weekend away with your loved one and give yourself a break. Make the plans you want to set as your personal goals upon reaching your millionaire/multi-millionaire goal. Is it the new house, autos, vacation? Make it BIG and think big about the goals and plans, visit the car dealer, go house looking, open house, etc.

Day 26-Date:

Identify target companies again, follow up with brokers, finders and follow up with your own company if that is applicable as to information gathering. Get the information questionnaire completed, in the acquisition target company you identified.

Day 27-Date:

Have business partners, if any, identify their area of responsibility relating to the acquisition prospects, and perfect what they will specifically do on each/with each prospect if acquired, or during the pricing phase. Call a meeting to discuss and finish all related discussions, make it today, TODAY. Have the meeting at a great opulent place to get you in the right mood. Identify how much more of an investment they can all make in order to be able to have a committed fund that is big. Determine ownership percentages for each partner and issue the stock certificates as applicable.

Day 28-Date:

Identify additional sellers and follow up regularly on all inquiries. Identify new newspapers to place classified ad, and start a simple web site (everybody can get this done easily-also check my web site for ideas) identifying your specific search.

Day 29-Date:

Follow up on any open items from any previous days.

Day 30-Date:

Do not allow any open items from day 29 to continue. Stop and finish all open items to date.

Day 31-Date:

If you do not have a target, continue daily until you do, if it is your employer, get the reply.

Day 32-Date:

Find target, get new target.

Day 33-Date:
Repeat day 32 until target or new target is available.

Day 34-Date:
What are you doing? Which target are you contemplating? What are your partners, if applicable doing and have they completed their assigned tasks?

Day 35-Date:
You are 10% to 50% of the way there!!! What did you do today?

Day 36-Date:
Continue searching, identifying, and pricing. Create E-mail letter relating to your search to be sent out to prospects. Buy mailing list or assemble one from data bases and library lists of corporations in your state or region.

Day 37-Date:
Prepare the mailing or e-mailing and send it out, take another day to finish, day 37.

Day 38-Date:
Finish up mailings and e-mailings from day 37. How many did you send, at least 250-350 I hope.

Day 39-Date:
Identify additional business brokers to contact using web search and yellow pages as well as business broker lists available state by state to make contact. Do same for day 40 and 41.

Day 40-Date:
Complete day 39 assignment.

Day 41-Date:
Complete day 39 assignment and start calling the names on the list.

Day 42-Date:

Complete the calls, and follow up on all new inquires, and related follow up as needed.

Day 43-Date:

Discuss your plans with your banker, preferably by taking him out to lunch, and make sure that he/she knows about your plans to acquire a business. Get him to suggest ways to increase your credit lines through loans that they offer or your home's equity, etc…

Day 44-Date:

Start making contact with the potential lenders, go see them and make a lunch date (they will probably pay anyway) and explain your plans, discuss any potential acquisitions that you priced to determine their general interest in the companies you reviewed to date. Get their version of how they would finance the purchase.

Day 45-Date:

Finish open items from day 44, and identify at least 4 lenders. Do not continue until you have at least 4 lenders identified and met personally.

Day 46-Date:

Determine if the lenders you have met with are likely to provide you the needed financing, or do you need more lenders to contact. If, yes make more contacts until you have a minimum of 4 lenders to work with.

Day 47-Date:

Repeat contacting brokers, looking for acquisitions. If you are working on the purchase of your present employer or a specific company on which you have now received due diligence information, review the information, study the Balance Sheet, the profits of the company and determine an Offer price.

Day 48-Date:

Prepare an Offer letter, the Letter of Intent (LOI), to present to the seller or your parent company, outlining the terms of your Offer and conditions. Make sure that in the body of the letter, or at the end of the letter containing your Offer, you insert the words "subject to obtaining sufficient financing to complete the contemplated Offer, and mutual execution of a Purchase and Sale Agreement". In addition, if the real estate now occupied by the company is owned by the seller, make sure that you propose its continued lease (see Day 50 below for additional lease ideas). You may check my web site and get some more ideas or get personal assistance, at your option.

USE THIS PROCESS FOR EVERY LOI YOU SEND, AND FOLLOW UP WITH THE DAY 49 INFORMATION AS WELL.

Day 49-Date:

Send or hand deliver your Offer. Make sure that you double check the Offer for typos, grammar and add to it any other important considerations, such as a description of your buying group, their experience in the business, or their past managerial or related information, which would show your interest in the purchase and future prospects of success. This is especially important if your Offer contains any provision that requires the seller to hold a Note, calling for the seller to receive future scheduled payments, for a portion of the Offer price.

Day 50-Date:

Wait patiently for response...NO.

Keep working on additional deals, and make as many Offers as possible on all companies as you can, you never know if the Offer you make will be accepted, or even if accepted, if you can ever reach the final stage of having the Purchase and Sale Agreement in an acceptable form. I have been in many situations where there was an agreement on the price, but then other matters were unresolved, and the deal broke down. For instance, the seller may want to lease to you the company's real estate, which he owns personally (or the parent company owns), and at the same ridiculous rate he has been charging the company to date. You will want a market price rate not the rate that he charged...you have to agree on a reasonable amount or that rental may be too expensive for you to pay over the terms of the lease. Another option that is worth while to have is the option of "first refusal to acquire the property" at either market value or at the same price as any Offer to acquire that the seller may have from a legitimate third party for the property during the time of your lease. The lease should be for a 5- or 10-year period, at a minimum, with as small a rental price escalation as possible, best tied to a formula of some type that you can live with. Another way is to have a NNN (triple net lease), which means that the tenant is responsible for all costs, operations, maintenance and increases in taxes on the property. The owner only provides the building, the tenant pays for everything else.

What did you do today, be specific, list exactly with names and specific work performed today.

Day 51-Date:
    Memo your work today.

Day 52-Date:
    Memo your work today.

Day 53-Date:
    Memo your work today.

Day 54-Date:
    Memo your work today.

Day 55-Date:
    Memo your work today.

Day 56-Date:
    Memo your work today.

Day 56-Date:
    Memo your work today.

Day 56-Date:

Write your frustrations and accomplishments to date. It is only coming up on the second month, look what you have accomplished so far!

Day 57-Date:

Take the time to celebrate accomplishments and do more of the things that worked, and less of the things that did not. Determine what were your best sources of leads, determine who are your best business brokers, etc…and stimulate them to get you some more deals.

Day 58-Date:

Continue what you have been instructed to do in the prior days. If you have an accepted Offer, start the process of preparing the information for your prospective lenders as shown in Chapter 6. If you do not have an accepted Offer, start the contact with the seller or his representative to check on the status of your Offer and get comments about your Offer. Do not expect that the seller will accept your Offer right away; it may be necessary to continue negotiations for some time and adjust price, terms or conditions.

Day 59-Date:

Review any Offers you may have outstanding, and check your pricing calculations, to make sure that they are accurate. In addition, consider having an alternative pricing plan for the acquisition if the seller makes a counter offer. If the counter offer relates to strictly wanting more money, take it under advisement for a few days. This will give you time to evaluate it with lenders, and come up with your own counter offer. In addition, if you decided with the lenders that they cannot lend you any more money for the Offer, use that to your advantage by telling that to the seller. Then, if you think that the seller's counter has merit, come back with the difference as a NOTE that the seller will get with future payments.

Day 60-Date:

Continue to evaluate any counter offers, and discuss with lenders to finalize. Do not contact the seller yet, let them wait for your response. I even suggest calling back to ask the seller his opinion about the forecasted earnings for the business, will they be as forecasted or lower, and why does he think that?

Day 61-Date:

Detail your work done today.

Day 62-Date:

Plan your call back to the seller in a few days. Work on other projects, Offers deal leads, record your progress as usual.

Day 63-Date:

Detail your work today, do all the things you have learned to do such as placing ads, calling intermediaries, etc.

Day 64-Date:

Detail your work today.

Day 65-Date:

Detail your work today, note that your work is basically the same every day! There is nothing out of the ordinary to do, it is the SAME every day, but you MUST do it every day, until you get a deal that you WILL BE ABLE TO ACQUIRE!!!!

Make a copy of the following blank numbered pages, and keep filling in the consecutive days from Day 66 to 365. You can also order or get at no cost the 365 Day Diary to keep as your personal record. Go to the web site for full information.

DO THE SAME THINGS YOU HAVE BEEN TAUGHT TO DO IN THIS BOOK. ALSO, IF YOU HAVE NOT BEEN ABLE TO ACQUIRE THE COMPANY YOU WORK FOR, TRY TO DO THE SAME FOR THE COMPANY THAT YOUR FRIENDS WORK FOR, YOUR RELATIVES WORK FOR, ETC......

You will acquire the business just as planned, but make sure that your days are filled with the required work. Go to my web site for help; in fact, you may finish your diary by day 70, or day 80 or day 100, instead of by day 365. From my own experience, it takes about 60 days or less to identify a company to acquire and make a bid, and negotiate an Offer or reject the deal.

Thus in the space of 365 days, you may be surprised to see that you may be able to acquire more than one company!

My partner and I acquired two companies with revenues approximating **$1,100,000,000 ($1.1 billion dollars)** in revenues within two weeks of each other, because we had so many deals in the Offer and bid stage. They just happened to come together that way due to the pressures on the part of one of the sellers to sell by December 31st of the year.

In fact, both of the deals described above came well within my suggested 365 day program outlined here in the book. You too will be amazed to see the deals coming together if you keep the diary and actually do something to make it happen. By this statement I do not mean one call a day, spending 5 minutes in total. If you use me as your coach by going to my web site, you will not get away with that type of daily work, you will be coached and motivated to make things happen, and quickly.

In addition, if you choose to utilize the web site, this will also allow you the opportunity to interact and directly to assist you, with things hanging up your process, or in helping you price the deal or any other problems you may experience. Use it as little or a lot, as you need it in your acquisition quest.

YOU WILL ACCOMPLISH YOUR GOAL IN LESS TIME THAN YOU THINK.

Watch and order the video, watch the suggested movie and take the time every day to document your accomplishments, you will accomplish the goal, you will!

NOW GO TO THE NEXT PAGE and make your copies for your own use to continue the daily diary, or order the DIARY to use for your daily progress and personal motivation.

Day_____-Date:
    List your activity today.

Day_____-Date:
    List your activity today.

Day_____-Date:
    List your activity today.

COPY THE PREVIOUS PAGE FOR YOUR USE IN CONTINUING THE ACTIVITY. If you want to share your diary and get coaching and motivational advice, share the same diary on my web site too. You will accomplish your goal in less days than you think, most likely before you get to 365!

The special hard bound diary and video is available to purchase or at no cost if you use any of the web site member services.

FINAL THOUGHTS

IMPORTANT MATTERS TO REMEMBER WHEN ACQUIRING A BUSINESS AND NEGOTIATING WITH THE SELLER, AND YOUR NEW LIFE AS A MILLIONAIRE/MULTI-MILLIONAIRE

You will be surprised to learn that the entire process of becoming financially successful is relatively easy and straight forward. You just needed guidance and coaching to fully understand the process.

There is nothing in this book that is difficult to understand, you do not need any special training, just follow the specific advice, and feel free to contact me and my associates directly for help.

Becoming a business owner, rather than being just an employee, is just steps away, if you know what steps to take to get there. My book will provide you the guidance and the follow-up is there for your availability, online as well.

Remember, there is nothing strange in this book, nothing you cannot do, even if you now work for a fast food franchise, and you want to own it, or one just like it!

Another "word of wisdom" for you is to remember that EVERY BUSINESS IS FOR SALE AT A PRICE. EVERY OWNER WILL SELL WHEN THERE IS REASON FOR THE OWNER TO SELL IT. **So, do not be afraid to contact business owners who are not sellers, such as competitors you do business with, etc......**

With that in mind, do not worry about dealing only with owners who are known to want to sell, such as through business listings, etc. Your direct contact with potential sellers, and your stimulation of potential sellers will be very effective through some of the ideas on the web site.

I can provide you with specific banker contacts, financing methods, or even assist you in pricing a transaction/acquisition you may be working on if you want my assistance; the full information is on my web site as well.

Sellers are just like you...except richer......or they may be a large company disposing of a subsidiary or division...maybe the subsidiary you and your co-workers now work for. You can own it, or you and your co-workers.

THEY WANT TO SELL YOU THE BUSINESS......DEAL WITH THEM AS YOUR FRIENDS, THEY LIKE YOU...THEY WANT YOU TO BUY THE BUSINESS, AND THEY ARE ALWAYS PREPARED TO HELP YOU BUY IT.

Take full advantage of their cooperation and have them assist all they can in meeting with you and your prospective lenders, describing the positive attributes of the business, and walking through the plant, offices or facilities.

Most importantly, remember, you are not only on your way to becoming a business owner, you are on your way to becoming a millionaire as well......

My wishes for your success......and in 365 days or less......

Remember, my coaching video is FREE with any of the web site memberships, my diary is free as well for your memorializing of your success in reaching the millionaire status.

Please feel free to share your success stories with me at any time.

If you are already a millionaire, my information will help you acquire larger and more profitable businesses.

Best of success in the next 365 days!!!!!!!

E-mail: info@sterlingcooper.us

SECTION TWO

For those who want to know more about the intricacies of the deal-making process, this section provides the information about specific means and methods behind the acquisition process. This is of course the textbook (if you really want to dig deeper) version of the process which is explained in its most simplified form in Section One.

This section deals with the intricacies of both privately owned companies as well as publicly traded companies. This book can be used to acquire both types, so I will cover each type of company as your particular approach may be to acquire a privately owned or a publicly traded company.

In addition, I will seek to explain in greater detail each type of acquisition as well as the methods used to finance the acquisition. Furthermore, other details of analyzing the target company and many other related matters will also describe the many ways to evaluate a potential acquisition in greater depth than described in SECTION ONE.

MERGERS

A *merger* is a combination of two corporations in which only one corporation survives and the merged corporation goes out of existence. In a merger, the acquiring company assumes the assets and liabilities of the merged company. A statutory merger differs from a *subsidiary merger,* which is a merger of two companies where the target company becomes a subsidiary of the parent company. The acquisition by General Motors of Electronic Data Systems, with its colorful CEO Ross Perot, is an example of a subsidiary merger.

A merger differs from a *consolidation,* which is a business combination whereby two or more companies join to form an entirely new company. All of the combining companies are dissolved and only the new entity continues to operate. In a consolidation, the original companies cease to exist, and their stockholders become stockholders in the new company. Despite the differences between them, the terms merger and consolidation, as is true of many of the terms in the mergers and acquisitions field, are sometimes used interchangeably. In general, when the combining firms are approximately the same size, the term consolidation applies; when the two firms differ significantly by size, merger is the more appropriate term. In practice, however, this distinction is often blurred, with the term merger being broadly applied to all combinations.

Another term that is broadly used to refer to various types of transactions is *takeover*. This term sometimes refers only to hostile transactions; at other times it refers to both friendly and unfriendly mergers.

REASONS FOR MERGERS AND ACQUISITIONS

There are several possible motives or reasons that firms might engage in mergers and acquisitions. One of the most common is expansion. Acquiring a company in a line of business or geographical area into which the company may want to expand can be a quicker way to expand than internal expansion. An acquisition of a particular company may provide certain synergistic benefits for the acquirer, such as where two lines of business complement one another. However, an acquisition may be part of a diversification program that allows the company to move into other lines of business.

Financial factors motivate some mergers and acquisitions. For example, an acquirer's financial analysis may reveal that the target is undervalued; the value of the buyer may be significantly in excess of the market value of the target, even when a premium that is normally associated with changes in control is added to the acquisition price.

MERGER FINANCING/PUBLIC AND PRIVATE COMPANIES

Mergers can be paid for in several ways. Transactions can use all cash, all securities, or a combination of cash and securities. Securities transactions may use the stock of the acquirer as well as other securities such as debentures. The stock may be either common stock or preferred stock. They may be registered, meaning they are able to be freely traded on organized exchanges, or they may be restricted, meaning they cannot be offered for public sale although private transactions among a limited number of buyers, such as institutional investors, is permissible. Smaller companies owned by just several stockholders are always private transactions.

Stock transactions may offer the seller certain tax benefits such as tax deferral that cash transactions of not provide. However, securities transactions require the parties to agree on the value of the securities. This may create some uncertainty and may give cash an advantage over securities transactions from the seller's point of view.

MERGER ADVISORS

When a company decides it wants to acquire or merge with another firm, it typically does so by utilizing the services of outside professionals. These professionals usually include investment bankers or advisors such as your author, financial advisors and attorneys.

Investment bankers may provide a variety of service, including helping to select the appropriate target, valuing the target, advising on strategy, and raising the requisite financing to complete the transaction. Merger advisory and financing fees are a significant component of the overall profitability of major investment banks.

Investment banks are often faced with the concern about conflicts between various departments of these large financial institutions, which may play very different roles in the merger process. Investment banks often have arbitrage departments that may accumulate stock in companies that may be taken over. If they purchase shares prior to the market being convinced that a company will be acquired, they may buy at a price significantly below the eventual takeover price, which usually includes a premium above the price at which that stock had been trading. This process, which is fraught with risks, is known as *risk arbitrage.* If an investment bank is advising a client regarding the possible acquisition of a company, it is imperative that a *Chinese wall* between the arbitrage department and the advisers working directly with the client be constructed so that the arbitragers do not benefit from the information that the advisers have but that is not yet readily available to the market. To derive financial benefits from this type of *inside information* is a violation of the law.

Given the complex legal environment that surrounds mergers and acquisitions, attorneys also play a key role in a successful acquisition process. Law firms may be even more important in hostile takeovers than in friendly acquisitions because part of the resistance of the target may come through legal maneuvering. Detailed filings with the Securities and Exchange Commission (SEC) may need to be completed under the guidance of legal experts.

LEVERAGED BUYOUTS

In an LBO a buyer uses debt to finance the acquisition of a company. The term is often for acquisition of public companies where the acquired company becomes private, however any purchase using assets of the company being acquired as loan collateral, can be considered an LBO. This is referred to as *going private,* because all of the public equity is purchased, usually by a small group or single buyer, and the company is no longer traded in securities markets. One version of a leveraged buyout is a *management buyout;* this is when the buyer of a company, or a division of a company, is the manager of the entity.

Most LBOs are buyouts of small and medium-sized companies or divisions of large companies. However, the largest transaction that staged Nabisco by Kohlberg Kravis & Roberts, chronicled in the book, "Barbarians at the Gate."

CORPORATE RESTRUCTURING

The term *corporate restructuring* referrs to asset sell-offs such as *divestitures.* Companies that have acquired other firms or who have developed other divisions through activities such as product extensions may decide that these divisions no longer fit into the company's plans. The desire to sell parts of a company may come from poor performance of a division, financial exigency, or a change in the strategic orientation of the company. For example, the company may decide to refocus on its *core* business and sell off non-core subsidiaries.

Other forms of corporate restructuring are cost and workforce restructuring. Many companies engage in *corporate downsizing* as they strive to become more efficient. This is encouraged by several factors, including the international competitive pressure of the globalization of world markets. It is not unusual to see companies that were reporting increased profits announce large-scale layoffs as they reacted to actions of competitors who were also taking steps to become more efficient.

Another form of corporate restructuring is *financial restructuring.* This refers to alterations in the capital structure of the firm, such as adding debt and thereby increasing financial leverage. Although this type of restructuring is important in corporate finance it is often done as part of the financing activities for mergers and acquisitions.

MERGER APPROVAL PROCESS

Most mergers and acquisitions are negotiated and friendly. This is the case of private companies but it may turn ugly if there are family members who have their own agendas for the company's future. The process usually begins when the management of one firm contacts the target company's management, often through the investment bankers of each firm. The management of both firms keep the respective boards of directors up to date on the progress of the negotiations, since mergers usually require the boards' approval. Sometimes this process works smoothly and leads to a quick merger agreement. A good example of this was the $19 billion acquisition of Capital Cities/ABC Inc., by Walt Disney Co. In spite of the size of this deal, there was a quick meeting of the minds by management of these two firms and a friendly deal was completed relatively quickly. In other instances, friendly negotiations can break down, leading to the termination of the bid or a hostile takeover.

Special Committees of the Board of Directors

The board of directors may choose to form a special committee of the board to evaluate the merger proposal. Directors who might personally benefit from the merger, such as when the buyout proposal contains provisions that management directors may potentially profit from the deal,(such as where it is proposed by one of the directors), should not be members of this committee. This process may be a good idea whether the company is privately owned or publicly traded; the more complex the transaction, the more likely that a committee will be appointed. This committee should seek legal counsel to guide it on legal issues such as the fairness of the transaction, the business judgment rule, and numerous other legal issues.

Fairness Opinions

It is common for the board to retain an outside valuation firm, such as an investment bank or a firm specializing in valuations, to evaluate the transaction's terms and price. This firm may then render a fairness opinion in which it may state that the offer is in a range that it determines to be accurate. These opinions may be somewhat terse and usually are devoid of a detailed financial analysis. Presumably, however, underlying the opinion itself is such a detailed financial analysis. As part of the opinion that is rendered, the evaluator should state what was investigated and verified and what was not.

Upon reaching agreeable terms and receiving board approval, the deal is taken before the shareholders for their approval, which is granted through a vote. The exact percentage necessary for stockholder approval depends on the articles of incorporation, which, in turn, are regulated by the prevailing state corporation laws. Following approval, each firm files the necessary documents with the state authorities in which each firm is incorporated.

MERGER NEGOTIATIONS

Except for hostile transactions, mergers are usually the product of a negotiation process between the managements of the merging companies. Typically the bidding firm or its advisor initiates the negotiations when it contacts the target's management to inquire whether the company is for sale and to express its interest in buying the target. This interest may be the product of an extensive search process to find the right acquisition candidates. However, it could be a recent interest that was inspired by the bidder's investment bank approaching it with a proposal that it believes would be a good fit for the bidder. For small-scale acquisitions, this intermediary might be a business broker or financial advisor.

Both the bidder and the target should conduct their own valuation analyses to determine what the target is worth. The value of the target for the buyer may be different from the value of that company to the seller (no big surprise here). In addition to the differing valuations that are a function of the different uses of the target assets, there may be differences in the future growth of the target that can cause the valuations to be different. If the target believes that it is worth substantially more than what the buyer is willing to pay, a friendly deal may not be possible. If, however, the seller is interested in selling and both parties are able to reach an agreement on price, a deal may be possible. Other important issues, such as financial and regulatory approvals, if necessary, would have to be completed before the negotiation process could lead to a completed transaction.

Disclosure of Merger Negotiations

For a time, was not clear what obligations publicly traded companies involved in merger negotiations had to disclose their activities. However, in the landmark *Basic Inc. V. Levinson* decision, the Supreme Court made it clear that a denial that negotiations were taking place when the opposite is the case is improper. Companies cannot deceive the market by disseminating inaccurate or deceptive information, even when the discussions are preliminary and do not show much promise of coming to fruition.

The Court's position reversed earlier court positions that had treated proposals or *negotiations* as being immaterial. The *Basic v. Levinson* decision does not go so far as to require companies to disclose all plans or internal proposals involving acquisitions. Negotiations between two potential merger partners, however, cannot be denied.

Given the requirement to disclose, a company's hand may be forced by the pressure of market speculation. The company's stock trading may pick up as speculation or rumors mount. It is often difficult to confidentially continue such negotiations and planning for any length of time. Rather than let the information slowly leak, the company has an obligation to conduct an orderly disclosure once it is clear that confidentiality may be at risk or that prior statements the company has made are no longer accurate.

Stock price movements may give rise to an inquiry from the exchange upon which the company trades or from the National Association of Securities Dealers (NASD). Although exchanges have come under criticism for being somewhat lax about enforcing these types of rules, an insufficient response from the companies involved may give rise to disciplinary actions against the companies.

SHORT-FORM MERGER

A short-form merger may take place in situations where the stockholder approval process is not necessary. Stockholder approval may be bypassed when the corporation's stock is concentrated in the hands of a small group, such as management, which is advocating the merger. Some state laws may allow this group to approve the transaction on its own without soliciting the approval of the other stockholders. The board of directors simply approves the merger by a resolution.

A short-form merger can occur only when the stockholdings of insiders are beyond a certain threshold stipulated in the prevailing state corporation laws. This percentage varies depending on the state in which the company is incorporated.

FREEZE-OUTS AND THE TREATMENT OF MINORITY SHAREHOLDERS

A majority of shareholders must provide their approval before a merger can be completed. A 51% margin is a common majority threshold; however various companies may have added specific requirements for a larger percentage to be effective such as 80%. When this majority approves the deal, minority shareholders are required to tender their shares, even though they did no vote in favor of the deal. Minority shareholders are said to be *frozen out* of their positions. This majority approval requirement is designed to prevent a *holdout problem,* which may occur when a small minority attempts to hold up the completing of a transaction unless they receive compensation over and above the acquisition stock price.

This is not to say that dissenting shareholders are without rights. Those shareholders who believe that their shares are worth significantly more than what the terms of the merger are offering can go to court to pursue their *shareholder appraisal rights.* There they can demand a cash settlement for the difference between the "fair value" of their shares and the compensation they actually received. Of course, corporations resist these maneuvers because the payment of cash for the value of shares will raise problems relating to the positions of other stockholders. Such suits are very difficult for dissenting shareholders to win.

I advised a client once to obtain the valuation of the true value of the shares and so many stockholders took me up on that offer, that this action caused the proposed buyer to cancel the transaction. We later made our own higher offer for the company which was accepted by its Board of Directors, and my buying group was successful in the acquisition. The original offer was for a $5.50 price per share, while our offer was at $13.50 a share (no wonder it was accepted).

PURCHASE OF ASSETS COMPARED WITH PURCHASE OF STOCK

The most common form of merger or acquisition involves purchasing the stock of the merged or acquired concern. An alternative to the stock acquisition is to purchase the target company's assets. In doing so, the acquiring company can limit its acquisitions to those parts of the firm that coincide with the acquirer's needs. When a significant part of the target remains after the asset acquisition, the transaction is only a partial acquisition of the target. When all the target's assets are purchased, the target becomes a corporate shell with only the cash or securities that it received from the acquisition as assets. In these situations, the corporation may choose to pay stockholders a liquidating dividend and dissolve the company.

ASSUMPTION OF THE SELLER'S LIABILITIES

If the acquirer buys all the target's stock, it then assumes the seller's liabilities. The change in stock ownership does not free the new owners of the stock from the seller's liabilities. Most state laws provide this protection, which is sometimes referred to as *successor liability.* One way the acquirer can try to avoid assuming the seller's liabilities is to buy only the assets rather than the stock of the target. In cases where a buyer purchases a substantial portion of the target's assets, the courts have ruled that the buyer is responsible for the seller's liabilities. This is known as the *trust funds doctrine.* The court may also rule that the transaction is a *de facto* merger - a merger that occurs when the buyer purchases the assets of the target, and, for all intents and purposes, the transaction is treated as a merger.

The issue of successor liability may also apply to other commitments of the firm, such as union contracts. The National Labor Relations Board's position on this issue is that collective bargaining agreements are still in effect after acquisitions.

ASSET SELLOFFS

When a corporation chooses to sell off all its assets to another company, it becomes a corporate shell with cash and/or securities as its sole assets. The firm may then decide to distribute the cash to its stockholders as a liquidating dividend and go out of existence. The proceeds of the assets sale can also be distributed through a *cash repurchase tender offer.* That is, the firm makes a tender offer for its own shares using the proceeds of the asset sale to pay for shares. The firm may also choose to continue to do business and use its liquid assets to purchase other assets or companies.

HOLDING COMPANIES

Rather than a merger or an acquisition, the acquiring company may choose to purchase only a portion of the target's stock and act as a *holding company,* which is a company that owns sufficient stock to have a controlling interest in the target.

If an acquirer buys 100% of the target, the company is known as a *wholly owned subsidiary.* However, it is not necessary to own all of a company's stock to exert control over it. In fact, even a 51% interest may not be necessary to allow a buyer to control a target. For companies with a widely distributed equity base, effective working control can be established with as little as 10 to 20% of the outstanding common stock. This may be the case with long-established family holdings that can be traced to a founding family member. While the family no longer holds a controlling interest such as in: Walgreens Drugs, Ford Motor, Dillard's Department Stores, Motorola, Standard Oil, Hess Oil, etc., they may continue to hold key positions in the company thus effectively controlling the business, even though they may only own a small percentage of the outstanding shares.

Advantages

Holding companies have certain advantages that can make this form of control transaction preferable to an outright acquisition. Some of these advantages are listed next.

- *Lower cost.* With a holding company structure, an acquirer can attain control of a target for a much smaller investment than would be necessary in a 100% stock acquisition. Obviously, a smaller number of shares to be purchased will permit a lower total purchase price to be set. In addition, since fewer shares are demanded in the market, there is less upward price pressure on the firm's stock and the cost per share may be lower. The acquirer can attempt to minimize the upward price pressure by buying shares gradually over an extended period of time. However, the assets of the target company cannot be used in this instance.
- *No control premium.* Since 51% of the shares were not purchased, the control premium that is normally associated with 51 to 100% stock acquisitions would not have to be paid.
- *Control with fractional ownership.* As noted, working control can be established with less than 51% of the target company's shares. This may allow the controlling company to exert certain influence over the target in a manner that will further the controlling company's objectives, such as becoming a member of the Board of Directors.
- *Approval not required.* To the extent that is allowable under federal and state laws, a holding company may simply purchase shares in a target without having to solicit the approval of the target company's shareholders. This has become more difficult to accomplish because various laws make it difficult for the holding company to achieve such control if serious shareholder opposition exists.

Disadvantages

Holding companies also have certain disadvantages that make this type of transaction attractive only under certain circumstances. Some of these disadvantages are listed here.

- *Multiple taxation.* The holding company structure adds another layer to the corporate structure. Normally, stockholder income is subject to double taxation. Income is taxed at the corporate level, and some of the remaining income may then be distributed to stockholders in the form of dividends. Stockholders are then taxed individually on this dividend income. Holding companies receive dividend income from a company that has already been taxed at the corporate level. This income may then be taxed at the holding company level before it is distributed to stockholders. This amounts to *triple taxation* of corporate income. If the holding company owns 80% or more of a subsidiary's voting equity, the dividends received from the parent company are not taxed. When the ownership interest is less than 80%, 80% of the dividends are not subject to taxation.
- *Antitrust problems.* A holding company combination may face some of the same antitrust concerns that an outright acquisition is faced with. If the regulatory authorities do find the holding company structure anticompetitive, however, it is comparatively easy to require the holding company to divest itself of its holdings in the target, or for the target to sell of certain subsidiaries.
- *Not 100% Owner.* Although the fact that a holding company can be formed without a 100% share purchase may be a source of cost savings, it leaves the holding company with other outside shareholders who will have some controlling influence in the company. This may lead to disagreements over the direction of the company.

JOINT VENTURES

Another type of business combination is a *joint venture*. This is when certain firms enter into an agreement to provide certain resources toward the achievement of a particular business goal. For example, one company could provide financing while another firm contributes physical assets or technological expertise. The venture would realize certain returns and they would be shared among the venture partners according to some prearranged formula. This has become particularly the case with large projects that may strain the capital or resources of one firm.

In recent years a number of international joint ventures have taken place in the automobile industry. U.S. companies have entered into agreements with Japanese or Chinese manufacturers to take advantage of certain comparative advantages these firms might enjoy, such as technological advantages and quality controls or labor costs. Some of the ventures provided for the establishment of manufacturing facilities in the United States to produce automobiles to be sold in the U.S. market under American manufacturers' brand names. The goal was to enable U.S. manufacturers to produce cars that offered some of the beneficial features of Japanese or German cars, such as quality, durability, and fuel economy, without having to invest the significant resources to develop this technology and manufacturing know-how. The foreign manufacturers would also be able to take advantage of the American manufacturers' brand names, distribution network, and other marketing advantages that American manufacturers enjoyed, such as good financing subsidiaries. In addition, the agreements using U.S. manufacturing facilities and U.S. workers would allow Japanese, German or Chinese manufacturers to avoid trade restrictions that might affect them if they were to sell directly to the U.S. market. One example of such an arrangement was the joint venture between Chrysler Motors and Mitsubishi Motors in which the companies agreed to jointly manufacture automobiles in Bloomington, Illinois.

It is difficult to determine the optimal level of profitability for each company. One important guide is the profitability of similar-size firms in the same industry. Several measures can be utilized, such as average industry profits or the industry average rate of return on equity. The company may come under increased scrutiny and pressure if it falls too far below the industry average. Often, one partner in a Joint Venture has the right to acquire the other partner under certain circumstances or at a pre-determined price.

LEVERAGED BUYOUT PROCESS

LBOs are acquisitions financed primarily with debt. They are usually cash transactions in which the cash is borrowed by the acquiring firm. Much of the debt may be secured by the assets of the corporation being taken private.

The target company's assets are used to provide collateral for the debt that is going to be incurred to finance the acquisition. Thus, the collateral value of these assets needs to be assessed. This type of lending is often called *asset-based lending (ABL LENDERS)*. Firms with assets that have a high collateral value can more easily obtain such loans; thus, LBOs are often easier to conduct in capital-intensive industries-firms that usually have more assets that can be used as collateral than non-capital intensive firms; LBO activity is more predominant in manufacturing than in non-manufacturing industries. LBOs are possible for firms that do not have an abundance of assets that can be used as collateral. Service industries are one example. They tend not to have as high asset values, but they may still be good LBO candidates if their cash flows are high enough to service the interest payments on the debt that will arise when the buyout is completed, and alternative lenders, other than ABL lenders are approached for financing.

The following is a step-by-step process of a hypothetical leveraged buyout in which a division of a public firm is taken private through a management buyout. Although process is presented in steps, to make it easier to understand, the exact order of the steps may vary somewhat depending on the particular circumstances of the layout.

Step 1.

The decision to divest is *made.* The management of Diversified Industries (DI) has observed that the chemicals division is performing poorly and has become a drain on the whole company. It is decided at a board of directors meeting that DI will divest itself of the chemicals division. The company does not want to be in the chemicals industry and would rather focus its resources on areas that show more promise. DI's managers are concerned about the welfare of the division's employees. They inform the management of the chemicals division of their plans and express their interest in remaining with the division after divestiture.

Step 2.

Management of the division makes the decision to purchase the division. After much deliberation, the managers of the chemicals division decide to attempt a buyout. The reasons can vary from a belief that the parent company never realized the true potential of the division to basic concerns about job security. They then determine the financial resources they can devote toward its purchase. The management of the overall company, as well as the management of the division, approach DI's investment bank to assess the availability of LBO financing.

Step 3.

A financial analysis of the division is *conducted.* A financial analysis of the chemicals division is conducted. The main focus of this analysis is to determine whether the division, on its own, is sufficiently creditworthy to support the assumption of the debt levels needed to finance the buyout. Several financial measures are often used to facilitate this assessment; three of the more frequently used measures for LBOs are highlighted here.

Division's book value of assets. This measure indicates the value of the division's assets carried on the firm's books. It may or may not accurately reflect the value of the division's assets.

Replacement value of assets. This is the cost to a purchaser of replacing the assets. It is a more accurate reflection of the true value of the division's assets, since it provides a better indication of the value the market places on these assets.

Liquidation value of assets. This measure indicates what a lender might receive if the assets were liquidated, such as in the case of a bankruptcy. It is one measure of the lender's protection in the event the division fails as an independent company. It is an imperfect measure, however, since assets sometimes sell at fire sale prices in liquidation proceedings.

Step 4.

The purchase/price is determined. Diversified Industries agrees on a sale price that is in excess of the value of the division's liquidation value of assets. This value should be considered a floor value because, presumably, DI could sell off the division's assets for at least this amount. How much above the liquidation value depends on the relative bargaining abilities of the groups involved in the transaction as well as the intensity of D1's desire to rid itself of the chemicals division. A firm may sometimes feel an obligation to the employees of the division and will allow them to buy the division at a price that is not too far above what would be considered a giveaway of company assets. However, the LBO sector sometimes features intense bidding contests for LBO targets. Such an atmosphere puts pressure on the management of the parent company to seek out the maximum value attainable through an auction process. I have participated in many such auctions, where to seller gives the appearance of having a fair auction, but somehow, mysteriously, the management group happens to be the highest bidder in a blind auction, usually by a token amount.

Step 5.

Investment by the division's management is determined. Once the purchase price has been determined, the managers of the division have to decide the extent of their own capital investment in the transaction.

This is often required as a condition of the lenders because managers who have a personal, financial stake in the future of the company will presumably help ensure the company's financial well-being and thereby theoretically protect the lenders' interests. Although the amount of this investment may be small compared with the total capital raised, it may constitute a significant part of the total wealth of the managers. Often, the management group invites private equity groups to provide a capital investment in return for an ownership interest, with the idea that this group can later exit its investment though an IPO (initial public offering of stock). This method will also provide for the potential of a significant increase in the value of the share-ownership of the entire stockholder group as the stock becomes publicly traded.

Step 6.

The lending group is assembled. At this point in the process, the investment banker puts together the lending group—the group of lenders who will supply the capital that is borrowed to pay for the LBO. Small transactions sometimes involve just one lender. In larger transactions, however, one lender may not want to commit to the full amount. Lenders seek protection against the risks of default by diversifying their assets. The effort to spread out the exposure to this particular LBO among several lenders is part of that process. LBO funds are an example of investors who wish to partake in the high returns available by investing in LBOs while retaining the protection provided by diversification. These investors pool together their resources to invest in a diversified group of leveraged buyouts. (LBO funds are discussed later in this chapter.) The process of assembling the debt capital can become more complicated for larger transactions.

External equity investment is acquired. The investment banker, in conjunction with the parties to the transaction, determines whether an additional outside equity investment is necessary. This may be necessary if sufficient debt is not available in the market for this type of transaction. It may also be a requirement of the lenders who may feel that the risk level of the transaction does not warrant the high percentage of debt relative to equity that would be necessary without outside private equity investors. Step 7 is performed in conjunction with steps 5, 6, and 8 since the results of this analysis will affect the investors' willingness to support the transaction.

Step 8.

Cash flow analysis is conducted. Once the relative components of debt and equity have been tentatively assessed, a cash flow analysis is conducted to determine whether the division's cash flow will be sufficient to service the interest payments on the debt. This is usually done by assuming restrictive budgets for the time period necessary to payoff the debt. These restrictions may come in the form of lower research and development and capital outlays. Often the cash flow analysis will be redone under different assumptions that will alter the financial structure of the deal, thereby requiring steps 5 through 7 to be repeated. Several repetitions of this iterative process may occur before the financial structure is agreed to.

Step 9.

Financing is agreed to. If the cash flows are sufficient to service the debt, the financing is agreed to and the deal is consummated.

The preceding scenario was explained within the framework of a management buyout. The process is similar, however, when the LBO is conducted by an outside entity such as a corporation. The key is the target's ability to raise and service the requisite debt financing

FINANCING FOR LEVERAGED BUYOUTS

Two general categories of debt are used in leveraged buyouts—secured and unsecured debt—and they are often used together. Secured debt, sometimes called *asset-based lending (ABL LENDING),* may contain two subcategories of debt: senior debt and intermediate-term debt. In some smaller buyouts these two categories are considered one. In larger deals there may be several layers of secured debt, which vary according to the term of the debt and the types of assets used as security. Unsecured debt, sometimes known as *subordinated debt and junior subordinated debt,* lacks the protection of secured debt but generally carries a higher return to offset this additional risk.

Within the category of secured financing there are two subcategories—senior debt and intermediate term debt.

Senior Debt

Senior debt comprises loans secured by liens on particular assets of the company. The collateral, which provides the downside risk protection required by lenders, includes physical assets such as land, plant and equipment, accounts receivable, and inventories. The lender projects the level of accounts receivable that the firm would average during the period of the loan. This projection is usually based on the amount of accounts receivable the firm has on its books at the time the loan is closed, as well as the historical level of these assets.

Lenders will commonly advance 85% of the value of the accounts receivable and 50% of the value of the target's inventories, excluding the work in progress. Accounts receivable, which are normally collected in short time periods such as 30 days, are more valuable than those of longer periods. The lender has to make a judgment on the value of the accounts receivable; similar judgments have to be made as to the marketability of inventories. The process of determining the collateral value of the LBO candidate's assets is sometimes called *qualifying* the assets. Assets that do not have collateral value, such as accounts receivable that are unlikely to be collected or pre-paid expenses, are called unqualified assets for collateral purposes.

Intermediate-term Debt

Intermediate-term debt is usually subordinate to the senior debt. It is often backed up by fixed assets such as land and plant and equipment. The collateral value of these assets is usually based on their liquidation value. Debt backed up by equipment typically has a term of several years. It ac be refinanced later. Loans backed up by real estate tend to have longer terms, typically 10-15 years. The relationship between the loan amounts and the appraised value of the assets varies depending on the circumstances of the buyout. Generally, debt can equal 80% of the appraised value of equipment and 50%-75% of the value of real estate. These percentages will vary depending on the area of the country and the conditions of the real estate market. The collateral value of assets, such as equipment and real estate, is based on the auction value of these assets, not the value that they carry on the firm's books. When the auction value is greater than the book value of the assets, the firm's borrowing capacity is greater than what its balance sheet would reflect. Lenders look for certain desirable characteristics in borrowers even when the borrower has valuable collateral. Some of these factors are as follows.

Desirable Characteristics of Secured LBO Candidates

There are certain characteristics which lenders look for in a prospective LBO candidate, as described below.

Stable cash flows.

One of the most important characteristics of LBO candidates is the existence of regular cash flows and strong assets as determined by examining the pattern of historical cash flows for the company, and its historical balance sheets. Statistical measures such as the standard deviation can be used to measure this variability. The more erratic the historical cash flows, the greater the perceived risk in the deal. Even in cases where the average cash flows exceed the loan payments by a comfortable margin, the existence of high variability can worry a lender. A business that has erratic financial results would need a reasonable and believable explanation of the possibility of predictable results in future years.

While historical cash flows are used to project future cash flows, the past may be an imperfect guide to the future. Market conditions change and the future business environment can be less favorable than what the company's historical data reflect. The lender has to make a judgment as to whether the past is going to be a reliable indicator of what the future will hold. Lenders and borrowers usually construct cash flow projections based on restrictive budgets and new cost structures. Such budget planning takes place for both secured and unsecured LBOs, but it is even more critical for cash flow LBOs. These budgets may include lower research and development expenditures and labor costs. The target attempts to find areas where costs can be cut-at least temporarily. These cost savings can be used to meet the loan payments on the LBO debt. The importance of cash flows to LBOs was underscored by a recent study that showed that buyout premiums were positively related to the firm's free cash flow. That is, the market is willing to pay higher premiums for greater cash flow protection certainty.

Stable and experienced management.

Stability is often judged by the length of time that management is in place. Lenders feel more secure when management is experienced; that is, if management has been with the firm for a reasonable period of time, it may imply that there is a greater likelihood that management will stay on after the deal is completed. Creditors often judge the ability of management to handle an LBO by the cash flows that were generated by the firms they managed in the past.

Room for significant cost reductions.

Additional debt used to finance an LBO usually imposes additional financial pressures on the target. These pressures can be somewhat alleviated if the target can significantly cut costs in some areas, such as fewer employees, reduced capital expenditures, elimination of redundant facilities, and tighter controls on operating expenses.

Equity interest of owners.

The collateral value of assets provides downside risk protection to lenders. The equity investment of the managers or buyers and outside parties also acts as a cushion to protect lenders. The greater the equity cushion, the more likely secured lenders will not have to liquidate the assets. The greater the managers' equity investment, the more likely they will stay with the firm if the going gets tough.

Ability to cut costs.

Many LBO candidates are inefficient and need cost restructuring. LBO deal makers work on finding areas where cost can be cut without damaging the business. When these cost cuts are focused on areas of waste or unnecessary expenditures, they can be of great benefit to the LBO candidate. The target can suffer, however, when the cuts are made in areas that will hurt the company in the future. Cuts in research and development, for example, may cause the company to fall behind its competitors and eventually lose market share. Industry factors may determine the extent to which research and product development expenditures can be cut. Reductions are often difficult to implement in rapidly evolving, high-tech industries, or in businesses with relatively high fixed costs that realistically can not be reduced, such as wages set by union agreements or pension costs mandated by law or contracts.

Limited debt on the firm's balance sheet.

The lower the amount of debt on the firm's balance sheet relative to the collateral value of the firm's assets, the greater is the borrowing capacity of the firm. If the firm's balance sheet is already encumbered by significant financial leverage, then it may be more difficult to finance the leveraged buyout. The prior debt limits the company's borrowing capacity. Even companies with low pre-LBO debt levels end up exhausting their borrowing capacity after the LBO.

I have been involved in LBO's whose largest asset that was being acquired was the cash balance on its balance sheet. Even then, lenders are often perplexed when a large cash balance is present since from a practical stand point they do not have a practical means of placing a lien on the cash balance.

Separable, non-core businesses.

If the LBO candidate owns non-core businesses that can be sold off to quickly "pay down" a significant part of the firm's post-LBO debt, the deal may be easier to finance. This may be important for both secured and unsecured LBOs. Problems can occur when debt is incurred based on an unrealistic sales price for non-core divisions (this can often occur since the selling parent company can force un unrealistically high purchase price on the divested division). The inability to sell components of the firm on a timely basis, at prices similar to those expected by investment bankers, was one of the main factors that caused the bankruptcy of the Campeau Corporation (which acquired some of the best known names in retailing). Deals that are dependent on the large-scale sell-off of most of the firm's businesses are referred to as *breakup LBOs*.

Other factors.

Each LBO candidate has a different product or service and a different history. The existence of unique or intangible factors can provide the impetus for a lender to provide financing when some ambivalence exists. A dynamic, growing, and innovative company can provide lenders with sufficient incentives to overlook some shortcomings. However, these factors, which are sometimes referred to as "the story," can only go so far in making up for deficiencies.

Costs of Secured Debt

The costs of senior debt vary depending on market conditions. Senior debt rates are often quoted in relation to other interest rates such as the prime rate. They often range between two and five points above the prime rate for a quality borrower with quality assets. The *prime rate* is the rate that banks charge their best customers. Less creditworthy borrowers will have to pay more. Interest rates, in turn, are determined by many economy-wide factors, such as the Federal Reserve's monetary policy or the demand for loan able funds. Therefore, rates on secured LBO financing will be as volatile as other interest rates in the marketplace. However, these rates will also be influenced by the lenders' demand for participation in this type of financing. LBO rates may fluctuate even more than other rates in the economy.

Sources of Secured Financing

Secured LBO financing is often obtained through the asset-based lending subsidiary of a major money center bank or through the thousands of ABL lenders.

Financing Gap

LBO lenders like financing buyouts in which the target company has significant assets that can be used as collateral. However, even then their value may not be sufficient to cover the total purchase cost of the target. In this case, a financing gap exists; that is, the financing needs of the leveraged buyout exceed the collateral coverage. At this point, the investment bank (or buyer group) must seek other sources of financing. These sources can be covered by equity, subordinated debt, or a loan that exceeds the collateral value of the assets. Equity capital may be raised by exchanging an ownership interest in the target to outside investors in exchange for financing. *Subordinated debt* is debt that has a secondary claim on the assets used for collateral. As a result of this inferior claim on assets, this debt usually has higher interest costs. Loans beyond the collateral value of the target's assets are often motivated by less tangible forms of security for the lender, such as the existence of dependable cash flows, which make it more likely that the debt payments will be met.

Unsecured LBO Financing

Leveraged buyouts are typically financed by a combination of secured and unsecured debt. The unsecured debt, sometimes referred to as subordinated and junior subordinated debt, is debt that has a secondary claim of the assets of the LBO target—hence the term *subordinated.* The term *mezzanine layer financing* is often applied to this financing because it has both debt and equity characteristics;

although it is clearly debt, it is equity-like in that lenders typically receive warrants that may be converted into equity in the target. Warrants are a derivative security offered by the corporation itself. They allow the warrant holder to buy stock in the corporation at a certain price for a defined time period.

When the warrants are exercised, the share of ownership of the previous equity holders is diluted. This dilution often occurs just at the time the target is becoming profitable. It is then that the warrants become valuable. In a management buyout, for example, managers may have held a very high percentage of ownership in the company. If the target becomes profitable in the future, management might have its share of ownership dramatically diluted by exercising the warrants by the junior subordinated lenders. Although such forms of debt may have undesirable characteristics for management, they may be necessary to convince lenders to participate in the LBO without the security of collateral.

It is important to be aware of the role of the warrants in computing the return to the providers of mezzanine layer financing. Their return is more than simply the interest payments they receive. The value of the equity derived from the exercise of the warrants, adjusted for the probability that the firm will be sufficiently profitable to justify exercising of the warrants, needs to be added to the interest payments to compute the return.

Cash Flow LBOs

The risk that a lender incurs when a loan is made is that the interest and principal payments may not be met. Collateral can be a source of protection in the event these payments are not made. Dependable cash flows, however, can also be an invaluable source of protection. The more regular the cash flows, the more assurance the lender has that the loan payments will be made.

Unsecured leveraged buyouts are sometimes called *cash flow LBOs*. These deals tend to have a more short-term focus, with a maturity of 3 to 6 years. In contrast, the secured LBOs might have a financing maturity of up to 10 years. Cash flow LBOs allow firms that are not in capital-intensive industries to be LBO candidates. This is most important in the U.S. economy, since the United States has become a more service-oriented economy. Many service industries, such as advertising, lack significant physical assets relative to their total revenue but have large cash flows. Cash flow LBOs are generally considered riskier for lenders. In return for the burden of assuming additional risk, lenders of unsecured financing typically require a higher interest rate as well as an *equity kicker*. This equity interest often comes in the form of warrants or direct shares in the target. The percentage of ownership can be as little as 10% or as high as 80% of the companies' shares. The percentage is higher when the lender perceives greater risk.

Just because the loan is not fully collateralized does not mean that the lenders are not protected by the firm's assets. Unsecured lenders are entitled to receive the proceeds of the sale of the secured assets after full payment has been made to the secured lenders. Unsecured LBOs started to become more common in the mid-1980s, when the demand for mergers, acquisitions, and LBOs drove up the premiums paid for targets. As premiums rose above the value of the target's assets, lenders were increasingly being requested to lend beyond the limits of the target's collateral. Michael Milken of the well known DREXEL BURNHAM firm pioneered the concept of financing LBO's with (Junk Bonds) unsecured or subordinated debt. The unsecured component received a higher return to compensate for assuming the greater risk. Most of the larger LBOs that attract so much media attention are largely unsecured deals.

The main advantage of mezzanine layer financing is the profit potential that is provided by either a direct equity interest or warrants convertible into equity to go along with the debt position of the lender. This added return potential offsets the lack of security that secured debt has. There are often several types of mezzanine layer financing in a leveraged buyout. The debt is structured in several layers, with each subordinate to another layer. Each layer that is subordinate to the layer before it in order of liquidation priority generally contains additional compensation for the lender to offset the lower degree of security.

EMPLOYEE STOCK OWNERSHIP PLANS

A large component of the dramatic growth of employee stock ownership plans (ESOPs) that occurred in the United States in the 1980s can be attributed to their role in mergers, acquisitions, and leveraged buyouts (LBOs). ESOPs are involved in mergers and LBOs in two main ways: as a financing vehicle for LBOs and as an anti-takeover device. Bidders and employees discovered that they could make a bid for a firm through an ESOP and realize significant tax benefits that would help lower the cost of the buyout. For their part, targets learned that ESOPs could provide them with an effective anti-takeover defense.

Employee stock ownership plans are allowable under the Employee Retirement Income Security Act of 1974 (ERISA), a law that governs the administration and structure of corporate pension plans. ERISA specified how corporations could utilize ESOPs to provide employee benefits. An ESOP provides a vehicle whereby the employer corporation can make tax-deductible contributions of cash or stock into a trust. These trust assets are then allocated in some predetermined manner to the employee participants in the trust. The corporation's contributions to the ESOP are tax deductible. Moreover, the employees are not taxed on the contributions they are entitled to receive until they withdraw them from the ESOP.

ESOPs are required to invest in the employer's stock. They can buy stock in subsidiaries of the employer's corporation if the employer corporation owns more than 50% of the subsidiary's stock. Unlike pension plans, ESOPs do not try to lower the risk level of their assets by diversifying. Although pension plans seek to invest in a variety of assets so as to lower risk, ESOPs are designed to hold only cash, cash equivalents, or the stock of the employer corporation.

TYPES OF PENSION PLANS

The ESOP is an alternative or a supplement to a corporate pension plan. The three main types of pension plans are defined benefit plans, defined contribution plans, and profit-sharing plans.

Defined Benefit Plans

In a defined benefit plan, an employer agrees to pay employees specific benefits upon retirement. These benefits may be defined in terms of a dollar amount per month or a percentage of the last year's salary, or several years' salary, according to preset formula. Government workers often have such plans.

Defined Contribution Plans

Employers guarantee a specific contribution, rather than a specific benefit, in a defined contribution plan. The employee's pension payments depend on the investment performance of the benefit fund. These funds may be managed by a union that oversees the investment of the funds. Defined contribution plans can be riskier for employees, since their pension payments will depend on the investment performance of the fund, which is not guaranteed by the employer. ESOPs are a defined contribution plan in which the contributions are the employer's stock as opposed to cash.

Profit-Sharing Plans

A profit-sharing plan is even riskier for employees than a defined contribution plan. Here the contributions made by the employer are a function of the company's profitability. The contributions are usually specified as a percentage of the firm's pretax profits.

CHARACTERISTICS OF ESOPS

The General Accounting Office (GAO) conducted a survey of firms that had ESOPs in place. It found that 91% of the respondents indicated that the primary reason for starting an ESOP was to provide benefits to employees; 74% cited tax incentives; and 70% mentioned improved productivity.

Using data derived from the GAO as well as other sources, however, it was discovered that half the plans were used to buy the company. In approximately one-third of ESOPs, employees owned a majority of the company, and in almost another one-third they owned less than 25% of the firm.

Employers with ESOPs contribute approximately 8 to 10% of their payroll to the ESOP each year.

LEVERAGED VERSUS UNLEVERAGED ESOPS

ESOPs can be divided into two groups: leveraged and unleveraged. Leveraged ESOPs, called LESOPs, are those that borrow, whereas unleveraged ESOPs do not borrow. Leveraged ESOPs are of more interest as a vehicle for leveraged buyouts. The size of the contributions that the corporation can make to the ESOP depends on whether it is a leveraged ESOP. Unleveraged ESOPs can make annual contributions of up to 15% of the payroll. With leveraged ESOPs, the corporation borrows to buy its own stock. The company then makes a contribution to the ESOP that is used to pay the principal and interest on the loan.

CORPORATE FINANCE USES OF ESOPS

The world of corporate finance has developed several innovative uses for ESOPs. Some of these uses are as described below.

Buyouts

ESOPs have been widely used as a vehicle to purchase companies. This technique has been used for both private and public firms. Over 60% of leveraged ESOPs have been used to buyout owners of private companies.

Divestitures

ESOPs have also been widely used as divestiture and sell-off vehicles; 37% of the leveraged ESOPs have been used as divestiture vehicles. For example, the Hospitals Corporation of America sold off 104 of its 180 hospitals to a new corporation, HealthTrust, which was owned by its employees through a leveraged ESOPs.

Rescue of Failing Companies

The employees of a failing company can use an ESOP as an alternative to bankruptcy. Several examples of this have occurred in the troubled steel industry. The employees of McLouth Steel, for example, exchanged wage concessions for stock in the company in an effort to avoid bankruptcy proceedings. Weirton Steel's rescue is another example.

Raising Capital

An ESOP can also be used to raise new capital for the corporation. The use of an ESOP as an alternative to a public offering of stock is discussed later in this book; 11 % of ESOPs have been used for this purpose.

VOTING OF ESOP SHARES

Voting the ESOP shares can be an important issue when the ESOP is used as a tool in mergers and leveraged acquisitions. *If* target corporation can try to use the ESOP as a white squire by placing stock in the plan. It then hopes that the ESOP shares will vote with management on major decisions such as approving mergers and other major transactions. Use of ESOPs as an anti-takeover defense is discussed in greater detail later in this chapter. We will see that the voting rights of the shares is an important determinant of the use of the ESOP as an anti-takeover defense.

In public corporations, employee shareholders in an ESOP hold shares that have voting rights. This may not be the case, however, for private corporations. Whether or not the ESOP employee participants in private corporations retain the right to vote their shares depends on the prevailing state laws, which vary from state to state. Some states provide for *limited voting rights,* which do not allow full voting privileges for the individual employee shareholders.

CASH FLOW IMPLICATIONS

Cash flows are critically important to the success of a leveraged buyout. ESOP stock contributions positively affect the cash flow of all corporations whether or not they are involved in a leveraged buyout.

Let us assume that a corporation makes a $1,000 stock contribution to an ESOP. Since the contribution is in the form of stock, there is no cash outlay. Tax laws allow the corporation a $500 *tax deduction.* which improves the firm's cash flow by the same amount. We should not conclude, however, that these cash flow benefits are costless. The benefits may be partially or completely offset by a dilution in the equity holdings of the non-ESOP stockholders. This may be reflected in lower earnings per share.

VALUATION OF STOCK CONTRIBUTED INTO THE ESOP

The cash flow of the corporation can be significantly improved by the tax benefits of the ESOP contribution. In deciding the size of the stock contribution, the company must first determine its value. For public corporations this is clear, since there is a readily available market value to use. The problem is less clear for private corporations. It becomes necessary to rely on the various techniques of securities valuation for privately held companies. The services of a business appraiser or an expert in business valuations may be utilized to determine the securities value. A valuation is particularly important in a LESOP to determine that accurate consideration was paid for the ESOP shares.

ELIGIBILITY OF ESOPS

The ESOP must fulfill certain requirements to qualify for tax deductibility benefits. It must include all employees 21 years old and over with one year of service during which they have worked 1,000 hours.

PUT OPTIONS OF ESOPS

Employees may receive a put option to sell their stock back to the employer corporation within 60 days of receiving it. If they do not choose to exercise this option in 60 days, they may receive another 60-day option in the following year. Put options may even have a life of up to five years. The put option may be waived if the corporation does not have sufficient retained earnings to purchase the stock. If retained earnings are not sufficient, the company can defer the put option to a year in which it does have sufficient retained earnings.

If a private company with an ESOP decides to go public in the future, the put option may be terminated. This is the case when the ESOP shares are included in the registration statement for going public.

DIVIDENDS PAID

Dividends paid by the employer corporation on the ESOP shares are charged against retained earnings. These dividend payments are a tax-deductible expense if they are paid in the following manner:

1. Dividends are paid directly to ESOP participants.
2. Dividends are paid directly to the ESOP, which distributes them to the ESOP participants within 90 days of the close of the plan year.
3. Dividends on the ESOP are used to make payments on an ESOP loan.

EMPLOYEE RISK AND ESOPS

By accepting part of their compensation in the form of stock in the employer corporation, workers take on an increased risk. They are, in effect, "putting more of their eggs in one basket." If the company fails, employees will lose not only their regular source of income but perhaps also the value of their pension.

Corporations can offset some of this risk by contributing convertible preferred shares instead of shares of common stock. The law requires that the shares be convertible in common stock to be eligible for the plan. Preferred shares have a higher priority in bankruptcy than common stock. If the value of the firm's stock increases, the employees will be able to participate in this growth by converting to shares of common stock. The risk-reduction benefits of using preferred stock instead of common stock are limited, given that both preferred and common stockholders tend to suffer significant losses in bankruptcy proceedings, although preferred shareholders do a little better than common stockholders.

SECURITIES LAWS AND ESOPS

Under federal securities laws, the sale of stock to an ESOP is not considered an issuance of securities to the public. When this stock is issued, it generally comes with a letter stating it is not subject to a sale to a third party. State corporation laws differ in their treatment of ESOPs. For example, New York laws do not require the registration of the donated securities, but they do require that the ESOP be registered as a securities dealer.

TAX BENEFITS OF LESOPS

One of the more valuable characteristics of LESOPs is their unique tax benefits. These are described next.

Deductibility of Interest and Principal Payments

If a corporation borrows directly from a bank, only the interest payments are tax deductible. However, if the LESOP borrows from a bank, or other lender such as an insurance company, both the interest and the principal payments are tax deductible. This significantly lowers the costs of debt capital.

Partial Interest Exclusion

In addition to the deductibility of both principal and interest payments, a corporation may be able to get a low-interest rate on ESOP loans—perhaps even lower than the prime rate. This is possible because the tax Code allows qualified lenders to be taxed only on 50% of the interest income that they receive from ESOP loans. To be a qualified entity, the lender must either be a commercial bank, a life or casualty insurance company, an investment bank, or other entity that is normally engaged in the creation of business loans.

As a result of competitive pressures, the interest exclusion given to lenders ends up being passed along, to varying extents, to borrowers. This can allow borrowers to borrow at rates that are significantly less than what they would achieve without an ESOP.

Other Tax Benefits of ESOPs

There are some additional tax benefits of ESOPs, as follows:

Employee/Shareholder Benefits

Like other types of pension plans, employee participants in an ESOP are not taxed on the benefits they receive until they actually receive distributions from the ESOP. In a merger or acquisition, if the target is not a public company, the target shareholders who tender their shares to an acquiring firm's leveraged ESOP may elect to defer the gain from the sale of the stock. Target shareholders are eligible for this deferment if certain conditions are met, such as the ESOP holding at least 30% of the value of the outstanding shares after the sale.

Employer Corporation Benefits

In addition to the benefits already discussed, a further tax benefit of ESOPs is that dividends paid to the ESOP are generally tax deductible. This helps avoid the double taxation of corporate income and gives this component of equity some of the same tax benefits that are enjoyed by debt financing.

It is even possible to pay no dividends on non-ESOP shares while paying dividends on ESOP stock. This can be done by creating a separate class of stock just for the ESOP that will receive these dividends.

THE BALANCE SHEET EFFECTS OF ESOPS

The debt that a leveraged ESOP incurs must be recorded on the firm's balance sheet. This corresponding reduction in shareholder equity must also be reflected on the firm's financial statements. The shares issued to the ESOP must be counted as outstanding shares for the purpose of computing earnings per share.

DRAWBACKS OF LEVERAGED ESOPS

There are certain drawbacks that offset the advantages, as described below.

Equity Dilution Effects

The ability of ESOPs to borrow while providing the borrower with attractive tax advantages that lower the ultimate borrowing costs is a clear advantage. However, to compare the after tax effects of borrowing directly from a bank with those of borrowing through an ESOP would be misleading. When a firm borrows through an ESOP, the employer firm is issuing equity while it is borrowing. From the original stockholders' viewpoint, the result is a dilution of equity. These new equity holders, the firm's employees, will share in any gains that the new debt capital can generate. They will still be there expecting to receive returns on their stock even after the loan is repaid. Therefore, a true analysis of the costs of borrowing through an ESOP will be accurate only if the equity dilution effects are considered. This is more difficult to do, since the equity dilution costs depend on the firm's future performance, which may be difficult to predict. The true equity dilution effects are based on the productivity of the new "capital," which derive from the ESOP's cost savings effects.

To reverse the equity dilution effects, the firm must repurchase the newly issued shares at a later date. When it does so, the discounted value of this expenditure can be used to derive a measure of the true costs of borrowing.

The ESOP can be structured so that there are smaller equity dilution effects. If the ESOP purchases currently outstanding shares instead of issuing new shares, equity will not be diluted.

Distributional Effects of ESOPs

Depending on the price the ESOP pays for the firm's shares, there may be distributional effects associated with the formation of the ESOP. If employees receive shares in the company at a below-market price, a redistribution of wealth may occur. Employees gain wealth at the expense of non-employee shareholders. If employees make other sacrifices, such as lower wages or benefits, which offset the gain on the below-market price shares, there may not be any distributional effects.

In a survey of 192 publicly held firms with ESOPs, it found that 48.2% of the firms reported an increase in employee compensation as a result of the ESOP and that 39.3% did not change their compensation. Only 6% reported a decline in employee compensation when the ESOP was adopted. There may be a redistribution of wealth from non-employee shareholders to employees. It would be shortsighted, however, to conclude that the total net effect is that non-employee shareholders lose. Some of the higher employees' compensation may be necessary to offset the increased risk of their total compensation package. In addition, productivity gains may be associated with the fact that employees are now owners of shares in the company.

Loss of Control

Another disadvantage of ESOPs, which is related to the equity dilution effects, is the loss of control by the non-ESOP stockholders. After shares have been issued to the ESOP, the non-ESOP stockholders experience reduced ownership and control of the corporation.

It is more difficult for management to expand its control when an ESOP owns much of the firm's stock. The Tax Reform Act of 1986 contained anti-discrimination provisions requiring that an ESOP's benefits cannot be controlled by a small group of managers. This law requires that the percentage of employees who are not highly compensated must comprise at least 70% of the shareholdings controlled by highly compensated employees. Highly compensated employees are defined as those who earn more than $75,000 or those who earn more than $50,000 and who are in the top 20% employee compensation bracket for that company. Given this restriction, it is more difficult for management to control a larger number of shares directly. This drawback may be partially offset by the workers tendency to vote with management on most issues.

ESOPS AND CORPORATE PERFORMANCE

Some proponents of ESOPs contend that ESOPs are beneficial for corporations because, as discussed, they help finance capital expenditures and facilitate improvements in labor productivity. ESOPs may also enhance worker productivity, if the workers view their ownership position as a reason to take a greater interest in their performance. With sufficient financial incentives, workers may be less resistant to productivity-enhancing changes such as mechanization or more efficient work procedures.

In a report to the chairman of the U.S. Senate Finance Committee, the General Accounting Office (GAO) found little evidence of such benefits. The study failed to find a perceptible difference in profitability between firms that had ESOPs and those that did not. Apparently, in the first year after adopting an ESOP, firms experienced a temporary increase in profitability; there were no noticeable long-term increases in profitability. The GAO study also compared labor productivity, as measured by the ratio of real value added to real compensation of ESOP firms, with non-ESOP firms. An examination of the productivity trend for ESOP firms appears to show an increase following the adoption of the ESOP.

Fiduciary Responsibilities and ESOPs

A fiduciary of an ESOP is an individual or other entity that exercises discretionary authority in managing and overseeing the plan. The investment in the employer stock must be "prudent." This is particularly relevant to LBO transactions. The Department of Labor may scrutinize a transaction if a company terminates a pension plan to finance a buyout where employees receive shares in a now highly leveraged company. It is acceptable that parties other than the employee, such as the employer corporation, receive benefits from formation of the ESOP. If, however, employee welfare is reduced by the transaction in an indisputable manner, the Labor Department may disallow the ESOP.

ESOPS AS AN ANTI-TAKEOVER DEFENSE

Much of the rising popularity of ESOPs is related to the use of this compensation vehicle as an anti takeover defense, rather than because of its tax advantages.

Delaware (where most corporations are incorporated) law provides that if a bidder purchases more than 15% of a firm's stock, the bidder cannot complete the takeover for three years unless:

1. The bidder purchases as much as 85% of the target's shares.

2. Two-thirds of the shareholders approve the acquisition (excluding the bidder's shares).
3. The board of directors and the shareholders decide to exempt themselves from the provisions of the law.

A Delaware corporation can establish an ESOP, which can act as its own white squire. The combined holdings of stock in the ESOP plus other "loyal" blocks of stock may prevent a bidder from ever reaching the 85% level necessary to complete the takeover. This defense was used most effectively in the Polaroid-Shamrock Holdings takeover battle.

The Polaroid court ruling imposed certain qualifications that restrict the indiscriminate use of ESOPs in takeover contests. The court ruled that the ESOP must be planned prior to the takeover contest.

Effectiveness of ESOPs as an Anti-takeover Defense

After controlling for the effects of other relevant factors, such as state takeover laws and other anti-takeover defenses, it was found that ESOPs significantly reduce the probability of a takeover. Interestingly, their results show that the defensive attributes of ESOPs compares favorably with even poison pills.

The frequency of adoption of anti-takeover defenses dropped dramatically after ESOPs were created or expanded. They found that some ESOPs were used as substitutes for other anti-takeover defenses such as poison pills.

ESOPS AND LEVERAGED BUYOUTS

One of the more dynamic ways in which LBOs can be structured involves the innovative use of ESOPs. Louis Kelso of Kelso and Company pioneered the use of this technique to purchase firms. (Kelso was also active in convincing legislators, such as Senator Russell Long, former chairman of the Senate Finance Committee, to support provisions of ERISA that would enhance the powers of ESOPs.) Using an ESOP as a corporate finance tool, Kelso helped the employees of small newspaper chain in Palo Alto, California, Peninsula Newspapers, to buy this business from the retiring owner of the chain. The plan enabled them to buy the company while enjoying significant tax benefits that lowered the cost of the purchase. Recently, a high profile LESOP was used to acquire the TRIBUNE Company, with high profile investor Sam Zell leading the deal.

In helping finance a leveraged buyout, the ESOP, or more appropriately the LESOP, arranges to borrow funds that will be used to finance the LBO. This can be done through a bank or a group of lenders. The larger the amount of funds required, the more likely the capital will come from a group of lenders. The LESOP borrows a certain amount of money from a bank (or group of lenders). The collateral for this loan will be the stock in the borrowing corporation. The loan may also be guaranteed by the parent corporation in the case of an LBO of a division of a company. The employer corporation makes tax-deductible contributions to the LESOP for the payment of the loan and principal.

The LESOP-LBO Process

All LBOs are somewhat different but tend to share many common characteristics. For the purposes of exposition, let's consider the case of a sell-off of a division in which the management of the parent company seeks to buy the division through an LBO. The steps by which this transaction could take place, using a LESOP, are as follows:

Step 1.

A new company is formed, which will be the division in an independent form.

Step 2.

The management of the division, which will constitute the new owners of that part of the parent company, may make an equity investment in the division. Up to this point, the division may be a corporate shell without assets.

Step 3.

An ESOP for the new company is established. The ESOP negotiates with a bank or other lenders for a loan and then becomes a LESOP. The new company agrees to make periodic payments to service the loan interest and principal. This loan can also be guaranteed by the original corporation, if that becomes a condition of the lenders.

Step 4.

The LESOP uses the proceeds of the loan to purchase the assets that will be put into the new company. These assets were allocated to the divested division when it was part of the parent company. After this transaction, the LESOP owns them.

Step 5.

The LESOP then sells the acquired assets to the new corporation for stock in the new company.

Step 6.

The new company makes periodic contributions to the LESOP, which the LESOP uses to repay the loan. These contributions have the great advantage of being tax deductible.

The deal can also be structured so that the LESOP uses the loan proceeds to purchase stock in the new corporation rather than to purchase assets. Under this scenario, the new corporation uses the proceeds of the sale to buy the assets of the parent corporation.

ESOPs can be used to lower the cost of the LBO by taking advantage of the tax deductions allowable under the law. In this way, they are an innovative means of completing an LBO. In a leveraged

ESOP, the securities that are purchased are placed in a *suspense* account. Shares that are in the suspense account are referred to as unallocated shares. These securities are allocated to the participants in the ESOP as the loan is repaid. The allocation is based on the compensation relevant to each participating employee.

SUMMARY

Employee stock ownership plans were originally developed to provide benefits to employees; however, they can also be a highly innovative corporate finance tool. When used as borrowing vehicles by corporations, ESOPs can provide the company with significant cash flow and tax benefits. These cash flow benefits can be enhanced when the company combines the tax benefits with a reduction in outstanding contributions to other benefits programs. Buyers of corporations have realized that this financing tool can give bidders cost advantages in raising the debt capital necessary to finance leveraged acquisitions. ESOPs, therefore, can be used by hostile bidders as well as by employee groups interested in acquiring their company.

Although ESOPs can be of great financing benefit to buyers of companies, they have also proved to be instrumental in creating a potent anti takeover defense for corporations. The value of this defense has been underscored by the fact that it has successfully withstood numerous legal challenges.

In addition to providing benefits to buyers of companies as well as to defending corporations in hostile contests, ESOPs also seem to generate positive shareholder wealth effects. Research studies support this conclusion, even though they also find that ESOPs are an effective anti- takeover deterrent. Even the smallest companies can have an ESOP. We have often dealt with small businesses that had ESOPS holding 30% of the shares (the minimum required for the selling stockholders to have the tax deferral).

CORPORATE RESTRUCTURING

Although the field of mergers and acquisitions tends to focus on corporate expansion, companies often have to contract and downsize their operations. This need may arise because a division of the company is performing poorly or simply because it no longer fits into the firm's plans. Restructuring may also be necessary to undo a previous merger or acquisition that proved unsuccessful. The pressures of large interest payments that were incurred to finance acquisitions or leveraged buyouts (LBOs) take their toll. For some of these companies, divestitures and sell-offs are among the few alternatives available to corporations to help pay down debt.

The methods used to value acquisition targets are also used by companies to determine whether a particular component of the firm is worth retaining. Both the divesting and the acquiring firm commonly go through a similar type of analysis as they view the transaction from opposite sides. Even though the methods are similar, the two parties may come up with different values because they use different assumptions or have different needs.

A corporation may be able to enhance the value of shareholder investments by pursuing a policy of corporate restructuring.

Corporate restructuring can take several different forms: divestitures, equity carve-outs, spin-offs, split-offs, and split-ups. A *divestiture* is a sale of a portion of the firm to an outside party. The selling firm is usually paid in cash, marketable securities, or a combination of the two. An *equity carve-out* is a variation of a divestiture that involves the sale of an equity interest in a subsidiary to outsiders. The sale may not necessarily leave the parent company in control of the subsidiary. The new equity gives the investors shares of ownership in the portion of the selling company that is being divested. In an equity carve-out, a new legal entity is created with a stockholder base that may be different from that of the parent selling company; the divested company has a different management team and is usually run as a separate firm.

A new legal entity is also created in a standard *spin-off.* Once again, new shares are issued, but here they are distributed to stockholders on a pro rata basis. As a result of the proportional distribution of shares, the stockholder base in the new company is the same as that of the old company. Although the stockholders are initially the same, the spun-off firm has its own management and is run as a separate company. Another difference between a spin-off and a divestiture is that a divestiture involves an infusion of funds into the parent corporation, whereas a spin-off normally does not provide the parent with a cash infusion.

In a *split-off,* some of the stockholders in the parent company are given shares in a division of the parent company, which is split off *in exchange* for their shares in the parent company. A variation on a split-off occurred when Dome Petroleum, which had purchased an equity interest in Conoco, exchanged its shares in Conoco for Conoco's Hudson Bay oil and gas fields.

In a *split-up,* the entire firm is broken up into a series of spin-offs. The end result of this process is that the parent company no longer exists, leaving only the newly formed companies. The stockholders in the companies may be different, since stockholders exchange their shares in the parent company for shares in one or more of the units that are spun off.

Sometimes a combination of a divestiture and a spin-off may occur. For example, Trans World Corporation (TWA) sold shares in TWA to the public equal to approximately 20% of the ownership of the airline. This is also referred to as a *partial public offering.* The remaining shares were distributed to existing TWA stockholders.

DIVESTITURES

Most sell-offs are simple divestitures. Companies pursue other forms of sell-offs, such as a spin-off or an equity carve-out, to achieve other objectives in addition to getting rid of a particular division. These objectives may be to make the transaction tax free, which may call for a spin-off.

The most common form of divestiture involves the sale of a division of the parent company to another firm or to you and the management team.

Involuntary versus Voluntary Divestitures

A divestiture can be either voluntary or involuntary. An involuntary divestiture may occur when a company receives an unfavorable review by the Justice Department or the Federal Trade Commission (FTC), requiring the company to divest itself of a particular division.

Reasons for Voluntary Divestitures

Poor Fit of Division

Voluntary divestitures are more common than involuntary divestitures and are motivated by a variety of reasons. For example, the parent company may want to move out of a particular line of business that it feels no longer fits into its plans or in which it is unable to operate profitably. This does not mean that another firm, with greater expertise in this line of business, could not profitably manage the division's assets. Divestitures then become part of an efficient market process that reallocates assets to those who will allow them to reach their greatest gain.

Reverse Synergy

One motive that is often ascribed to mergers and acquisitions is synergy. Synergy refers to the additional gains that can be derived when two forms combine. When synergy exists, the combined entity is worth more than the sum of the parts valued separately. In other words, 2 + 2 = 5. *Reverse synergy* means that the parts are worth more separately than they are within the parent company's corporate structure. In other words, 4 - 1 = 5. In such cases, an outside bidder might be able to pay more for a division than what the division is worth to the parent company. For instance, a large parent company is not able to operate a division profitably, whereas a smaller firm, or even the division by itself, might operate more efficiently and, therefore, earn a higher rate of return.

Reverse synergy occurred when the Allegis Corporation was forced to sell off its previously acquired companies, Hertz Car Rental and Weston and Hilton International Hotels. Allegis had paid a high price for these acquisitions based on the belief that the synergistic benefits of combining the travel industry companies with United Airlines, its main asset, would more than justify the high prices. When the synergistic benefits failed to materialize, the stock price fell, setting the stage for a hostile bid from the New York investment firm Coniston Partners. Coniston made a bid based on its analysis that the separate parts of Allegis were worth more than the combined entity, which was very true.

Poor Performance

Companies may want to divest divisions simply because they are not sufficiently profitable. The division could fail to pay a rate of return that exceeds the parent company's *hurdle rate*—the minimum return threshold that a company will use to evaluate projects or the performance of parts of the overall company. A typical hurdle rate could be the firm's cost of capital.

A division could decline for many reasons. The industry as a whole might be in a state of decline. For example, high labor costs, caused by a unionized labor force, may make the division uncompetitive in the world market. This occurred when Swift and Company decided that it would have to sell its fresh meats division. (See the case study later in this chapter.) Beset with a high-cost, unionized labor force, this division could not compete with its non-unionized competitors, and Swift and Company decided to sell it off.

Management may be reluctant to sell a poorly performing division, since they may have to admit that they did a poor job of managing it or, in the case of a prior acquisition, that the purchase was a mistake. They may then hold on to the division for a longer time than what would be dictated by its performance.

Capital Market Factors

A divestiture may also take place because the post-divestiture firm, as well as the divested division, has greater access to capital markets. The combined corporate structure may be more difficult for investors to categorize. Certain providers of capital might be looking to invest in steel companies but not in pharmaceutical firms. Other investors might seek to invest capital in pharmaceutical companies but may feel that the steel industry is too cyclical and has low-growth potential. These two groups of investors might not want to invest in a combined steel/pharmaceutical company, but each group might separately invest in a stand-alone steel or pharmaceutical firm. Divestitures might provide greater access to capital markets for the two firms as separate companies than as a combined corporation.

Similarly, divestitures can create companies in which investors would like to invest but that do not exist in the marketplace. Such companies are sometimes referred to as *pure plays*. Many analysts argue that the market is incomplete and that there is a demand for certain types of firms, which is not matched by a supply of securities in the market. The sale of those parts of the parent company that become pure plays helps complete the market.

The separation of divisions facilitates clearer identification and market segmentation for the investment community. New investment dollars can then be attracted.

An example of a capital market induced spin-off involves Koger Properties, Inc. which historically consisted of two distinct businesses. These two businesses were development and construction and property ownership and management. The development and construction business traditionally had provided investors with relatively volatile, high risk opportunities. As a result, earnings were quite sensitive to the availability and cost of capital for real estate development, and to the strength of the national and local economies. But the ownership and management of the rental office properties, while also involving risks to the investor, was not as sensitive to those factors because completed, leased properties have established rental income and generally are financed through long term mortgage indebtedness having fixed equal monthly payments of principal and interest. Koger Properties, Inc.'s management felt that the development aspect of the company was never fully reflected in the marketplace. Accordingly, management believed that it was in the interest of stockholders for the firm's two business activities to be conducted by separate and independent companies.

Cash Flow Factors

A sell-off produces the immediate benefits of an infusion of cash from the sale. The selling firm is selling a long-term asset, which generated a certain cash flow per period, in exchange for a larger payment in the short run. Companies that are under financial duress are often forced to sell off valuable assets to enhance cash flows. Beset with the threat of bankruptcy, Chrysler Corporation was forced to sell off its prized tank division in an effort to stave off bankruptcy. International Harvester (now known as Navistar) sold its profitable Solar Turbines International Division to Caterpillar Tractor Company, Inc., to realize the immediate proceeds of $505 million. These funds were used to cut Harvester's short-term debt in half, saving the company.

Abandoning the Core Business

The sale of a company's core business is a less common reason for a sell-off. An example of the sale of a core business was the sale by

Greyhound of its bus business, which my company tried to acquire. The sale of a core business is often motivated by management's desire to leave an area that it believes has matured and presents few growth opportunities. Usually, the firm has already diversified into other, more profitable areas, and the sale of the core business can help finance the expansion of these more productive activities.

DIVESTITURE AND SPIN-OFF PROCESS

Each divestiture is unique and takes place in a different sequence of events.

Step 1.

Divestitures or the Spin-off Decision. The management of the parent company must decide whether a divestiture is the appropriate course of action. This decision can be made only after a thorough financial analysis of the various alternatives has been completed. The method of conducting the financial analysis for a divestiture or spin-off will be discussed later in this chapter.

Step 2.

Formulation of a Restructuring Plan. A restructuring or reorganization plan must be formulated, and an agreement between the parent and the subsidiary may be negotiated. This plan is necessary in the case of a spin-off that will feature a continuing relationship between the parent and the subsidiary. The plan should cover such details as the disposition of the subsidiary's assets and liabilities. In cases where the subsidiary is to keep certain of its assets while others are to be transferred back to the parent company, the plan may provide a detailed breakdown of the asset disposition. Other issues, such as the retention of employees and the funding of their pension and, possibly, health care liabilities, should also be addressed.

Step 3.

Approval of the Plan by Shareholders. The extent to which approval of the plan is necessary depends on the significance of the transaction and the relevant state laws. In cases such as a spin-off of a major division of the parent company, stockholder approval may be required. If so, the plan is submitted to the stockholders at a stockholders' meeting, which may be the normally scheduled shareholders' meeting or a special meeting called just to consider this issue. A proxy statement requesting approval of the spin-off is also sent to stockholders. The materials submitted to stockholders may address other issues related to the meeting, such as the amendment of the articles of incorporation.

Step 4.

Registration of Shares. Shares issued in a spin-off must be registered with the Securities and Exchange Commission (SEC). As part of the normal registration process, a prospectus, which is part of the registration statement, must be produced. The prospectus must be distributed to all shareholders who receive stock in the spun-off entity, (this refers to public companies).

Step 5.

Completion of the Deal. After all these preliminary steps have been taken, the deal can be consummated. Consideration is exchanged, and the division is separated from the parent company according to a prearranged timetable.

Involuntary Spin-offs

When faced with an adverse regulatory ruling, a firm may decide that a spin-off is the only viable way to comply. The classic example of such an involuntary spin-off was the mammoth spin-off of AT&T's operating companies. As a result of an antitrust suit originally filed by the Justice Department, the government and AT&T reached an agreement providing for the breakup of the large telecommunications company. Only our government is stupid enough to continually want to destroy our large successful businesses. In other countries large businesses are nurtured and supported, instead of destroyed. The final settlement agreement, provided for the reorganization of the 22 operating companies within AT&T into seven regional holding companies. These holding companies would be responsible for local telecommunications service, and the new AT&T would maintain responsibility for long-distance communications.

The spin-off of the 22 operating companies would still allow AT&T shareholders to have the same number of shares in the post-spin-off company. These shares represented ownership rights in a much smaller telecommunications company. For every ten shares that each shareholder had in the original AT&T, shareholders received one share in each of the seven regional holding companies.

The AT&T spin-off is an extreme form of an involuntary spin-off, given the sheer size of the transaction. The spin-off resulted in a dramatic change in the nature of the telecommunications industry in the United States. Most spin-offs, however, are not on this scale and are not a response to a regulatory mandate. AT&T set history again when it engaged in a three way split-off that separated the company into three separate firms. Now many of these have merged into each other, and AT&T is back together again.

Defensive Spin-offs

Companies may choose to spin off divisions to make it less attractive to the bidder. For example, Diamond Shamrock's board of directors approved a restructuring plan that provided for spinning off two core businesses and forming a new entity, called Diamond Shamrock R&M, and distributing R&M stock to its shareholders.

Defensive spin-offs, or other types of sell-offs, are a drastic takeover defense. They may be challenged in the courts by the bidder and possibly by shareholders. If they are determined to limit the auction process and reduce shareholder value, they may be voided. The wealth effects of these defensive sell-offs will be discussed later in this chapter. Tax Consequences of Spin-offs One of the advantages that a spin-off has over other types of sell-offs is that the transaction may be structured so that it is tax free. For example, the shares in the regional Bells that stockholders received did not result in any additional tax liabilities for those shareholders. The IRS treated the distribution of shares in the AT&T spin-off as neither a gain nor a loss. Voluntary spin-offs are also often treated as nontaxable transactions. If the spin-off occurs for valid business reasons, rather than for the purpose of tax avoidance, Section 355 of the Tax Code allows for the transaction to be nontaxable. Among the Tax Code's requirements for a tax-free spin-off are the following:

1. Both the parent company and the spun-off entity must be in business for at least five years prior to the restructuring.
2. The subsidiary must also be at least 80% owned by the parent company.

Employee Stock Option Plans

For employees holding shares under an employee stock option plan (ESOP), the number of shares obtainable by option holders may also need to be adjusted following a spin-off. The adjustment is designed to leave the market value of shares that could be obtained following the spin-off at the same level. This is usually done by increasing the number of shares that can be obtained with a given option. Those option-holding employees in the parent company who become employees in the spun-off entity have their stock options changed to become options in the new company. Here again, the goal is to maintain the market value of the shares that can be obtained through conversion of the employee stock options.

THE WEALTH EFFECTS OF SELL-OFFS

A major motivating factor for divestitures and spin-offs is the belief that reverse synergy may exist. Divestitures, spin-offs, and equity carve-outs are basically a "downsizing" of the parent firm. Therefore, the smaller firm must be economically more viable by itself than as a part of its parent company. Several research studies have analyzed the impact of spin-offs by examining the effect on the stock prices of both the parent company and the spun-off entity. This effect is then compared with a market index to determine whether the stocks experience extra-normal performance that cannot be explained by market movements alone. Spin-offs are a unique opportunity to analyze the effects of the separation, since a market exists for both the stock of the parent and the spun-off entity.

The research in the field of sell-offs, whether they are spin-offs or other forms of asset sales such as equity carve-outs, presents a picture of clear benefits for shareholders.

Rationale for a Positive Stock Price Reaction to Sell-offs

When a firm decides to sell off a poorly performing division, this asset goes to another owner, who presumably will value it more highly because he or she can utilize this asset more advantageously than the seller. The seller receives cash (or sometimes other compensation) in place of the asset. When the market responds positively to this asset reallocation, it is expressing a belief that the firm will use this cash more efficiently than it was utilizing the asset that was sold. Moreover, the asset that was sold may have attracted a premium above market value, which should also cause the market to respond positively.

The selling firm has a few options at its disposal when contemplating the disposition of the newly acquired cash. The firm can pay the cash to stockholders in the form of a dividend, or it may repurchase its own shares at a premium. Either option is a way the selling corporation can give its stockholders an immediate payout. If the seller retains the cash, it will be used for internal investment to expand in one of its current areas of activity or for an acquisition. The choice of another acquisition may give stockholders cause for concern.

Another argument in favor of the value-increasing effects of sell-offs is that the market might find it difficult to evaluate highly diversified companies. The validity of this argument is a matter of considerable debate, since it implies that the market is somewhat inefficient. If the market is inefficient in evaluating these types of firms, then the sale of one or more divisions might facilitate categorization of the parent company. The greater ease of categorization and evaluation would encourage investors looking to invest in certain types of companies.

SUMMARY

Corporate restructuring is often warranted when the current structure of the corporation is not yielding values that are consistent with market or management's expectations. It may occur when a given part of a company no longer fits into management's plans. Other restructuring may prove necessary when a prior acquisition has not performed up to management's expectations. The decision to sell may be difficult, because it requires management to admit that the firm made a mistake when it acquired the asset that is being sold. Once the decision to sell has been made, management must then decide how this will be implemented.

Managers may consider several of the different options discussed in this chapter, such as a straightforward sale or divestiture or the sale of an equity interest in a subsidiary to outsiders, which is an equity carve-out. In both cases a separate legal entity is created, and the divested entity is run by a new management team as a stand-alone company. An alternative that also results in the creation of a separate legal entity is a spin-off. Here shares are issued on a pro rata basis and distributed to the parent company's shareholders, also on a pro rata basis. When the transaction is structured so that shares in the original company are exchanged for shares in the parent firm, the deal is called a split-off. A split-up occurs when the entire firm is broken up and shareholders exchange their shares in the parent company according to a predetermined formula.

Empirical research has found that a significant amount of sell-offs are associated with positive shareholder wealth effects for parent company shareholders. This implies that the market agrees that the sale of part of the company will yield a higher return than the continued operation of the division under current operating policies. The market is indicating that the proceeds of the sale of the firm can be utilized more advantageously than the division that is being sold. The market also has responded with a positive stock price response for shareholders in the divested or spun-off entities. Even the price performance of buyers (if they are publicly traded) of divested firms enjoy positive stock market valuation increases.

The positive market response to restructuring paints this form of corporate change in a favorable light. Other forms of corporate downsizing, such as large-scale employee layoffs, also are quite common. Although this type of restructuring has been criticized, because it is often associated with employee duress, it is partially responsible for the improvement in U.S. productivity.

RESTRUCTURING IN BANKRUPTCY

Reorganization through the bankruptcy process is a tool of corporate finance that, in certain instances, provides unique benefits that are unattainable through other means. This chapter explores the different forms of bankruptcy and discusses the circumstances in which a company would use either of the two broad forms of corporate bankruptcy that are available: Chapter 7 and Chapter 11. Chapter 7, liquidation, will be appropriate for the more severely distressed companies. Chapter 11 reorganization, however, is the more flexible corporate finance tool that allows, the company to continue to operate while it explores other forms of restructuring. In addition, Chapter 11 allows companies to continue to operate while a reorganization plan is developed and approved.

TYPES OF BUSINESS FAILURE

Filing for any form of bankruptcy is a drastic step that is only pursued when other more favorable options are unavailable. Bankruptcy filing is an admission that a company has in some way failed to achieve certain goals. The term *business failure* is somewhat ambiguous and can have different meanings depending on the context and the users. There are two main forms of business failure: economic failure and financial failure. Each has a very different meaning.

Economic Failure

On the two broad types of business failure, economic failure is the most ambiguous. For example, it could mean that the firm is generating losses; that is, revenues are less than costs. However, depending on the users and the context, it could also mean that the rate of return on investment is less than the cost of capital. It could also mean that the actual returns earned by a firm are less than those that were forecast. These uses of the term are very different and cover situations in which a company could be unprofitable to cases where it is profitable but just not as much as what was expected.

Financial Failure

Financial failure is less ambiguous that economic failure. It means that a company cannot meet its current obligations as they come due. The company does not have sufficient liquidity to satisfy its current liabilities. This can occur even when the company has a positive net worth with the value of assets exceeding its liabilities.

CAUSES OF BUSINESS FAILURE

Dun and Bradstreet conducted a study of the causes of business failure. They found that the three most common factors, in order of frequency, were economic factors, such as weakness in the industry; financial factors such as insufficient capitalization; and weaknesses in managerial experience, such as insufficient managerial knowledge. This last factor highlights the role of management skills in preventing bankruptcy and is one reason that workout specialists focus so strongly on managerial skills when working on a company turnaround.

Dun and Bradstreet also analyzed the average ages of the businesses that failed. They found only 9% of the failures were in business for one year or less. Just under one-third were in business for three years or less while half existed for up to five years. This we can conclude that if the business makes it past the five year mark, it is likely to survive.

My personal preference is to always consider acquiring a long established business, even if it one that may be on the brink of financial disaster, if it has the potential to be turned around if its existing debt is restructured.

REORGANIZATION VERSUS LIQUIDATION

The purpose of the reorganization section of the bankruptcy code is to allow a *reorganization plan* to be developed that will allow the company to continue to operate. This plan will contain the changes in the company that its designers believe are necessary to convert it to be a profitable entity. If a plan to allow the profitable operation of the business cannot be formulated, the company may have to be liquidated, with its assets sold and the proceeds used to satisfy the company's liabilities.

CHAPTER 11 REGORGANIZATION PROCESS

While the Chapter 11 process varies somewhat depending on the particular circumstances of the bankruptcy, they have certain important common characteristics outlined below.

Bankruptcy Petition and the Filing

The reorganization process is started with the filing of a bankruptcy *petition for relief* with the bankruptcy court. In the petition, the debtor lists its creditors and security holders. Also included are standard financial statements, including an income statement and balance sheet. The court then sets a date when the creditors can file their *proofs of claim.* The company then attempts to put together a reorganization plan while it continues its operations. Contrary to what the layperson might think, there is no financial test that is performed by the court at this time to determine whether the debtor is truly financially insolvent.

The petition is usually filed in the federal district in which the debtor has its home office. After the petition is filed, a case number is assigned, a court file is opened, and a bankruptcy judge is assigned to the case.

Debtor in Possession

Following the bankruptcy filing, the bankrupt company is referred to as the *debtor in possession.* This is a new legal entity; however, practically, it is usually the same company with the same management and employees. From the creditors' point of view, this is one of the problems of the bankruptcy process; that is, the same management that led the company into its financial troubles is usually still running the business while a reorganization plan is being developed.

If the creditors strongly oppose the management of the debtor staying in control of the business, they may petition the court and ask that a trustee and examiner be appointed. For example, if concerns exist about fraudulent actions or incompetence of the debtor's directors or management, the court may agree. A trustee is charged with overseeing the operations of the company while it is in bankruptcy. An examiner may be appointed to investigate specific issues. If the court denies a request for a trustee, an examiner is usually appointed.

Automatic Stay

When the petition is accepted by the court, an automatic stay is granted. This is one of the main benefits that the debtor receives in the Chapter 11 process. During the automatic stay, a halt is placed on any pre-petition legal proceedings as well as on the enforcement of any pre-filing judgment. Creditors are unable to pursue a lien on the debtor's assets or to collect money from the debtor. Parties seeking relief from the stay may petition the court and request a hearing. If the creditors can convince the court that the assets that are being used as collateral for obligations due them are not necessary for the continued operation of the company, or the debtor has no equity interest in the assets, they may be able to get relief from the stay.

Time Line in the Reorganization Process

Within 10 days of the filing of the Chapter 11 bankruptcy petition, the debtor is required to file a schedule of assets and liabilities with the court. This schedule needs to include the names and addresses of each creditor. The next important date is the *bar date* which is the date when those creditors who have disputed or contingent claims must file a *proof of claim.* This is a written statement that sets forth what is owed by the debtor to the particular creditor. Failure to file by this date results is forfeiture of the claim. It is automatically assumed, however, that other claimholders have filed a proof of claim.

Following the bar date, the next important dates are those associated with the filing and approval of the reorganization plan.

Duties of the Debtor in Possession

After the filing of the petition, the court establishes certain schedules, which feature various reporting requirements. For example, the debtor has to file monthly financial statements 15 days following the end of each calendar month. In addition to the court rules as set forth on the federal law, each federal district may have its own additional reporting requirements.

Creditors' Committees

A creditors' meeting is usually held within 20 to 40 days of the bankruptcy filing. The meeting is called by the U.S. Trustee and is usually held at its office. The debtor and its principal officers must be present at this meeting. All the creditors can attend this meeting and can ask the debtors specific questions of concern to them.

In larger filings, a creditors' committee is formed. This committee is usually composed of the largest creditors, assuming they are interested in being represented. Along with the U.S. Trustee, the creditors' committee monitors the actions of the debtor, ensuring that it does not do anything that would adversely affect the creditors' interests. The creditors' committee can retain counsel, accountants, and other financial experts to represent the creditors' interests during the reorganization process. The costs of professionals are borne by the debtor, and can at times be a significant expense to the debtor, but a bonanza to the professionals.

The bigger the bankruptcy, the more likely there may be more committees, such as an equity holders' committee, or different types of creditors' committees such as a bondholders' committee, representing the various forms of debt that might exist (and each one with an army of lawyers billing all that they can get away with).

One example of a mega-bankruptcy that had several committees was the Campeau bankruptcy. This featured the bankruptcy of Campeau's two major subunits, Federated Department Stores, Inc. and Allied Stores Corp. In this proceeding there were several committees, including a bondholders' committee and two trade creditors' committees. The court attempted to appoint a cross section of similarly situated creditors on each committee. In smaller bankruptcies, creditors may have little interest in the committees. In the Campeau bankruptcy, the U.S. Trustee's office was flooded with bondholders who were interested in serving on the committee.

In the bankruptcy of United Airlines, the attorney fees alone exceeded the sum of $350 million.

Debtor's Actions and Its Supervision

During the reorganization process, the debtor can continue to operate the business. The law requires that the debtor obtain the bankruptcy court's approval before its takes any extraordinary actions, such as selling assets or property that is not part of the normal business operations.

My company has participated in many auctions held for subsidiaries of large companies that were in bankruptcy; these have often been very stable businesses which were being disposed of by the parent company who filed for the bankruptcy protection.

Others were poorly performing companies that were usually available as bargains, to those willing to face the challenge of tuning them around financially.

Technically, the supervision of the debtor is the responsibility of the judge and the creditors. They can acquire resources, such as legal and accounting or other financial expert assistance, to help them with this. Practically, neither the judge nor the creditors usually have the resources or time to closely supervise the debtor. Even if the debtor does something that the creditors don't like, the debtor may be able to convince the judge that some actions are necessary for the survival of the company; that is, if the court does not allow the debtor to take these actions, the company may go under. Thus, the judge is put in the difficult position of making this decision with limited information. If the judge rules against the debtor and is wrong, he risks the company going out of business and all the duress and employee suffering this might cause. For this reason, the debtor is usually granted significant leeway and will only be opposed when its proposed actions are clearly objectionable.

Exclusivity Period

After the filing of the bankruptcy petition and the granting of the automatic stay, only the debtor has the right to file a reorganization plan. This period, which is initially 120 days, is known as the *exclusivity period.* It is rare, however, particularly in larger bankruptcies, to have the plan submitted during that time frame. It is common for the debtor to ask for one or more extensions. Extensions are only granted for cause; however, they are not difficult to obtain, and at times have this process delayed by years.

Under early versions of the bankruptcy law, only the debtor could file a reorganization plan. Current versions of the Code, however, allow the creditors to prepare and file their own reorganization plan if they do not like the one the debtor put forward.

The end of the exclusivity period is a sign that control in the bankruptcy process is shifting from the debtor to the creditors. Contrary to what one might think, there is no specific time limit when the Chapter 11 process must come to an end. If the judge determines that sufficient progress toward the submission and approval of a plan is not being made, however, he can try to take steps to move the process along.

Obtaining Post-petition Credit

One of the problems a near bankrupt company has is difficulty in obtaining credit. If trade creditors are concerned that a company may become bankrupt, they may cut off all additional credit. For companies that are dependent on such credit to survive, this can mean that a bankruptcy filing is accelerated.

To assist bankrupt companies in acquiring needed credit, the Code has given post-petition creditors an elevated priority in the bankruptcy process. That is, post-petition claims have an elevated priority over pre-petition claims. It is ironic that creditors may be unwilling to extend credit unless the debtor files for bankruptcy so that the creditor can obtain the elevated priority status.

Reorganization Plan

The reorganization plan, which is part of a larger document called the disclosure statement, looks like a prospectus. For larger bankruptcies, this is a long document. It contains the plans for the turnaround of the company. The plan is submitted to all the different creditors and equity holders' committees. The plan will be approved when each class of creditor and equity holders approves it. Approval is granted if one-half in number and two-thirds in dollar amount of a given class approve the plan. Once the plan is approved, the dissenters are bound by the details of the plan.

A confirmation hearing follows the attainment of the approval of the plan. It is not supposed to be a pro-forma proceedings, even if the vote is unanimous. The presiding judge must make a determination that the plan meets the standards set forth by the Bankruptcy Code. After the plan is confirmed, the debtor is discharged of all pre-petition claims and other claims up to the date of the confirmation hearing. This does not mean that the reorganized company is a debt-free entity. It just means that it has new obligations now that are different from the prior ones. Hopefully, the post-confirmation capital structure is one that will allow the company to remain sufficiently liquid to meet its new obligations and generate a profit.

Cramdown

The plan may be made binding on all classes of security holders, even if they all do not approve it. This is known as a *cramdown*. The judge can conduct a cramdown if at least one class of creditors approves the plan and the "crammed down" class is not being treated unfairly. In this context, unfairly means that no class with inferior claims in the bankruptcy hierarchy is receiving compensation without the higher-up class being paid 100% of its claims. This order of claims is known as the *absolute priority rule,* which states that claims must be settled in full before any junior claims can receive any compensation.

The concept of a cramdown comes from the concern by lawmakers that a small group of creditors could block the approval of a plan to the detriment of the majority of the creditors. By giving the court the ability to cram down a plan, the law reduces the potential for a holdout problem.

Fairness and Feasibility of the Plan

The reorganization plan must be both fair and feasible. Fairness refers to the satisfaction of claims in order of priority as discussed in the last section. Feasibility refers to the probability that the post-confirmation company has a reasonable chance of survival. The plan must provide for certain essential characteristics, such as adequate working capital and a reasonable capital structure that does not contain too much debt. Projected revenues must be sufficient to adequately cover the fixed charges associated with the post-confirmation liabilities along with the other operating expenses.

Partial Satisfaction of Pre-petition Claims

The plan will have a new capital structure that, it is hoped, will be one that the company can adequately service. This will typically feature payment of less than the full amount that was due the claim holders. For example, the Penn Central Railroad, in a bankruptcy process that took a whopping eight years, produced a confirmed plan that gave holders of secured bonds 10% of their claims in cash. The cash was generated by the sale of assets. The remaining 90% was satisfied by 30% each in new mortgage bonds, preferred stock, and common stock. This provided Penn Central with a lower amount of financial leverage because the secured bond debt was 10% discharged by the cash payment, and 60% was converted to preferred and common equity.

BENEFITS OF THE CHAPTER 11 PROCESS FOR THE DEBTOR

The U.S. Bankruptcy Code provides great benefits to debtors. The debtor is still left in charge of the business and allowed to operate relatively free of close control. Some are critical of what they perceive as a process that overly favors the debtor at the expense of the creditors' interests. The bankruptcy law, however, seeks to rehabilitate the debtor so that it can become a viable business and productive member of the business community.

COMPANY SIZE AND CHAPTER 11 BENEFITS

The fact that debtors enjoy unique benefits while operating under the protection of the bankruptcy process is clear. Smaller companies, however, may not enjoy the same benefits that the process bestows on the larger counterparts. 69% of the larger companies, those with revenues in excess of $100 million, survived the process and were viable afterward, whereas only 30% of the smaller firms, those with revenues under $25 million, were able to do so.

The reason for the size differential in survival rates is that larger companies are in a better position to handle the additional unique demands placed on a Chapter 11 debtor. For example, the bankruptcy process is very demanding on management time. Prior to the bankruptcy, management was presumably devoting all of its time to managing the business and still was not successful. Now management has to devote its time to managing the business and dealing with the time demands that the bankruptcy litigation imposes. This task may be more difficult for smaller companies, where management is not as deep as in larger firms.

Although the additional expenses of the bankruptcy process may be relatively small compared with a larger company's revenue base, such expenses may be an additional burden that a smaller business cannot handle. Direct costs average 3.1% of the book value of the debt, plus the market value of the equity. Professional fees can be very high-particularly in the larger bankruptcies. For example, in the Johns Manville bankruptcy, professional fees equaled almost $200 million, while I previously gave the example of $350 million in fees for the United bankruptcy. For a small firm, with a thin capitalization, percentages may be much higher than the average reported. For these reasons, Chapter 11 may be an excellent choice for some large companies but may not be a good idea for smaller businesses.

PREPACKAGED BANKRUPTCY

A new type of bankruptcy emerged in the late 1980s; now it accounts for one-fifth of all distressed restructurings. This option is also significantly less costly, and consumes a much shorter time frame.

In a prepackaged bankruptcy, the firm negotiates the reorganization plan with its creditors prior to an actual Chapter 11 filing. Ideally, the debtor would like to have solicited and received an understanding with the creditors that the plan would be approved following the filing. In a prepackaged bankruptcy, the parties try to have the terms of the reorganization plan approved in advance. This is different from the typical Chapter 11 reorganization process, which may feature a time-consuming and expensive plan development and approval process where the terms and conditions of the plan are agreed only after a painstaking negotiation process.

The first major prepackaged bankruptcy was the Crystal Oil Company, an oil and natural gas exploration company located in Louisiana. The total time between the bankruptcy filing and the company's emergence was only three months. During this time, the company negotiated a new capital structure in which it reduced its total indebtedness from $277 million to $129 million. As is typical of such debt restructurings, the creditors received other securities, such as equity and convertible debt and warrants, in exchange for the reduction in the original debt.

Benefits of Prepackaged Bankruptcy

The completion of the bankruptcy process is usually dramatically shorter in a prepackaged bankruptcy than in the typical Chapter 11 process. Both time and financial resources are saved. This is of great benefit to the distressed debtor, who would prefer to conserve financial resources and spend as little time as possible in the suspended Chapter 11 state. In addition, a prepackaged bankruptcy reduces the holdout problem associated with voluntary non-bankruptcy agreements. In such agreements the debtor often has to receive the approval of all of the creditors. This is difficult to do when there are many creditors-particularly many small creditors. One of the ways a voluntary agreement is accomplished is to pay all of the small creditors 100% of what they are owned and pay the main creditors, who hold the bulk of the debt, an agreed upon lower amount.

It was noted earlier that approval of a Chapter 11 reorganization plan required creditors' approval equal to one-half in number and two-thirds in dollar amount. With the imminent threat of a Chapter 11 filing, creditors know that once the filing is made these voting percentages, as opposed to unanimity, will apply. Therefore, if the threat of a Chapter 11 filing is real, the post-bankruptcy voting threshold will become the operative one during the prepackaged negotiation process.

Pre-Voted versus Post-Voted Pre-Packs

The voting approval for the prepackaged bankruptcy can take place prior to or after the plan is filed. In a "pre-voted pre-pack" the results of the voting process are filed with the bankruptcy petition and reorganization plan. In a "post-voted pre-pack" the voting process is overseen by the Bankruptcy Court after the Chapter 11 filing. In a study of 49 prepackaged bankruptcies, it was found that pre-voted pre-packs spend less time in bankruptcy court but devote more time in pre-filing negotiations. Pre-voted pre-packs also had lower direct costs as a fraction of assets and had higher recovery rates for non-equity obligations.

Tax Advantages of Prepackaged Bankruptcy

A prepackaged bankruptcy may also provide tax benefits. This is because net operating losses are treated differently in workouts than in bankruptcy. For example, if a company enters into a voluntary negotiated agreement with debt holders whereby debt holders exchange their debt for equity and the original equity holders now own less than 50% of the company, the company may lose its right to claim net operating losses in its tax filings forfeiture of these tax-loss carry-forwards can have adverse future cash flow consequences. In bankruptcy, however, if the court rules that the firm was insolvent, as defined by a negative net asset value, the right to claim loss carry-forwards may be preserved. It is estimated that the present value of future taxes saved by restructuring through a prepackaged bankruptcy, as opposed to a workout, is equal to 3% of total assets.

If a debtor company reaches a voluntary agreement whereby creditors agree to car certain percentage of the debt, say one-third, this amount is treated as income for tax poses, thus creating a tax liability. A similar debt restructuring in bankruptcy, how does not create such a tax liability.

WORKOUTS

A *workout* refers to a negotiated agreement between the debtors and its creditors outside the bankruptcy process. The debtor may try to extend the payment terms, which is called *tension,* or get creditors to agree to accept a lesser amount than what they are owed, is called *composition.* Workouts are different from a prepackaged bankruptcy in that workout, the debtor has either already violated the terms of the debt agreements or is to. In a workout, the debtor tries to convince creditors that they would be financially off with the new terms of a workout agreements than with the terms of a formal bankruptcy.

When I started to buy my first companies, almost all were purchased through or with a workout plan, allowing me to have a smaller creditor obligation.

Benefits of Workouts

The main benefits of workouts are cost savings and flexibility. Workout agreement generally cost less to both the debtor and the creditors in terms of the resources the participants have to devote to the agreement process. In addition, the participants in a workout are not burdened by the rules and regulations of Chapter 11 of the Bankruptcy Code. There they are free to create their own rules, as long as the parties agree to them. They also the public scrutiny, such as from opening accounting records to the public, that, occur in a bankruptcy filing. Workouts may also help the debtor avoid any business disruption and loss of employees and overall morale that might occur in a bankruptcy.

With these benefits come certain risks. The key risk is the holdout problem discussed earlier. If this problem cannot be circumvented, a bankruptcy filing may be the only alternative.

CORPORATE CONTROL AND DEFAULT

When a firm defaults, it typically loses control, which is passed to its creditors. Creditors may then acquire seats on the defaulting firm's board of directors and may even require that there be a change in management. Creditors may also receive an ownership position in the debtor in exchange for other consideration, such as a reduction in the amount owned.

LIQUIDATION

Liquidation is a distressed firm's most drastic alternative, which is usually only pursued when voluntary agreement and reorganization cannot be successfully implemented. Here the company's assets are sold and the proceeds used to satisfy claims. The sales are made pursuant to the regulations that are set forth under Chapter 7 of the Bankruptcy Code. The priority of claims are as described below.

1. Secured creditors. If the amount owed exceeds the proceeds from the sale of the asset, the remainder becomes an unsecured claim.
2. Bankruptcy administrative costs.
3. Post-petition bankruptcy expenses.
4. Wages of workers owed for three months prior to the filing (limit per employee).
5. Employee benefit plan contributions owed for six months prior to the filing (limit per employee).
6. Unsecured customer deposits (limit).
7. Federal, state, and local taxes.
8. Unfunded pension liabilities (limit related to book value of preferred and common equity; any remainder becomes an unsecured claim).
9. Unsecured claims.
10. Preferred stockholders (up to the par value of their stock).
11. Common stockholders.

INVESTING IN THE SECURITIES OF DISTRESSED COMPANIES

Investing in the securities of distressed companies can offer great profit potential, but only if the buyer is willing to assume significant risks. Distressed securities are defined as the bonds or stocks of companies that have defaulted on their debt obligations or have filed for Chapter 11. The K-Mart bankruptcy is a great example as it later acquired Sears.

SUMMARY

The world of bankruptcy changed dramatically in the 1980s as companies began to discover the creative corporate finance uses of Chapter 11 of the Bankruptcy Code. Chapter 11 reorganization became a method of corporate restructuring that under certain circumstances can bestow significant benefits to the distressed company. By formulating a reorganization plan, the company can restructure its liabilities as well as engage in other forms of restructuring, such as selling off assets to fund the plan. The Chapter 11 company obtains an automatic stay once entering Chapter 11, and creditors are held at bay by the court while the debtor and, possibly, the creditors structure a reorganization plan.

The reorganization plan must be approved by creditors prior to being approved by the court. Initially, only the debtor can propose a reorganization plan. This time period is called the exclusivity period. At the end of this period, which is initially 120 days but is often extended by the court, the creditors can propose an alternative plan if they oppose aspects of the debtor's plan. The plan must be fair and feasible as determined by the court. If all classes of creditors fail to approve the plan, it may be crammed down on the dissenting class, as long as there is one class that approves of it.

In the late 1980s prepackaged bankruptcies became popular and remain till today. This is where approval of a plan is obtained prior to entering bankruptcy. The bankruptcy process is significantly shorter in a prepackaged bankruptcy. Therefore, there is less disruption to the debtor's business, and both debtors and creditors can gain from this form of reorganization. There also may be tax advantages that this alternative may pose that are not available in workouts. Workouts are voluntary agreements that do not involve a bankruptcy filing.

Trading in the securities of bankrupt companies, both bonds and equity, can be a high risk way of implementing a takeover. The purchasers of the securities may participate in the bankruptcy process in an effort to win control of the post-bankrupt company. Although this method may enable a company to be taken over relatively cheaply, it is highly unpredictable and fraught with risk for these investors.

FINANCIAL ANALYSIS AND VALUATION

Many financial documents need to be analyzed when conducting a valuation of a potential target. The analysis should focus on both the acquirer and the target. The acquirer needs to ascertain the value of the target to determine the proper offering price and whether the target meets the acquirer's financial standards. The target, in turn, needs to know what its company is worth. Presumably, this will tell the acquirer's management and board of directors whether the offer is in the stockholders' best interest. As part of this analysis, a series of key financial statements will be examined. Each acquisition candidate will present its own unique characteristics that make it different from other firms. These novel aspects may be discerned after considering information other than what is contained within the four corners of the standard financial statements. Therefore, the framework of financial statement analysis presented in this chapter is a basic model that may be followed in an analysis of a merger or an acquisition. It is a minimum and should be supplemented by additional analysis that is required due to the unique aspects of each transaction.

The discussion of financial statement analysis is not meant to be comprehensive. Rather, it is designed to highlight some of the basic financial issues that need to be considered in business valuations for mergers and acquisitions. A more thorough and detailed discussion can be found in most good corporate finance textbooks.

The three most basic financial statements are the balance sheet, the income statement, and the statement of cash flows. Publicly held companies prepare these statements on a quarterly and annual basis. The quarterly statements are available in the 10Q quarterly reports that are filed with the Securities and Exchange Commission (SEC). The annual statements are available in the firm's 10K and Annual Report.

HOSTILE VERSUS FRIENDLY DEALS: ACCESS TO FINANCIAL DATA

One of the significant differences between friendly and hostile deals is the bidder's access to detailed financial data. In a friendly transaction, the bidder and the target may work closely together to reach an agreement. Often this involves the target releasing detailed internal financial data that the bidder requests. The target does this to be able to sell the company for a certain goal price. In a hostile deal, the target usually only gives the bidder the minimum information required by the law. This may mean that the bidder has to conduct its valuation analysis using publicly available information, such as the financial statements that are required to be disclosed by securities laws. This puts the bidder at a disadvantage, particularly when the offer is for a multidivisional target that may not disclose much detail on the performance of specific divisions. This may be important, since the bidder may be planning on selling off some divisions and using the proceeds to reduce the takeover financing obligations. Without detailed internal financial data, the bidder may have to estimate the performance of the divisions.

The bidder may try to force the target to provide such data by trying to have the court compel it to do so. Sometimes the bidder may indicate that, without any supporting financial data, it is unwilling to pay a price that the target indicates it is worth. This puts pressure on the target's board to release the information, lest the bidder withdraw its offer and shareholders incur losses. Although the target's board and management may truly want the bidder to withdraw the offer, the target's position is made more difficult, because if a bidder's offer is withdrawn, ostensibly due to the target's unwillingness to comply with "reasonable" information requests, the target could become the object of a shareholders' lawsuit.

I have had several occasions where faced with this situation, the target company does not want to disclose its financials or its stockholder list. My group has had a landmark case in the Delaware courts which forced the target company to make the information available, since it was determined that it was for a proper purpose.

BALANCE SHEET

The balance sheet, sometimes called the statement of financial position, is basically a snapshot of a firm's financial position at a given moment in time. The statement constructed on a different date may present a very different picture of the firm's financial position. This may be important for an analyst to bear in mind if he or she suspects that the seller is attempting to present an inaccurate picture of value to inflate the purchase price. The seller may attempt to temporarily alter the makeup of the balance sheet to try to receive a higher purchase price for the firm. In such instances, buyers must critically scrutinize the balance sheet to detect inaccuracies or inconsistencies. The balance sheet reflects information on the resources and assets owned by the company along with the firm's various obligations. The name *balance sheet* comes from the equality between assets and liabilities and stockholder equity. These two parts of the balance sheet are, by definition, always in balance, since the difference between assets and liabilities is the value of stockholders' equity.

Assets = liabilities + stockholders' equity

The balance sheet is constructed so that current items appear before non-current items. A review of the items that normally appear in a balance sheet is presented below.

Assets

Current assets can be converted into cash within a year. Among the assets included here are cash, marketable securities, accounts receivable, inventories, and prepaid expenses.

Cash. Obviously, this is the seller's most liquid asset. Firms concerned about being the object of a hostile bid may attempt to keep their cash reserves as low as the normal operation of the business will allow to prevent the cash from being used to finance the offer. Therefore, potential targets need to monitor their liquidity position. This became an issue in when Kirk Kerkorian, a substantial shareholder in Chrysler Corporation, tried to use Chrysler's large cash position to possibly finance the takeover of the automobile manufacturer. Chrysler rebuffed his overtures, contending that such larger cash reserves were necessary due to the cyclical nature of the industry.

Marketable Securities. These are short-term investments of excess cash. Typical investments are Treasury securities, certificates of deposit (CDs), or other money market securities. Like cash, these very liquid assets can also be used to finance the target's own acquisition.

Accounts Receivable. These items reflect the amount of money the company expects to collect from sales. They include an allowance for bad debts based on the firm's historical collection efforts. The accounts receivable and the allowance for bad debts are usually shown separately, with the net accounts receivable shown in the far-right column of the balance sheet. Acquirers may want to *qualify* the target's accounts receivable through an aging analysis and only include those receivables that have a reasonable likelihood of being collected.

Inventories. Inventories include items such as work in progress, raw materials, and finished goods. Inventories are typically the least liquid asset of the firm. Goods that are finished are naturally considered more liquid than work in progress. Only those inventories that are marketable should be included in a valuation analysis. That is, obsolete inventories need to be identified and eliminated.

Prepaid Expenses. These items have already been paid in advance. Examples are insurance premiums or rent.

Other Assets. This category comprises items such as long-term investments, including the stocks or bonds of other companies. For firms that are active in takeovers, this category may be an important one. The value of these investments will depend on their liquidity and the size of the holdings. The greater the liquidity, the more valuable the asset. If the company holds a large amount of the available stock of a company that is traded on the over-the-counter market with a relatively small daily trading volume, then the value of this asset may be questionable.

Plant and Equipment. Plant and equipment consists of the tangible, capital assets of the firm. They are usually valued at cost, minus accumulated depreciation, and include land, buildings, machinery, and other tangible assets the firm may own, such as computer equipment, vehicles, and furniture. A buyer may attempt to revalue these assets at market prices rather than the book values that the balance sheet reflects. Quick sales of some of these assets may enable a buyer to pay down some of the debt assumed in a leveraged transaction. An inaccurate valuation of the market value of such assets may cause a buyer to assume more debt than the combined firms can handle. Investment banks were/are the object of criticism for presenting an overly optimistic picture of the market value of the assets of merger partners and leveraged buyout (LBO) candidates, which later filed for bankruptcy.

Liabilities

Current liabilities consist of those obligations that the firm has to pay within one year. Among the liabilities included are accounts payable, notes payable and accrued expenses.

Accounts Payable. These are the amounts owed by the firm to suppliers for credit purchases. For each accounts payable, there should be a corresponding accounts receivable on the supplier's balance.

Notes Payable. Notes payable are outstanding obligations, such as loans to commercial banks or obligations to other creditors.

Accrued Expenses. These are expenses for items that have been used to generate sales for which the firm has not paid. The firm may or may not have been billed for these goods or services.

Long- Term Debt. Long-term debts are debt obligations for which payment does not have to be made within one year. This might be, for example, the value of the bonds that the firm may have issued or term loans from financial institutions. The balance sheet should include, where relevant, the long-term obligations of the company, such as capital lease obligations, pension liabilities, and estimated liabilities under warranty agreements. Some explanation of these items may be contained in footnotes.

Depending on the company's accounting practices, there may also be a description of deferred federal income taxes. This will be affected by tax law changes that will determine the firm's ability to shelter income through accelerated depreciation write-offs and other tax-avoidance methods. Buyers have to be careful to detect the presence of hidden liabilities. These are the potential obligations of the seller that may not be explicitly highlighted on the firm's balance sheet. Such liabilities might include future environmental liabilities or losses from pending litigation. These hidden liabilities have become a greater cause for concern in certain industries, such as the chemicals industry, asbestos mining or manufacturing and lately, sub-prime mortgages and financial derivatives.

Stockholders' Equity

This part of the balance sheet shows the owner's claims on the firm's assets after taking into account the obligations to creditors who have a prior claim before equity holders. It includes the ownership interests of both preferred and common stockholders.

Preferred Stock. The company mayor may not have issued preferred stock. Preferred stock is more like debt than equity, in that it usually pays a fixed dividend that must be paid before dividends are paid to common stockholders. Given its debt-like characteristics, this does not enhance the company's financial appearance.

Common Stock. Common stock represents the claims of ownership of the corporation. In the event of bankruptcy, common stockholders have the last claim on the corporation's assets. Several different classes of common stock can exist. The issuance of different classes of common stock with different voting rights is another anti-takeover defense. The common stock is listed on the balance sheet at par value, an arbitrarily assigned value for the common stock that is used primarily for accounting purposes. It may also be used as an indicator of the value of the stock in the event of liquidation. It does not, however, have a useful relationship to the market price of the stock of a publicly held company.

Paid in Capital in Excess of Par. This is the amount of money received for the sale of the common stock that was in excess of the par value.

Retained Earnings. Retained earnings represent the earnings of the corporation not paid out in dividends. The retained earnings on the balance sheet are not a supply of available cash that is put into a bank account and used to pay bills. This amount is really just a bookkeeping entry to account for the earnings not paid out as dividends (and can be paid out in the future as dividends to stockholders) and has no real tangible value as cash.

Certain states would not allow a distribution to stockholders of amounts that are greater than the retained earnings and capital stock, such as in a recapitalization of the company, or the payment of a leveraged dividend.

Issues Related to Understanding Balance Sheets

The balance sheet is important in mergers because it provides an indication of what the company's assets and equity are worth while also showing what the business owes. However, the values of the assets, liabilities, and equity cannot be literally taken from the balance sheet without further scrutiny. A few of the issues that should be considered are as follows:

1. *Time element.* Balance sheets reflect the company's position at an instant in time. The time period chosen will therefore affect the value reflected on the balance sheet.
2. *Cash versus non-cash assets.* The only item on the balance sheet that is actual cash is the one listed as cash. Although the other assets are denoted in dollars, they are not cash. They may be, for example, receivables or inventories, but they cannot be used at the moment to directly pay bills.
3. *Inventory accounting.* The value of the inventory will be affected by the type of accounting method used-FIFO (first-in, first-out) or LIFO (last-in, first-out). The FIFO method assumes that the items the firm uses from its inventory are the oldest items in the inventory, whereas LIFO assumes that the items used are the newest. In a world of rising prices, FIFO will show lower costs and higher profits and will also result in a higher tax bill.

Areas to Consider in Analyzing Balance Sheets

The merger analyst needs to focus on numerous areas when reviewing balance sheets. The following is a sample of a few of these. It is important to remember that each merger or acquisition presents its own unique issues. Therefore, the items mentioned here are merely provided as examples of some that may be relevant.

1. *Understated liabilities.* Beware when the firm has the discretion to estimate its own liabilities. Firms that are offering themselves for sale may want to understate liabilities to increase the value of the firm. Companies may estimate the potential liabilities in various areas such as litigation, health care, and pension liabilities. The bad debt policy of the firm should be examined, particularly if the firm has increased its sales by selling to a *riskier* category of customers while not increasing the allowances for bad debts.

2. *Low-quality assets.* It should be determined that the valuation of all major assets on the balance sheet accurately reflects the value these assets might command in the marketplace or their value to an acquirer. Assets that can be affected by changing government policies, such as pollution control equipment, or assets that are related to the sale of products that may become obsolete have to be examined more closely. Unfortunately, publicly available documents, such as annual reports, lack the detail necessary to determine the market value of some assets. This may be a problem for hostile bidders who may have to rely solely on public documents.

3. *Overstated receivables.* A receivable is only as good as its likelihood of being paid. Receivables from firms that are in financial difficulty or that are subject to return policies may have to be revalued. In the garment industry, for example, if stores believe that a manufacturer may go out of business, they may not pay the receivables. Slow collection of receivables and deteriorating liquidity may cause factors, financing sources that many manufacturers depend on, to freeze credit. This can quickly bring an end to the company. Receivables from firms that are affiliated with the parent company may have been "manufactured" to overstate the parent's value. In general, transactions with affiliates are usually worth closer scrutiny.

4. *Inventory.* Changes in the level of inventory from period to period need to be considered. A rapid buildup of inventory may signal a

decreased marketability for the product. This is often the case, for example, in the toy business. These products can quickly go from being valuable to near valueless.

5. *Valuation of securities.* For firms that have substantial assets in marketable securities, an analysis of the firm's portfolio needs to be conducted. The marketability of each security in the portfolio should be determined. The increased volatility of the securities markets has heightened the need to be cautious in valuing such assets. Substantial holdings of the debt or common stock of firms that are traded in thin markets may be of questionable value, unless ownership in these firms is one of the acquirer's goals. The riskiness of the securities portfolio should comport with the risk preferences of the acquirer. The more marketable the securities and the smaller the holdings, the more likely the acquirer can sell them without incurring a significant cost.

6. *Intangible assets.* Intangible assets, such as goodwill, though difficult to value, may be quite valuable. The name of an established business with a sound reputation in the marketplace may be valuable, even though it is intangible. Assets such as patents may only be as valuable as the company's ability and will to defend them through costly litigation. Patents can sometimes be copied without incurring significant legal liability. When this is likely, careful consideration must be given before paying a high price for these assets.

7. *Real estate assets.* Real estate assets have been a motivation for many takeover battles, such as the Campeau takeover of Federated Stores and Olympia and York's attempted takeover of Santa Fe-Southern Pacific. The valuation of these assets is subject to the vicissitudes of the real estate market. The importance of an accurate valuation of these assets is one reason that the real estate expert has became a more important part of the takeover valuation team in merger and takeover proposals.

8. *Valuation of divisions.* The valuation of divisions of companies became crucial in highly leveraged takeovers. The value that a division, subsidiary, or major asset might bring in the market will only be known after it has actually been sold. This problem can be

prevented if the sale of certain assets can be prearranged with a third party. My partner and I pioneered this process in our takeovers of department store properties. We simply arranges for a pre-purchase of certain assets, which then reduced our purchase price, or allowed us to pay down the acquisition debt. One problem with working with public documents such as annual reports is that it is difficult to get a detailed breakdown of the performance of separate divisions. Such information is hard to acquire in a hostile takeover. Sometimes an acquirer will resist increasing its bid unless the target provides the detailed information necessary to do a full evaluation.

INCOME STATEMENT

The income statement measures the net results of the firm's operations over a specific time interval, such as a calendar year or a fiscal year. A fiscal year is an accounting year that ends on a day other than December 31. The balance sheet and income statement are usually presented together. Most large companies typically prepare monthly statements for management and quarterly statements for stockholders. The balance sheet is usually prepared for the last date of the time period covered by the income statement. The income statement is sometimes referred to as the profit and loss statement. Items that appear in an income statement include:

Net Sales. Net sales are usually listed first on the income statement. Net means the sales after returns on goods shipped and other factors such as breakage. Cost of goods sold is deducted from net sales to determine the net operating profit.

Cost of Goods Sold. Cost of goods sold refers to the company's cost for the goods and services sold. For manufacturing firms, this includes labor, materials, and other items, such as overhead.

Gross Profits. Gross profits are the difference between sales revenues and the cost of goods sold. Gross profit divided by sales revenues is the gross profit margin, or gross margin.

Operating Expenses. Operating expenses are deducted from gross profits to determine *operating profit.* The main categories of operating expenses are selling expense, general and administrative expense, and depreciation expense.

Operating Profit. Operating profit is also called earnings before interest and taxes (EBIT). Operating profit is often considered a good measure of managerial success. It reflects the profit derived from management's operating activities, not financing decisions or governmental tax obligations. It is often considered a good indicator of the target management's performance. Operating profit can be placed in perspective by considering it as a percentage of sales and comparing it with similarly sized firms in the same industry.

Interest Expense. Interest expense is deducted from operating profit to determine earnings before taxes (EBT).

Taxes. Taxes are deducted from the EBT at the relevant tax rate for the corporation. The result is earnings after taxes.

Earnings Available for Common Stockholders. Preferred stock dividends are deducted from earnings after taxes to determine the income available for distribution to common stockholders as dividends.

Earnings per Share (EPS). EPS is calculated by dividing the earnings available to common stockholders by the number of shares of common stock outstanding.

Issues Related to Understanding Income Statements

Although there are many issues that are important to focus on when reviewing income statements, two that very often are relevant to valuations are depreciation policies and inventory valuation.

Depreciation

Depreciation refers to the charging of a portion of the cost of certain capital assets against revenues. Different methods of depreciation will result in different levels of taxable income for the same revenue stream. More rapid depreciation will show a lower taxable income. The Generally Acceptable Accounting Principles (GAAP) set forth the accepted methods of writing off an asset. The two primary methods are straight-line depreciation and accelerated depreciation. The same amount of depreciation is allowed under each method, but the timing of the write-off is different.

Valuing Inventory

The valuation of inventory will affect the value of cost of goods sold in the income statement. This factor, already discussed in the context of balance sheet analysis, will affect profitability on the income statement. If a firm wants to appear more profitable, it may do so by using FIFO rather than LIFO inventory accounting. When we bought a department store chain, we had millions in added value of the inventory by using LIFO inventory valuation.

In private companies, the inventories are often significantly understated by the owners so as to show much lower earnings than actual. This presents particular problems upon acquisitions, since the buyer wants to show the actual inventory for his financing sources, yet the financing sources see lower amounts in the financial statements.

Areas to Consider in Analyzing Income Statements

Just as with the balance sheet, there are various areas that the merger analyst needs to focus on when reviewing income statements. Perhaps the most important is earnings quality. Also important is the related area of revenue recognition.

Quality of Earnings

The quality of earnings may be suspect for a wide variety of reasons. Some firms in industries that have been experiencing hard times have resorted to accounting manipulations to generate income. An example of this occurred in the thrift industry. Savings and loan associations (S&Ls) treated as income a stock dividend paid to them by the Federal Home Loan Mortgage Association (Freddie Mac), an institution owned by the thrifts, as income. The Financial Accounting Standards Board (FASB) stated that this was like paying yourself money. The financial difficulties of the thrift industry motivated many mergers as the industry sought to consolidate. The acquiring and merging firms had to examine the earnings and expected earnings of their merger partners to ascertain whether they were truly of high quality.

Another example of such low-quality earnings occurs in the utilities industries, where the firms are allowed to claim income from projects under construction Allowance for Funds Used During Construction (AFUDC) as earnings, even though the cash from the projects that are not even completed may not be realized until future reporting periods. In some cases, such as the WPPSS bankruptcy, some of these revenues were never realized, since some power plants were never built.

We are of course all familiar with the most famous of all the manipulator of earnings: ENRON CORPORATION and its multi-billion dollar financial collapse.

Generally, the greater the non-cash component of earnings, the lower their quality. This is especially true when there are extraordinary earnings other than from the normal operations. The concern about earnings quality has placed greater emphasis on the cash flow statement and less focus on the income statement.

There was a time when department store operators received most of their earnings from their credit card finance operations and dispositions of their valuable real estate assets.

Revenue Recognition

A related point is that firms can alter the income that appears on their income statement through various accounting manipulations. For example, companies can recognize revenues for services that have not been performed and, in fact, may be performed in later time periods.

This has the effect of increasing the profits in the current time period. The most infamous was the case of Z-Best Corporation which claimed non-existent multi-million dollar cleaning contracts which inflated their purported earnings.

STATEMENT OF CASH FLOWS

The FASB issued Financial Accounting Standard 95 (FAS 95), which required that, all firms issue a statement of cash flows instead of a statement of changes in financial position. This statement would provide analysts and investors with valuable information on the cash receipts and cash payments of the firm. It shows the impact of the firm's operations, investment, and financial decisions on its cash position. Analyzing the statement of cash flows enables the merger analyst to assess the firm's ability to generate future cash flows that can be used to service the debt that might result from a merger or an LBO. The ability to generate sufficient cash flows may determine whether the firm can survive a leveraged transaction. More basically, firms have been forced into bankruptcy when their cash position deteriorated, even though their net income remained positive. High interest payments heightened the need to accurately predict the firm's ability to generate stable cash flows.

A classic example was W. T. Grant and Company, which filed for bankruptcy. The firm had been profitable for the years prior to the bankruptcy filing and showed a positive net income in all those years. Deterioration in cash flows, however, brought about the demise of this established company. This was the case with many large companies, as they suddenly do not generate true cash for operations.

The statement of cash flows adjusts net income to remove the non-cash effects such as accruals of future cash receipts, gains and losses on sales of assets, and depreciation. In doing so, the statement of cash flows becomes a valuable measure of a firm's ability to generate cash, after taking into account the firm's cash needs. The difference between cash flows and net income can indicate the quality of earnings. The smaller this difference, the higher the quality of earnings.

Example of Cash Flows Statement

Investing Activities
Inflows

Receipts from collections or sales of loans made by the enterprise and of other entities' debt instruments (other than cash equivalents) that were purchased by the enterprise.

Receipts from sales of equity instruments of other enterprises and from returns of investment in those instruments.

Receipts from sales of property, plant, and equipment and other productive.
assets

Outflows

Disbursements for loans made by the enterprise and payments to acquire debt instruments of other entities (other than cash equivalents).

Payments to acquire equity instruments of other enterprises.

Payments at the time of purchase or soon before or after purchase to acquire property, plant, and equipment and other productive assets.

Financing Activities
Inflows

Proceeds from issuing equity instruments.

Proceeds from issuing bonds, mortgages, notes, and from other short or long-term borrowing.

Outflows

Payments of dividends or other distributions to owners, including outlays to reacquire the enterprise's equity instruments.

Repayments of amounts borrowed.

Other principal payments to creditors who have extended long-term credit.

Operating Activities

Inflows

Cash receipts from sales of goods or services, including receipts from collection or sale of accounts and both short- and long-term notes receivable from customers arising from those sales.

Cash receipts from returns on loans, other debt instruments of other entities, and equity securities-interest and dividends.

All other cash receipts that do not stem from transactions defined as investing or financing activates, such as amounts received to settle lawsuits; proceeds of insurance settlements, except for those that are directly related to investing or financing activities, such as from destruction of a building; and refunds from suppliers.

Outflows

Cash payments to acquire materials for manufacture or goods for resale, including principal payments on accounts and both short and long term notes payable to suppliers for those materials or goods.

Cash payments to other suppliers and employees for other goods or services.

Cash payments to governments for taxes, duties, fines, and other fees or penalties.

Cash payments to lenders and other creditors for interest.

All other cash payments that do not stem from transactions defined as investing or financing activities, such as payments to settle lawsuits, cash contributions to charities, and cash refunds to customers.

Depreciation and Cash Flows

The income statement and the statement of cash flows differ in how they treat depreciation. All non-cash charges, those that do not involve a cash outlay, are added back to the net after-tax income to determine the cash flow. One of the major categories of non-cash charges is depreciation. These charges are tax shields that minimize taxes but distort the firm's true cash. Basically, depreciation is neither a source nor a use of funds.

Free cash flows can be projected into the future after taking into consideration the firm's future capital investment needs. Including capital investment enables free cash flows to be more than a short-term measure of the firm's health. Using free cash flows, as it is defined above, the analyst can measure both the quality of the firm's future earnings and the firm's ability to maintain its future competitive position.

ANALYSIS OF FINANCIAL STATEMENTS AND COMPUTER PROGRAMS

Having discussed the basics of financial statements, we can now analyze them to determine the firm's financial condition. The analyst's main tool is a spreadsheet program such as Lotus, Quattro Pro, or Excel, which allows the user to perform a great number of financial calculations very rapidly. It also permits a complete set of calculations to be redone instantly after certain changes have been enacted. Of course you can do it my way with a pencil and a 12-column analysis pad.

The various other software packages available are really large macro programs that use spreadsheet programs. The user loads the spreadsheet program and asks the program to use the financial programs written on this software package. One software package that provides good summary data for financial analysis, using Lotus, is Financial Calculator. Among its many other functions, this package instantly provides a large array of financial ratios after the user inputs the balance sheet and income statements. However, this package and others lack the flexibility to alter the framework to deal with the unique aspects of each merger. In effect, the user is locked into a standard framework that may not be that appropriate to the case at hand. Another such program is FINSOLVE. It also uses Lotus to perform a variety of standard financial computations, such as financial statement analysis. In addition, Lotus offers various add-on templates to its Windows version that compute financial ratios and even attempt to value businesses.

Other software packages do even more intricate analysis. One such program is ValuSource. This program does a complete valuation analysis that includes financial statement analysis but also goes so far as to do a complete valuation. It contains source data, such as comparable transaction data and risk premium data, using add-on data sets that are purchased separately.

FINANCIAL RATIO ANALYSIS

Financial ratio analysis, one of the main tools of financial analysis, permits an easy comparison with similar firms, such as those in the same industry and of a similar size. Ratio analysis standardizes the financial data that help reduce the effect of factors such as sheer size. In doing so, the financial performance of acquisition candidates in the same industry that are of very different sizes can be better compared.

The more commonly used financial ratios can be divided into the following categories:

• Liquidity ratios
• Activity ratios
• Financial leverage ratios
• Profitability ratios

Liquidity Ratios

Liquidity ratios measure the firm's ability to satisfy its current obligations as they come due. The two principal liquidity ratios are the current ratio and the quick ratio.

$$\text{Current ratio} = \frac{\text{Current assets}}{\text{Current liabilities}}$$

Current assets = cash plus all assets that can be converted into cash within a year. These include short-term marketable securities, accounts receivable, and inventories.

Current liabilities = all the financial obligations that are expected to be paid within a year. These include accounts payable, notes payable, and the current part of the long-term debt.

Working capital = Current assets - Current liabilities

The current ratio measures the firm's ability to meet its short-term obligations using assets that are expected to be converted into cash within a year. The quick ratio removes inventories from current assets because they may not be as liquid as some of the other current assets. The more liquid a firm is, the higher the current and quick ratios. The greater the liquidity of a firm, the lower the probability it can become *technically insolvent,* which means that the firm cannot meet its current obligations as they come due. The more liquid the firm before a takeover, the more likely it will not face liquidity problems if it assumes additional post-merger costs, such as higher interest payments. If, however, the firm is only marginally liquid at the time of the merger, it may experience liquidity problems following the merger, unless it can rely on the other merger partner for additional liquidity. Generally, the more illiquid part of the current assets is the inventories. If the analyst would like to have a more stringent measure of liquidity, the quick ratio can be used. When there are questions about the liquidity of the company's inventories, greater reliance is placed on the quick rather than the current ratio. In such circumstances, other measures, such as the activity ratios, need to be carefully examined.

Activity Ratios

Activity ratios reflect the speed with which various accounts are converted into cash. Activity ratios are an important supplement to liquidity ratios because liquidity ratios do not provide information on the composition of the firm's various assets.

Average Collection Period

$$\text{Average collection period} = \frac{\text{Accounts receivable}}{\text{Annual credit sales}/360}$$

The average collection period indicates the number of days an account remains outstanding. For example, if the average collection period is 60 days, it takes the firm an average of 60 days to collect an account receivable.

As with all financial ratios, activity ratios make sense only in relation to the firm's collection policy. If the firm requires customers to pay within 30 days and the average collection period is 60 days, the ratio is a negative indicator. But if the firm allows customers to pay within 90 days, and the average collection period is 60 days, the ratio looks good. Further analysis would still have to be done to see whether the early payment was a result of cash discounts for early payment, which would cut into the company's profitability.

In a merger it is important to determine whether the collection and credit policies of the two firms are similar. If they are not, and if the acquirer plans to institute stricter payment and credit policies, then the impact of the policies on the target's sales needs to be projected. If the target has large sales only because it is extending credit to those customers with weaker credit ratings, then the compatibility of the two firms and their credit policies needs to be examined further. This would be important in mergers of retail firms that have significant credit sales. Moreover, the profitability of the target, after the acquirer's credit policies are instituted, may be below what might be necessary to meet the cost of capital associated with the acquisition.

Inventory Turnover

$$\text{Inventory turnover} = \frac{\text{Cost of goods sold}}{\text{Average inventory}}$$

The inventory turnover ratio reveals how often the inventory of the firm turns over in a year. The cost of goods sold is derived from the income statement, whereas the average inventory is taken from the balance sheet. Given that the balance sheet reflects the firm's position on a given day, it might be useful to derive the average inventory by taking the beginning year inventory from the previous year's balance sheet and averaging that with the current year's amount. A better way would be to determine the inventory levels on a monthly basis and average these amounts. This would help reduce the impact of seasonal influences. The more seasonal the business, the more care needs to be exercised in interpreting the inventory turnover ratio.

The appropriate amount of inventory turnover is highly dependent on industry norms. A ratio of 30 may be normal for a retail food store, whereas an aircraft manufacturer may be quite pleased with a value of 1.

Although the inventory turnover value should be compared with industry averages, care should be exercised not to place too much weight on the pure number without further analysis. A high inventory turnover is normally a good sign, but this need not always be the case. For example, a firm could have a very high inventory turnover level by holding smaller than appropriate inventories. A high inventory turnover could be a result of shortages, or it could be related to the firm's credit policies, whereby the firm is lowering its profit margins and is, in effect, "giving the product away" to move inventory. Therefore, inventory levels need to be placed in perspective with the firm's average inventory levels and the average for the industry.

Generally, a low inventory turnover is a bad sign for a potential target, for it may be indicative of illiquid or inactive inventories. If the acquirer believes that the inventories are indeed marketable, then it must also have an answer to the question, Why was the manufacturer of the inventory unable to sell these goods in a manner that was comparable with competitors? If the answer is mismanagement and if the acquirer believes it can solve this problem, then the low inventory turnover should not be of as great a concern.

Fixed Asset Turnover

$$\text{asset turnover} = \frac{\text{Sales Total}}{\text{Net fixed assets}}$$

Fixed asset turnover reflects the extent to which a firm is utilizing its fixed assets to generate sales. This ratio is important to an acquirer who is contemplating acquiring a capital intensive firm. However, the analyst should take great care when comparing this ratio to industry averages. The fixed asset turnover value derived from the ratio shown in the preceding equation is very sensitive to several factors that may vary by company.

The fixed asset ratio is based on the historical cost of assets. Firms that have acquired their assets more recently may show a lower fixed asset turnover because the dollar value of their fixed assets is higher, and this value enters into the denominator of the ratio. The greater the rate of inflation over the period of asset acquisition, the more this ratio can lead to deceptive results.

Other factors that can affect the fixed asset turnover are the firm's depreciation policies and the use of leased rather than purchased assets. If the assets were recently acquired, a lag may occur between the acquisition of the assets and the resulting generation of sales from the use of these assets. Therefore, a recent acquisition may increase the denominator of the ratio but have little immediate effect on the numerator. Consideration of the industry norms relating to the investment-sales lag should be given before any judgment is made with regard to a target's use of fixed assets. A fixed asset turnover of 1.90, for example, means that a firm turns over its fixed assets 1.9 times a year.

Total Asset Turnover

$$\text{Total asset turnover} = \frac{\text{Sales}}{\text{Total assets}}$$

This ratio shows how effectively a firm uses its total resources. The caveats that apply to the use of the fixed asset turnover also apply here. A total asset turnover ratio of 1.60, for example, means that the firm turns over its assets 1.60 times a year.

Financial Leverage Ratios

Given the large amounts of debt frequently associated with takeovers, financial leverage ratios become a most useful financial analysis tool for the merger analyst. The financial leverage or debt ratios indicate the degree of financial leverage that the firm has assumed. Financial leverage refers to the amount of debt the firm has used relative to the equity in its total capitalization.

In takeovers, the analyst must compute the financial leverage ratios based on different assumptions regarding the total debt used to finance the acquisition. These resulting debt levels are then compared with industry norms and standards to reveal how the merged firm compares with other firms in the industry. A takeover often results in a firm being well above the industry average.

When the acquirer has plans to "pay down" the debt following the acquisition by assets sales, the financial leverage ratios should be projected for several years to determine the impact of the debt retirement. In this case, the analyst would like to determine how long it takes until the leverage ratios return to industry norms.

Debt

<u>Total debt</u>
Debt= Total assets

The debt ratio is usually computed by adding together short-term and long-term debt. It is also sometimes computed by using total liabilities rather than just formal debt. The debt ratio indicates the firm's ability to service its debt. Obviously, creditors want this ratio to be low. An acquirer may consider a target firm with a relatively larger amount of marketable fixed assets and a low debt ratio to be an ideal takeover target. Such a firm may have much unused borrowing capacity and may be vulnerable to a takeover. Companies with low debt ratios relative to the industry, recognizing their own vulnerability, may load up on debt. This is ironic, since doing so may adversely increase the risk level of the company. A debt ratio of 0.65, for example, means that the firm has financed 65% of its assets by using debt.

Debt to Equity

$$\text{Debt to equity} = \frac{\text{Long-term debt}}{\text{Total equity}}$$

The debt to equity ratio is one of the more often quoted financial leverage ratios. Preferred stock is commonly added to long-term debt in the computation because preferred stock payments are somewhat fixed. A firm cannot be forced into receivership if preferred stock payments are not made. It is usually assumed, however, that the firm has every intention of making these payments when the debt is issued. Therefore, they usually are treated as fixed. This is why preferred stock is more like debt than equity and is often categorized with fixed income securities.

It is difficult to judge a good debt to equity ratio without analyzing the firm's cash flows. Firms with very stable cash flows can more predictably handle higher debt levels. If an acquirer is considering taking over a target and financing the acquisition primarily with debt, a cash flow analysis needs to be conducted. If the cash flows are volatile, an added element of risk is introduced. A debt to equity ratio of 0.67, for example, shows that the firm's long-term debt is only 67% as large as its equity.

Debt to Total Capitalization

$$\text{Debt to Total Capitalization} = \frac{\text{Long-term debt}}{\text{Long-term debt} + \text{Stockholders' equity}}$$

This ratio determines the proportion of total capitalization, which is the firm's permanent financing, that long-term debt represents. A low debt to total capitalization ratio is usually taken to be a desirable attribute in a target. Generally, firms with lower debt to total capitalization ratios are considered better credit risks because a larger equity cushion exists to protect creditors. Such firms can become takeover targets because of a greater, unused borrowing capacity.

In addition to the leverage ratios discussed, coverage ratios are often used to measure the firm's ability to meet its interest payments and other fixed payments. These ratios are the times interest earned ratio and the fixed charge coverage ratio.

Times Interest Earned

$$\text{Times interest earned} = \frac{\text{EBIT}}{\text{Interest charges}}$$

As noted earlier, earnings before interest and taxes (EBIT) is also called operating profit. The times interest earned ratio is a good measure of the firm's ability to meet its debt obligations. It is a particularly important measure for creditors, since it tells them how much operating profit can shrink and the firm is still able to meet its debt obligations. For this reason, it has great relevance to firms that are planning to finance an acquisition through debt.

The pre-merger and the post-merger times interest earned ratios are calculated to determine whether earnings are sufficient to meet the expected debt payments. Generally, a ratio between 3 and 5 is considered good. Firms in more volatile or cyclical industries may need to have higher ratios.

Fixed Charge Coverage

$$\text{Fixed charge coverage} = \frac{\text{EBIT}}{\begin{array}{l}\text{Interest payments} + \text{Lease payments} + \\ \text{Preferred stock dividends before tax} + \\ \text{Before-tax sinking fund payments}\end{array}}$$

This ratio, along with variations, is used when there are other significant fixed payments in addition to interest payments. Since the inability to meet other fixed obligations could easily force the firm into receivership, the fixed charge coverage may be a better way to measure this type of risk.

Profitability Ratios

These ratios allow the firm to measure profit in relation to sales volume. The purpose of an acquisition should be to generate profits. Profit-minded acquirers invest a given amount of capital to obtain the right to an expected future stream of profits. These profitability ratios allow the acquirer to determine the target's profitability relative to that of its competitors and other firms.

$$\text{Gross profit margins} = \frac{\text{Sales} - \text{Cost of goods sold}}{\text{Sales}}$$

$$= \frac{\text{Gross profit}}{\text{Sales}}$$

$$= \frac{\text{EBIT}}{\text{Sales}}$$

$$= \frac{\text{Earning after taxes}}{\text{Sales}}$$

The gross profit indicates how much is left, on a percentage basis, after payments are expended for goods. The operating profit margin measures what is left before the impact of the financing decisions and governmental tax liabilities. The net profit margin is an after tax measure of the firm's profitability. It measures what is left after all payments, including taxes, are made. There is no standard net profit margin; there are great differences across industries. Although the net profit margin is often cited as a measure of a corporation's success, good net margins differ considerably across industries. A net margin as low as I may be considered acceptable for a high-volume business like a retail food store, whereas a net profit margin of 10% would be low for a jewelry store.

The merger analyst should review the historical trend in the firm's gross, operating, and net profit margins. An upward trend is usually considered a sign of financial strength, whereas a decline generally signifies weakness. A deterioration in those margins, if it causes the stock price to sag, may make a firm vulnerable to a hostile takeover. Falling stock prices combined with highly marketable assets can present an opportunity to leveraged buyers, who may be able to sell assets quickly to payoff the debt while keeping the remaining assets that they acquired at bargain prices.

Return on Investment

$$\text{Return on investment} = \frac{\text{Earnings after taxes}}{\text{Total assets}}$$

The return on investment ratio is sometimes also called the total asset ratio. This ratio measures how effectively management can generate after-tax profits by using the firm's available assets. It has a number of drawbacks, including the fact that it is a book value ratio. If the assets are not carried on the books at accurate values, then the ratio may not be very meaningful. This was the same drawback of the total asset turnover ratio. Merger analysts are more concerned with market values than with book values. Therefore, this ratio may serve as a rough guide to the true return that the firm is receiving on its assets. If the market value of the assets is significantly greater than the book value, then the return on investment may overstate the effectiveness of the firm's management. Buyers should understand that this high return does not mean that they could buy the target's assets and achieve a similar return. A low return on investment, however, does not mean that the target's assets could not be better utilized by the buyer.

Return on Equity

$$\text{Return on equity} = \frac{\text{Earnings after taxes}}{\text{Stockholders' equity}}$$

This ratio is usually calculated by including both preferred stock and common stock in the denominator. It is a measure of the kind of return the company's owners are earning. The return on equity is an often-cited measure of performance used by both investors and management. Since equity, like total assets, is a balance sheet item, it may not accurately reflect the value of equity during the full year. An average of quarterly values can help offset this drawback. The return on equity also suffers from the fact that it is a book value, not a market value. Ironically, a high return on equity does not mean that shareholders will receive a high return on their investment. This problem is greater when there is a larger divergence between the market value of the equity and the book value. One solution to this problem is for the analyst to reconstruct the return on equity by substituting the market value for the book value of equity.

The return on equity is greatly influenced by the degree of financial leverage the firm employs. For example, if a firm is willing to increase its level of debt by borrowing to purchase income-generating assets, then it can increase after-tax earnings while stockholders' equity remains constant. A naive analyst might interpret this as an up-and-coming company and a good takeover target. The higher return on equity, however, does not come without a price. The cost of this higher return on equity is the additional risk the firm assumes when it increases its financial leverage.

Market-based ratios

If securities markets are relatively efficient, adverse information contained in the financial statements should be reflected in the market-based ratios. These ratios contain the market's assessment of the financial well-being of the firm as well as the market's projection of the company's future ability to provide stockholders a profitable return on their investment.

SUMMARY

The analysis described based on financial statements that are normally available publicly to the merger analyst by virtue of legal filing requirements for publicly held companies. In addition, various financial ratios commonly used to measure the financial well-being of a company were discussed. The value of much of this financial analysis depends on the quality of the available financial data. Friendly transactions and of course privately negotiated ones, tend to feature greater disclosure between the two parties. In a hostile takeover, however, the target will only disclose the minimum as required by federal disclosure laws and any other disclosure requirements imposed by litigation.

I hope that this deeper insight into the realm of acquisitions of every type has provided you with a greater and complete understanding of all the underlying analysis required for an acquisition.

If you brake down the numbers, step by step in every stage of the analysis of any acquisition, it is really easy to understand.

Anyone can buy the business they work for individually, or in concert with other managers, or together with a private equity group willing to assist in the acquisition if they are provided an opportunity to own some stock in the new company.

Use my step-by-step method, and feel free to make contact with me and my associates relating to anything you may need help with relating to a proposed acquisition.

E-mail: info@sterlingcooper.us

My best wishes to you in your acquisition endeavors.

APPENDIX LISTING

APPENDIX 1.

LIST OF BUSINESSES TO ACQUIRE

When I checked last with several of the well-known sources of business information, there were approximately 13,000,000 businesses of every type in the United States, and millions more in the English speaking world.

You will, as your goal, own a business with a revenue base of at least $2,000,000 to $25,000,000 or more, using this step by step program. If you were creative at ways of raising capital outlined in Chapter 1, and you were able to raise $1-$3 million, you may be able to acquire a business with as much as $50-$100 million in revenues or more.

The business you choose to buy should be, in order of likely importance:

1   The business you now work for, since you are experienced in running it or potentially running it and should be able to get your co-workers to buy it and contribute capital to do so.
2   Any business for which you have a passion for and some experience, or a present competition of the business you work for.
3   Any business similar to or in the broad sense in your "industry", such as manufacturing, trucking, retailing, or whatever the business you work for, is categorized to be in.
4   Any business, if you intend to work with and retain the existing management personnel to work for you/with you after the acquisition.

You may easily obtain a fairly reliable list of businesses of the size you may desire, for business list providers such as INFO USA, Dun & Bradstreet, Wards and Hoovers or the Thomas Directory. Others may also be known to you as well.

These lists will provide you with the leads to start with on your search. In addition you will be able to search by zip code, by state and by other criteria you may set up.

Do not limit yourself to close proximity of your present residence. Maybe consider the exotic location you always wanted such as a mountain resort, or a tropical location, maybe both.

These list providers will also have available the specific SIC (Standard Industrial Classification) for literally every business you may possibly consider, so take advantage of this free service to obtain the free lists. Then identify your search criteria and GO.

APPENDIX 2

INFORMATIONAL QUESTIONNAIRE

COMPANY:

CONTACT PERSON FOR QUESTIONS AND PHONE

WITH THIS CONFIDENTIAL REPORT PLEASE ATTACH THE FOLLOWING:

1. Auditors letters (item #8)
2. Appraisals of real estate (item #12)
3. All current litigation (item #27)
4. Description of ESOP (item #34)
5. Copy of policy manual (item #35)
6. Table of organization (item #59)
7. Photos of plant and products (item #60)
8. One month's management reports (item #61)
9. Financial projections (item #61)
10. Three year financial (item #63)
11. Equipment list (item #73 c)
12. Accounts payable (item #75)
13. Employment contracts (item #83 i)
14. If public company:
    a. Current form 10K
    b. Last form 10Q issued
    c. Last 3 years copies of form 8K
    d. Last 2 years annual reports and proxy statements
15. If an item is not applicable to your business, indicate "N/A".

PLEASE USE ADDITIONAL SHEETS AND REFERENCE ALL ANSWERS BY QUESTIONS NUMBER.

NOTE: THIS INFORMATION MAY BE USED IN THE PREPARATION OF INFORMATION, BROCHURES, ETC., TO LENDERS, ADVISORS, AND OTHER AUTHORIZED PERSONS.

Date _____

NAME OF COMPANY:

1 State of incorporation_____when _____
2 Authorized capital stock and par value. $_____
   Shares $_____par
3 Currently issued and outstanding_____shares
   $_____total value, including paid-in capital.
4 Are your state franchise and business taxes paid to date or current?

   _____

   Remarks:

5. List of states where the corporation is registered as a foreign corporation or transacts business:

   1 List the names of subsidiaries: Name State Incorporated Percentage Owned
   2 Independent auditors name and address:
   3 Do you have auditors' letters to management for the past three years?_____If so, please enclose.
   4 Up to what year has the IRS audited your corporate tax returns? _____
   5 Do you have a line of bank credit? ___
      How much is the open line and commitment fee?____
      What collateral is pledged?
      1 Are compensating balances required as part of your loan arrangement?_____
      2 Give complete description of real estate owned.

13. Are you (as a corporation or personally - please specify) guarantor of any bank loans or similar obligations? If so, explain:

(a) Are any stockholders guarantors of corporate loans? If yes, explain:

3 Does your company own any patents or trademarks? If so, please briefly describe:

15. List your stockholders:

Name   % held   Shares

16. How much capital do you need within the next 90 days?

If you need none, what are your projected needs for the next 12 months?

1 How are your creditor relationships?

2 Do you pay your bills in: 30 days_____60 days_____90 days_____more than 90 days _____

3 Do you need additional equipment?_____If yes, what type and cost? _____

20. List any outside business interests of key employees and or stockholders.

(a) How much annual income do they derive from these sources?

4 Explain the responsibility flow in the area of invoice, receipt, verification, authorization for payment and payment signature.

5 How do you control your internal cost and cash controls to monitor any potential cash misapplication?

(a) Any of your employees ever been fired for such offense?

How much was involved? _____

23. Are employees who handle deposits/disbursements bonded or insured? _____

What coverage limits? _____

24. Do you employ an accounts receivable financing or factoring plan? _____

If yes, briefly describe the program (i.e. with whom, at what rate, percent advanced, age of qualified receivables, chargebacks, cash collateral, etc.)

1 How long would the selling shareholder like to stay employed?

_____

2 If selling shareholder continues to be employed by the company, all conflicts of interest or time commitments must be eliminated. Can this be done immediately?

27. List on an attached page ALL current litigation by classification as follows: a) claims against the company, b) claims on behalf of the company.

(a) Are there any reserves established for claims and litigation?

3 Has the company or any of its officers ever been found guilty of a felony in the operation of the business?

Foreign illegal payments?

1 Are there any present local, state or federal investigations of any kind in progress against the company?

2 Do you have in-house counsel?

1 Are you in compliance with current governmental regulations with such departments as OSHA, FTC, EEOC, SEC, DOT and EPA? If not in compliance, explain:

32. What unions represent your various employees?

UNION EMPLOYEE GROUP CONTRACT EXPIRATION

33. Are your employee relations generally good?

If not, explain any current grievances or litigations:

2 Do you have an ESOP?_____If so, please enclose.

3   Do you have a company policy manual?_____If so, please enclose.

36. How many employees:

FYE Mgt. Clerical Plant Sales Other Total

20___

20___

20___

Current ____

4   What specialists do you employ, i.e. consultants?

5   Do you expect all key employees to stay after a sale? _____ Who will not stay?

6   What trade associations do you belong to? (As a company and as an individual.)

7   What insurance coverage do you carry and in what amounts?

INSURANCE INSURANCE AMOUNT OF MONTHLY TYPE
CARRIER COVERAGE RATE

Fire _____ ____Product _____

Liability _____ General Liability _____ _____

_____ Other _____ _____

_____   Other _____ _____

_____   Other_____ _____

_____   _____ _____

(a) Describe your claim experience. (By type of claim.)

1   What key man insurance is carried?

2   What type of security measures do you institute at office, plant and equipment storage facilities, and are employees bonded?

3   How much theft and vandalism do you estimate in a year period?

44. Do you conduct job safety programs for your employees?

(a) How many employees were injured in your operation last year?

_____

(b) What types of workman's compensation claims have you experienced during the past two years?

(c) What is your overall workman's compensation costs per $100.00 or payroll?

(d) Were there any fatalities?

4 List company owned cars, planes, yachts, condos?

How much is your usage? (specify)
List appraised value of each:

1 How is your sales operation organized?

    47. Do you have any contractual customer relationships?

    Will you briefly describe:

2 Approximately how many customers and approximately what % of your business, have you served continuously for at least the past two years?

3 In submitted a price proposal, or contract bid, on any project at this time, what % of profit do you figure. Do you provide discounts for favored customers, for specific lines, and/or specific geographic territories? How do you establish pricing in your company?

4 When you figure overhead into a price, do you include total overhead? _____

5 List special services that you provide that are unique, different, or not easily duplicated by your competitors, or by potential new entrants into your market:

6 What are your major sales territories?

    53. Are there any large contracts, significant new customers, or new markets that you project adding during the next 12 months? _____

Explain:

7   Do you have any government contracts?_____If so, what percent of your total business is from the government? _____

8   Are there any large contracts, existing customers, or present markets that you expect to lose, terminate or abandon during the next 12 months? _____

9   Do you do business with agents? _____

TYPE OF PROJECT DISCOUNT OR PROFIT MARKUP

Explain:

If yes, approximately what % of your revenue do you do with agents? _____

What is the average contractual % that you pay to the agents? _____

1   Do you have in-house computer(s)? _____ If yes, which model(s) _____ and what do you use it for?

2   What type of telephone system/communications do you employ?

What is the cost of the system?_____
What special features? _____ Do you own, lease, rent, or otherwise finance your communication system or portions of your communications system?

_____
Are all of your facilities on the same communication system?

_____
If not, are the systems in use mutually compatible? _____
How many on your EDP staff? _____

1   Enclose the table of organization with a brief description of the senior officers' duties.

2   Enclose photos, if available, of the plant and products. Also enclose all company's brochures.

3   Enclose one month's management reports used to operate the business.

    62. Enclose, if available, financial projections for this year and the next year.

    FINANCIAL STATEMENT

    63. Enclose 3 year statements including the notes to the financials.

    (a) If your statement is a consolidation of several companies then enclose a consolidating statement.

    (b) If no consolidating statement is available then indicate all intercompany transactions.

4   Are these 3 year statements certified?_____If not, have you ever had certified statements?

5   How often do you prepare in-house financials?

6   What is the normal time delay from the end of the month and the time you receive your financials?

7   At the end of any of the last 3 years have the accountants made any material year-end adjustments? _____

If so, explain:

BALANCE SHEET

68. Cash

    a. Is cash encumbered in any way? _____

    b. If a negative balance is reflected on current statements, is this due to a bank overdraft facility or checks drawn but not mailed?

    c. If this is an overdraft facility, what is the amount of the line?_____

69. Accounts Receivable

    a. Please enclose an aging schedule. The last page reflecting aging totals is all that is necessary.

    b. Does any customer represent more than 5% of the total?
       If so, list the names and the percentage.

    c. Are receivables pledged for any loans?

70. Investments

    a. Indicate type and amount.

71. Inventory

    a. Indicate how valued, i.e. LIFO, FIFO or other.
    b. When was last physical taken?
    c. Are there any obsolete items included in total?
    d. If work in process is indicated separately, how valued?
    e. During the manufacturing state or in storage of the inventory are there any environmental problems? If so, please explain:

72. Prepaid Expenses

    a. List for two years the major items in this category and amounts.

73. Property, Plant and Equipment

    a. Property - when was it acquired?
    b. Plant - What condition is it in? _____

    How much spent over the last 3 years? _____
    c. Equipment - Is it competitive with others in the industry?
_____

If not, what changes are needed and what is the replacement costs? Enclose an equipment list showing date of purchase, description, cost and fair market value.

74. Other

    a.   List major categories and amounts.

75. Accounts Payable

    a.   Enclose an aging schedule if payables are not current.

76. Loans Payable

    a.   List all loans separately, amounts, terms, and what collateral supports these loans.

77. Taxes

    a.   Are all taxes current?_____If not, list type and amounts past due.

78. Accrued Expenses

    a.   List major categories and amounts.

79. Long Term Debt

    a.   List all debt separately, amounts, terms, and what collateral supports these debts.

80. Net Worth

   a. Have any dividends been paid in the last 2 years?_____If so, when and how much?

81. Other Balance Sheet Items

   a. Describe any other items listed on Balance Sheet but not indicated in any category above.

PROFIT AND LOSS STATEMENT

82. Income

   a. List major categories and amounts, or major customers.
   b. What is your policy on refunds and or allowances?
   c. When do you recognize income?
   d. If there was more than a 5% change from last year, explain.

83. Expenses

   a. If any item materially changed from last year, explain.
   b. Indicate what licenses are needed to operate.
   c. Over what life do you depreciate your plant and equipment?
   d. Are there any unusual expenses recorded on the books?

   _____

   If so, what are they and the amount?

   e. What is the salary and bonus arrangement for the principal officers of the company?
   f. What fringe benefits do the principal officers receive?
   g. What compensation does the Board of Directors receive?

    h. Are there any family members of the principal shareholder employed? _____

If so, indicate their names, their duties and compensation received.

    i. Are there any employment contracts?_____If so, enclose a copy.

    j. Has the company a union? _____

If so, summarize the contract terms and expiration date.

    k. Has the company a pension or profit sharing plan? If so, summarize the terms. Is the pension plan over or under funded and to what amount?

    l. If the land and plant is leased, what are the terms of the lease?

    m. Is any equipment leased by a related party? Indicate items and amounts.

If owned by a related party, indicate to whom.

84. Other Income and Expenses

    a. If any item materially changed from last year, explain.

    b. Explain any unusual items.

85. Profit or Loss

    a. If a loss, or a reduced profit for any period - explain reason.

    b. If a loss, or a reduced profit for any period - explain what steps are being taken to reverse this condition.

    c. If the company is experiencing an increase in profits, explain what the company is doing differently.

    d. When was the company's last price increase?

Is the company's price structure competitive in the industry?

    e. Who are your major competitors?

    f. Indicate by product line, cost of goods sold, and retail price.

    g. What is your current average daily business production volume?

    h. What is the capacity of the plant? Can it be utilized for more than one shift?

86. Your added comments

APPENDIX 3.

GUARANTEE OF CONFIDENTIALITY

THE UNDERSIGNED, individually and in his corporate capacity, represents that he has requested and is receiving confidential information for the sole purpose of evaluating the potential purchase of a business.

THE UNDERSIGNED warrants that the information now or hereafter provided, will not be disclosed to any person, company, or firm not directly involved in the undersigned's consideration of the purchase of the business.

Dated this_____day of_____, 20_____

By:_____
(Name and Title)

NAME OF BUSINESS

APPENDIX 4.

CASH FLOW PLANNER Date Prepared:_____
Prepared By: _____

Fill In Month	Month 1	Month 2	Month 3	Month 4
Cash In	Budget	Actual	Budget	Actual
Cash from sales Current				
30 days				
60 days				
90 days				
Other:				
Total cash received				
Cash Out				
Production/purchasing costs				
Selling expenses				
Administration expenses				
Long term loan repayment				
Interest on debt				
Other				

Total cash paid out				
Monthly Cash Flow Summary				
Cash flow surplus (deficit)				
Monthly				
Year to date				
Cash available (or required)				
- beginning of month				
- end of month				

SAMPLE CASH FLOW FORM

APPENDIX 5.

LENDERS LISTING

Contact us for this information and additional related topics.

E-mail: info@sterlingcooper.us

APPENDIX 6.

SAMPLE FINANCING PROPOSAL

See Chapter 6.

APPENDIX 7

SAMPLE ACQUISITION PROPOSAL LETTER

RE: NAME OF COMPANY TO BE ACQUIRED

Dear Mr./Ms. (SELLERS' NAMES):

We are finished with our evaluation of your fine company, from a financial standpoint, and would like to propose the purchase of all the outstanding shares, including the assumption of all the assets and liabilities, as follows:

1 Purchase price of
2

This Offer is subject to completion of our due diligence, and execution of a definitive purchase agreement, and expires within 15 days of the date of this letter unless we hear from you to discuss it further, AND IS SUBJECT TO RECEIPT OF A FINANCING COMMITMENT SUFFICIENT TO FUND THE TRANSACTION.

Our Offer is being made on behalf of an entity which will be formed specifically for this acquisition, for who I will be the exclusive representative relating to this transaction.

The proposed purchase consideration is based on the information you provided relating to this company, and includes all known information made available to us as of the dates last contained on said information. Our Offer is subject to change upon receipt of updated financial or factual information, discovery of any additional unknown information during the due diligence process, receipt of financing commitment or any material changes in the financial condition of the company from the date of the information that was provided for us as a basis for solicitation of this Offer.

As part of our continuation of the due diligence process, I am enclosing a 24-page form to be completed at your convenience, **only if it is your desire to go forward with this proposed transaction.** This process will allow us to start our due diligence information gathering and completion process toward the preparation of a draft purchase agreement without having to send on-site personnel at this time, and allow us to move toward the timely conclusion of this proposed purchase transaction.

Page 2.

This Offer is a non-binding indication of value, from a financial standpoint, and is subject to the terms and conditions as outlined in this letter. Any changes or revisions of the Offer may only be made in writing by me. In addition, under no circumstances are you authorized to publicize this Offer without our specific written permission.

Looking forward to your response.

Your very truly,

YOUR NAME, address and phone
Or your present letterhead

APPENDIX 8.

SAMPLE CORPORATE FORMS

Contact us for this information and additional related topics.

E-mail: info@sterlingcooper.us

APPENDIX 9.

365 DAY PROGRESS CHART

Day 1	Day 2	Day 3	Day 4	Day 5
Day 6	Day 7	Day 8	Day 9	Day 10
Day 11	Day 12	Day 13	Day 14	Day 15
Day 16	Day 17	Day 18	Day 19	Day 20
Day 21	Day 22	Day 23	Day 24	Day 25
Day 26	Day 27	Day 28	Day 29	Day 30
Day 31	Day 32	Day 33	Day 34	Day 35
Day 36	Day 37	Day 38	Day 39	Day 40
Day 41	Day 42	Day 43	Day 44	Day 45
Day 46	Day 47	Day 48	Day 49	Day 50
Day 51	Day 52	Day 53	Day 54	Day 55
Day 56	Day 57	Day 58	Day 59	Day 60
Day 61	Day 62	Day 63	Day 64	Day 65
Day 66	Day 67	Day 68	Day 69	Day 70
Day 71	Day 72	Day 73	Day 74	Day 75
Day 76	Day 77	Day 78	Day 79	Day 80
Day 81	Day 82	Day 83	Day 84	Day 85
Day 86	Day 87	Day 88	Day 89	Day 90
Day 91	Day 92	Day 93	Day 94	Day 95
Day 96	Day 97	Day 98	Day 99	Day 100
Day 101	Day 102	Day 103	Day 104	Day 105
Day 106	Day 107	Day 108	Day 109	Day 110
Day 111	Day 112	Day 113	Day 114	Day 115
Day 116	Day 117	Day 118	Day 119	Day 120
Day 121	Day 122	Day 123	Day 124	Day 125
Day 126	Day 127	Day 128	Day 129	Day 130
Day 131	Day 132	Day 133	Day 134	Day 135
Day 136	Day 137	Day 138	Day 139	Day 140
Day 141	Day 142	Day 143	Day 144	Day 145
Day 146	Day 147	Day 148	Day 149	Day 150
Day 151	Day 152	Day 153	Day 154	Day 155
Day 156	Day 157	Day 158	Day 159	Day 160
Day 161	Day 162	Day 163	Day 164	Day 165
Day 166	Day 167	Day 168	Day 169	Day 170
Day 171	Day 172	Day 173	Day 174	Day 175

Day 176	Day 177	Day 178	Day 179	Day 180
Day 181	Day 181	Day 183	Day 184	Day 185
Day 186	Day 176	Day 188	Day 189	Day 190
Day 191	Day 192	Day 193	Day 194	Day 195
Day 196	Day 197	Day 198	Day 199	Day 200
Day 201	Day 202	Day 203	Day 204	Day 205
Day 206	Day 207	Day 208	Day 209	Day 210
Day 211	Day 212	Day 213	Day 214	Day 215
Day 216	Day 217	Day 218	Day 219	Day 220
Day 221	Day 222	Day 223	Day 224	Day 225
Day 226	Day 227	Day 228	Day 229	Day 230
Day 231	Day 232	Day 233	Day 234	Day 235
Day 236	Day 237	Day 238	Day 239	Day 240
Day 241	Day 242	Day 243	Day 244	Day 245
Day 246	Day 247	Day 248	Day 249	Day 250
Day 251	Day 252	Day 253	Day 254	Day 255
Day 256	Day 257	Day 258	Day 259	Day 260
Day 261	Day 262	Day 263	Day 264	Day 265
Day 266	Day 267	Day 268	Day 269	Day 270
Day 271	Day 272	Day 273	Day 274	Day 275
Day 276	Day 277	Day 278	Day 279	Day 280
Day 281	Day 282	Day 283	Day 284	Day 285
Day 286	Day 287	Day 288	Day 289	Day 290
Day 291	Day 292	Day 293	Day 294	Day 295
Day 296	Day 297	Day 298	Day 299	Day 300
Day 301	Day 302	Day 303	Day 304	Day 305
Day 306	Day 307	Day 308	Day 309	Day 310
Day 311	Day 312	Day 313	Day 314	Day 315
Day 316	Day 317	Day 318	Day 319	Day 320
Day 321	Day 322	Day 323	Day 324	Day 325
Day 326	Day 327	Day 328	Day 329	Day 330
Day 331	Day 332	Day 333	Day 334	Day 335
Day 336	Day 337	Day 338	Day 339	Day 340
Day 341	Day 342	Day 343	Day 344	Day 345
Day 346	Day 347	Day 348	Day 349	Day 350
Day 351	Day 352	Day 353	Day 354	Day 355
Day 356	Day 357	Day 358	Day 359	Day 360
Day 361	Day 362	Day 363	Day 364	Day 365

APPENDIX 10.

CHECKBOOK FORM

EXPENSE CATEGORY	LAST MONTH TOTAL	THIS MONTH TOTAL
Payroll Expense	$_____	$_____
Advertising Expense	$_$_____ Utilities	Expense
	$_____	$_____
Legal Expense	$_____	$_____
Office Expense	$_____	$_____
Postage/Shipping	$_____	$_____
Auto Expense	$_____	$_____
Travel Expense	$_____	$_____
Expense	$_____	$_____
Expense	$_____	$_____
Expense	$_____	$_____
Expense	$_____	$_____
Expense	$_____	$_____
TOTAL	$_____	$_____

This month's total is not more than total monthly projected revenues

APPENDIX 11.

MEDICINE FOR TROUBLED COMPANIES

A troubled company is like a losing army. Its generals and grand plans are in disarray, the organization panics and casualties mount.
SYMPTOMS OF TROUBLE

1 The company is losing money from operations - cash is going out.

2 Cash shortages become routine. Vendors are paid in 90 days to 120 days, while the company is borrowing against new receivables. Paydays virtually empty out the cash, or actually overdraw the company's accounts.

3 Loss of market share in its markets, while competition gains.

4 Quality employees are leaving or have left, and new ones are not being recruited.

5 Physically the company facilities are deteriorating. Paint is peeling, parking lots are filthy. The only maintenance that is being done is breakdown repair.

6 Emotions are low. Morale of employees is low - pessimistic attitudes prevail.

7 Vendors are refusing shipment and credit standing is low.

8 Inventories are low or dated.

9 Markdowns are used as product lure, instead of advertising and inventory level of quality products is slowly decreasing.

STEP-BY-STEP GUIDE FOR NURSING TROUBLED COMPANIES

STEP 1 - HOLD ON AND CONTROL CASH. Take daily personal responsibility for cash disbursements and income. Place all cash into the highest possible yielding transfer accounts. Pay only what must be paid. Payroll, utilities, key suppliers and withholding taxes.

STEP 2 - LISTEN, AND MAKE EMPLOYEES TALK. Don't give orders yet. Gather data and information on which you can rely to make decisions, such as: where is the best deal on a product; highest markups; less competitive product line, etc.

STEP 3 - LISTEN TO FIRST-LEVEL EMPLOYEE SUPERVISORS. See all in person. Ask what's wrong with the company? Who are the key employees, and why? Who are the suppliers that will allow better price or terms? Who are the customers? Last - what would you do if you were me?

STEP 4 - INVOLVE ALL EMPLOYEES. Let everyone help you. In this way you will find the good people quickly. Decisions at the individual level are best. Motivate cash incentives and "Company Man" mentality.

STEP 5 - IDENTIFY EXCESS ASSETS, AND GET RID OF THEM, RAISE CASH. Every fixed asset, every spare piece of equipment should be evaluated. An auction or publicized sale will always bring in cash quickly. Fastest cash is for real estate and obsolete merchandise.

STEP 6 - IDENTIFY LOSERS, GET RID OF THEM IMMEDIATELY. Everyone generally knows if there is a division, product line or "loser" operation within the company. Stop the bleeding - at once. Close it or sell it. Don't think about it, just do it. Everyone quickly realizes you're serious.

STEP 7 - FIND THE POSITIVES. Key products, history, sales, whatever. Use them, move from a position of strength. Boost your public image and employee morale. News releases, advertising, etc., especially TV ads. Heavy concentration on Thursday is good.

STEP 8 - FIND THE "STARS". Now that you have your data, employee "rap sessions", etc., find your star performers and give them authority, while watching closely.

STEP 9 - MAKE A PLAN. Establish a corporate plan, objective and short term goals ONLY. Fire anybody who tries to give you a plan over 12 months in duration. Look for results, weekly (daily on special events) and discuss results with all employees.

STEP 10 - RAISE NEW CASH. Sell stock, sell inventory - go to STEP 5.

STEP 11 - BUY ON CONSIGNMENT, SUBLEASE SPACE OR DEPARTMENTS. Why use your cash, when plenty of merchandise is available? Sublease space to others, or lease departments at as close to 20% of sales as possible.

STEP 12 - SHOW A PROFIT. Is there anything else?

GUIDELINES - DON'T EVER FORGET

   A. Collect receivables.
   B. Get rid of "dead inventory".
   C. Sell useless assets.
   D. Sell real estate and lease-back.
   E. Keep up your image.

APPENDIX 12.

DRAFT STOCK PURCHASE AND SALE AGREEMENT

This Agreement, dated as of the _____ day of_____, 20 , by_____, (the "Seller/s"), and _____, a _____ corporation (hereinafter called "Buyer"); Buyer may form a new corporation solely for this transaction, solely to complete this transaction, with a name different than indicated in this Agreement.

W I T N E S S E T H:

WHEREAS, Seller/s owns all of the issued and outstanding shares of capital stock of_____, a _____ corporation (hereinafter called "Company"); and,

WHEREAS, Seller/s desires to sell to Buyer and Buyer desires to purchase from Seller/s all of the outstanding stock of Company (such shares of stock are hereinafter referred to as the "Company Stock"), all subject to the terms and conditions hereinafter provided;

NOW, THEREFORE, for and in consideration of the mutual agreements hereinafter contained, Seller/s and Buyer agree as follows:

1. <u>TRANSACTIONS TO BE EFFECTED AT THE CLOSING</u>. Subject to the terms and conditions of this Agreement, including the Schedules and/or Exhibits hereto (hereinafter the "Agreement"), at the Closing (as hereinafter defined),

    1.1. <u>Sale and Purchase of Company Stock</u>. Seller/s shall sell to Buyer, and Buyer shall purchase all of the Company Stock. Seller/s shall deliver certificates representing all of the Company Stock with endorsements and/or stock powers executed in a form reasonably requested by Buyer as necessary or desirable to effectively transfer title of said stock to Buyer.

1.2. <u>Total Consideration</u>. Buyer shall pay the amount of $_____ (hereinafter the "Total Consideration") in the following manner to Seller/s:

1.2.1. <u>Cash</u>. Buyer shall deliver a check in readily available funds in a form acceptable to the Seller/s in the amount of $_____ at closing.

1.2.2 <u>Non-Competition Agreement</u>. Seller/s shall receive $_____ for an agreement not to compete with Company. The Seller/s agrees to enter into this agreement in the form attached hereto as Exhibit 1.2.2.

1.3. <u>Other</u>.
   (a) Buyer shall receive possession of the minute book, stock ledger, corporate seals, and all other books and records of Company.
   (b) Seller/s and Buyer shall execute such other documents as are contemplated by this Agreement or necessary to complete the transactions hereunder.

1.3.1. All Seller/s unconditionally agree not to engage in any business that competes with Buyer or in the alternative must be in or serve a geographical area that is outside the business territory or the acquired business. Additionally, Seller/s will not divulge any business secrets, customers or methods used by the Company to any other persons for any reason.

1.4. <u>Closing</u>. The closing of the sale to Buyer provided for hereunder (the "Closing") shall take place at the time that the Buyer receives a satisfactory financing proposal to fund the contemplated transaction and shall be at the place as Seller/s and Buyer may mutually agree upon (the "Closing Place"). Both parties will use their best efforts to conclude this transaction as quickly as possible, subject to EPA clearance and no material discrepancies being discovered in the due diligence process.

2. REPRESENTATIONS AND WARRANTIES OF SELLER/S.
Seller/s represents and warrants unto Buyer the following:

2.1. Organization of Company. Company is a duly organized and existing corporation under the laws of the State of _____, in good standing therein, with full corporate power and authority to carry on its business as currently conducted and in good standing in each jurisdiction in which Company is required to be qualified as a foreign corporation.

2.2. Ability to Carry Out the Agreement. Except as set forth in Schedule 2.2 hereto, neither Seller/s nor Company is bound by any restriction of any kind or character which would prohibit or otherwise be breached or violated by the entering into or performance of this Agreement by Seller/s or the consummation of the transactions contemplated hereby. The entering into, execution, delivery and performance of this Agreement by Seller/s, and the consummation of the transactions contemplated hereby, will not, with or without notice, lapse of time or the occurrence of any other event, result in the acceleration of any obligation under any agreement or other instrument to which Company or its properties are subject.

2.3. Validity of Agreement and Authority. This Agreement has been duly executed and delivered by Seller/s and is a valid and binding obligation of Seller/s enforceable in accordance with its terms. The performance by Company of any of its obligations required by this Agreement and of all actions that Seller/s has agreed to cause it to take under this Agreement has been duly authorized by all necessary corporate action of Company.

2.4. <u>Financial Statements</u>. Buyer has been furnished with financial statements of Company for the years ended_____, and latest quarterly statements dated_____, (the "Financial Statement"), which are attached as Exhibit 2.4. The Financial Statement, (i) have been prepared in accordance with generally accepted accounting principles, applied on a consistent basis with prior periods, (ii) include all reserves, allowances and adjustments related to the assets, liabilities, and owner's equity carried on the books and records of Company and/or necessary for a fair presentation of the financial conditions and results of operations of Company; (iii) are in accordance with the books and records of Company, (iv) are true and complete in all respects and fairly reflect the financial condition, assets, liabilities (whether accrued, absolute, contingent or otherwise), and results of operations of Company for the periods therein specified, and (v) contain and reflect reserves which are adequate to cover all liabilities and all losses and costs.

2.5. <u>Compliance with Laws and Litigation</u>. Company has complied with all applicable federal, state, local and foreign laws and regulations, or those of any agency thereof, with respect to the conduct of its business. Except as listed in Schedule 2.5, there is no action, suit, investigation, or proceeding pending or threatened against Company before any court, arbitrator, or administrative or governmental body.

2.6. <u>Agreements, Contracts and Commitments</u>. Except as disclosed in Schedule 2.6, Company is not a party to, nor is it or any of its properties otherwise subject to, any oral or written agreement. Except as disclosed on Schedule 2.6, Company is not in default under any agreements to which it is a party or by which it or its properties is bound; there have been no claims of defaults and there are no existing facts or conditions which (with or without notice, lapse of time or the occurrence of any other event) will result in a default under any agreements to which it is a party or by which it or its property may be bound.

2.7. Conduct of Business. Except as set forth on Schedule 2.7, since the last dated Financial Statement, there has not been:

   (a) any adverse change in the financial condition, assets, liabilities or business properties or results of operations or business prospects of Company;

   (b) any damage, destruction or loss, whether or not covered by insurance, affecting the business or properties of Company; or

   (c) any sale, assignment, license or transfer by Company, of any patents, Trademarks, logos, copyrights, licenses, designs or other similar intangible assets.

2.8. <u>No Misstatements or Omissions</u>. No covenant, representation or warranty by Seller/s made in this Agreement or in any document, statement or certificate furnished to Buyer, or in connection with the transactions contemplated hereby, contains or will contain any misstatement of fact, or omits or will omit to state a fact necessary to make the statements or facts contained herein or therein not misleading. There is no fact known to Seller/s or Company that adversely affects or in the future may adversely affect the business, operations, affairs, prospects or condition of Company, or any of its properties or assets, that has not been set forth in this Agreement or otherwise disclosed in writing to Buyer prior to the Closing Date.

2.9. <u>Company Stock</u>.

   (a) The Company Stock constitutes all of the issued and outstanding shares of Company Stock and said shares are validly authorized, issued and outstanding, fully paid, not pledged and non-assessable.

   (b) There are no outstanding options, warrants, or rights of any kind to acquire any capital stock of the company.

   (c) Seller/s has full and absolute right and power to transfer and convey to Buyer such Seller/s's stock in the

Company, free and clear of all liens, encumbrances, warrants, options, equities and claims.

2.10. <u>Financing/Use of Assets</u>. Seller/s specifically acknowledges that he has knowledge of the fact that Buyer will/may buy, sell or pledge the assets of the Company to a financing source, in any fashion he desires to complete the acquisition contemplated herein, and specifically waives any and all claims, protests, and defenses with respect to such use of assets, including but not limited to any intercompany transfers that might be necessary in the future, to cause compliance with this agreement.

<u>Broker's Fees</u>. Seller/s warrant that there is no obligation or liability to pay any fees or commissions to any broker, finder or agent with respect to the transactions contemplated by this agreement.

3. <u>COVENANTS, REPRESENTATIONS AND WARRANTIES OF BUYER</u>. Buyer covenants, represents and warrants unto Seller/s the following:

3.1. <u>Organization of Buyer</u>. Buyer is a duly organized and existing corporation under the laws of its state of incorporation and in good standing therein.

3.2. <u>Propriety of Corporate Action</u>. All corporate and other proceedings to be taken on the part of Buyer to authorize it to execute and deliver and perform its obligations under this Agreement have been duly and properly taken; the execution and delivery by Buyer of this Agreement and the performance by it of its obligations hereunder will not conflict with or violate any provision of any charter, bylaw, mortgage, lien, lease, contract, agreement, judgment, order or decree to which it is a party or otherwise bound; and this Agreement is the valid and binding obligation of Buyer.

4. COVENANTS OF SELLER/S PENDING THE CLOSING.
Seller/s agrees, represents, warrants, and covenants to and with the
Buyer that during the period from the date hereof through the Closing
Date and except as required by the provisions of this Agreement or as
Buyer and Seller/s may agree in writing:

4.1. Conduct of Business. Seller/s shall cause Company to carry
on its business and conduct business operations in all respects in
the same manner as previously conducted and to make no purchase
or sale, nor introduce any new method of management or
operation, with respect to its business or the assets or liabilities
thereof, except in the ordinary course of business and in a manner
consistent with prior practice and not in violation of any of the
representations, warranties or covenants contained in this
Agreement.

4.2. Satisfy Conditions Precedent. Seller/s together with Company
shall promptly perform all acts and take all measures necessary to
satisfy the conditions precedent to the Closing and shall not take
any action inconsistent thereto.

4.3. Compliance with Law. Seller/s shall cause Company to
comply with all applicable laws and regulations; to obtain and
renew, if required, all governmental permits, licenses or
authorizations required for the conduct of its business or the use of
its assets; to notify, to the extent necessary, all governmental
regulatory authorities in each jurisdiction in which it does business
of the transactions contemplated herein; and to obtain the issuance
by each such authority of such permits, licenses, authorizations and
other forms as may be required to enable Company to continue to
maintain and enjoy its business and the permits, licenses,
authorizations and forms now held by it and to assist Buyer in
obtaining any such issuance(s) required to be obtained by it.

4.4. Obtain Consents. Seller/s shall cause Company to obtain all
necessary consents to the transactions contemplated by this
Agreement required in any of its contracts, agreements or leases.

4.5. Maintain Business. Seller/s shall cause Company to maintain and preserve intact in all respects its business organization and the goodwill associated therewith, to retain present customers and suppliers so that such customers and suppliers will be available to Company on the Closing Date; and to maintain relationships with its present customers and suppliers and others so that such relationships will be preserved on the Closing Date.

4.6. Information to Buyer, Etc. Subsequent to the date of execution of this Agreement and prior to the Closing Date, Seller/s shall afford Buyer and its representatives reasonable access from time to time to Company and all its records and correspondence (with the right to make copies thereof) as Buyer or any such representative may reasonably request and to allow Buyer and its representatives to contact and communicate with Company's customers and other persons having business dealings with Company, but only with Seller/s's prior approval. It is further hereby agreed that all such access, investigations, contacts and inquiries shall be conducted by Buyer and its representatives so as not to interfere unreasonably with the normal conduct of Company's business and that, if the transactions contemplated by this Agreement are not consummated for any reason whatsoever, Buyer and its representatives shall keep confidential any information (unless ascertainable from public or published information or trade sources) obtained from Company (or such customers or other persons) concerning Company's operations or business. Seller/s will fully cooperate with Buyer's financing sources, and execute or cause to be executed any documents necessary for the financing source in order to expedite the closing.

5. CONDITIONS PRECEDENT TO THE OBLIGATION OF SELLER/S. The obligations of Seller/s to consummate the transactions contemplated by this Agreement are subject to the fulfillment of each of the following conditions prior to or at the Closing:

5.1. Covenants, Representations and Warranties are Correct. The covenants, representations and warranties of the Buyer made hereunder shall be deemed to have been made at and as of the Closing and shall then be true in all material respects and all undertakings and agreements required by this Agreement to be performed or complied with by the Buyer prior to or at Closing shall have been performed or complied with in all material respects; and Seller/s shall have been furnished a certificate of Buyer dated the Closing Date certifying to that effect.

5.2. Resolutions. Seller/s shall have delivered to Buyer a copy of appropriate corporate resolutions of the Company authorizing the execution of this Agreement and approving the transactions contemplated hereby together with a certificate of the Secretary or an Assistant Secretary of the Company with respect to the due adoption and continued force and effect of such resolutions.

6. CONDITIONS PRECEDENT TO BUYER'S OBLIGATIONS. The obligation of Buyer to consummate the transactions contemplated by this Agreement is subject to the fulfillment of each of the following conditions prior to or at the Closing:

6.1. Covenants, Representations and Warranties are Correct. The covenants, representations and warranties of Seller/s made hereunder shall be deemed to have been made again at and as of the Closing and shall then be true in all material respects, and all undertakings and agreements required by this Agreement to be performed or complied with by Seller/s prior to or at the Closing shall have been performed or complied with in all material respects; and Buyer shall have been furnished with certificates of appropriate officers of Seller/s, dated the Closing Date, certifying to that effect.

6.2. Resolutions. Buyer shall have delivered to Seller/s a copy of appropriate corporate resolutions of Buyer authorizing the execution of this Agreement and approving the transactions contemplated hereby together with a certificate of the Secretary or an Assistant Secretary of Buyer with respect to the due adoption and continued force and effect of such resolutions.

7. POST CLOSING COVENANTS OF SELLER/S AND BUYER.

7.1. Additional Transfer Documents. From time to time after the Closing, at the request of Buyer and without further consideration, the Seller/s shall execute and deliver to Buyer such certificates and other instruments of sale, conveyance, assignment and transfer, and take such other action, as may be required by Buyer, to complete the transactions contemplated by this Agreement.
7.2. Responsibility for Payment of Taxes After Closing. The Buyer and Company shall by responsible for and shall pay any federal or state income taxes of Company or any successor thereto for all periods commencing on and/or subsequent to the Closing Date.
7.3. Authority. Parties agree that the Buyer has full authority to operate the Company as it so deems without any interference from the Seller/s.

8 SURVIVAL OF WARRANTIES. All covenants, representations and warranties hereunder of Seller/s and/or Buyer shall survive the Closing and the consummation on the Closing of the sale to Buyer provided for hereunder, notwithstanding any investigation which may have been made by or on behalf of Seller/s or Buyer, and shall be effective notwithstanding the form of any instrument, conveyance, assignment or transfer executed by any of them pursuant hereto.

9. INDEMNIFICATION.

9.1. Seller/s and Buyer. Seller/s and Buyer agree to indemnify each other in respect of any and all claims, losses and expenses which may be incurred by such other party (the "Indemnified Party") arising out of:

(a) any misrepresentation or breach of any covenant, representation, warranty, agreement or undertaking pursuant to this Agreement or in any certificate delivered hereunder on the part of either party;

(b) any failure by either party to perform or otherwise fulfill any undertaking or other agreement or obligation arising under this Agreement;

(c) any and all actions, suits, proceedings, claims, liabilities, demands, assessments, judgments, costs, and expenses, including reasonable attorneys' fees, occasioned by and reasonably paid as a direct result of any of the foregoing.

9.2. Right to Offset. If the facts giving rise to a right to indemnification hereunder shall involve any actual or threatened claim or demand against Seller/s, the Buyer may offset any claims against Seller/s against any payments to be made to Seller/s pursuant to this Agreement or any Exhibit hereto and such withholding shall not be a breach hereof or thereof. Buyer and Seller/s agree to use their best efforts to first settle any differences prior to arbitration.

9.3. Failure to Deliver All Stock at Closing. The Seller/s agrees that in the event Seller/s shall not transfer all of Seller's stock or fail to close in any way, Seller/s shall pay an amount to reimburse the Buyer for time, expense and effort expended by Buyer, and those engaged by Buyer, in this transaction.

9 APPLICABLE LAW. This Agreement shall be construed and the rights and duties of the parties determined hereunder in accordance with the internal law of the State of Illinois and Seller/s and Buyer agree that jurisdiction and venue shall be proper in the Circuit Court of Cook County, Illinois or in the United States District Court for the Northern District of Illinois, Eastern Division.

10 ARBITRATION. Any dispute or claim involving this Agreement shall be settled by an arbitration in Chicago, Illinois under the rules of the American Arbitration Association. The arbitrator shall have no authority to change any provisions of this agreement; the arbitrator's sole authority shall be to interpret or apply the provisions of this Agreement. The decision of the arbitrator shall be final and binding and the exclusive remedy for any alleged breach of this Agreement. Judgment upon the award rendered by the arbitrator may be entered in any court having jurisdiction.

11 NOTICES. All notices, requests, permissions, waivers and other communications hereunder shall be in writing and shall be deemed to have been duly given if signed by the respective persons giving them (in the case of any corporation the signature shall be an executive officer thereof) and received by the other persons.

(a) If to Seller/s, to:

Attn.:
Copy to:

(b) If to Buyer, to:

Such names and addresses may be changed by a notice given pursuant to this Section 12.

1 ENTIRE AGREEMENT. This Agreement, including the Schedules and Exhibits attached hereto or furnished hereunder, all of which are a part hereof, contains the entire understanding of the parties hereto and their Affiliates with respect to the subject matter contained herein and therein, and supersedes and cancels all prior agreements with respect hereto and thereto.

14. PARTIES IN INTEREST AND ASSIGNMENT. Except for the assignment by Buyer of all or any portion of its rights and obligations hereunder to an affiliate of Buyer, in which event such affiliate shall be responsible for the obligations of Buyer under this Agreement and the assignment, this Agreement shall not be assignable or otherwise transferred in whole or in part. The representations, warranties and covenants contained in this Agreement shall inure to the benefit of and be binding upon the Buyer and Seller/s and their successors and permitted assigns and not benefit or create any responsibility or liability to any other persons.

2   SEVERABILITY. The parties intend that, to the fullest extent permitted by law, the invalidity of any portion of this Agreement shall not affect the validity, force and effect of the remaining portions hereof.

IN WITNESS WHEREOF, the parties hereto have executed this Agreement on the date, month and year first set forth above at Chicago, Illinois.

SELLER/S

Date _____

BUYER

Date _____

APPENDIX 13.

CORPORATE DOCUMENTS AND LAWS AND BASIC FORMS TO USE

When to skip this material

If you are well organized and feel you understand the purpose of your articles, bylaws and minutes, or have purchased a corporate book kit, you'll be all set.

ORGANIZE YOUR CORPORATE RECORDS

Anyone who sets up a corporation needs to be able to quickly locate key organizational documents.

If you have not already done so, the best approach is to set up a corporate records book that contains the key documents. You can do this on your own with a three-ring binder, or by using a customized corporate kit designed for the purpose; available through many sources.

Your corporate records book should contain:

- articles of incorporation
- bylaws
- minutes of the first directors' meeting
- stock certificate stubs or a stock transfer ledger showing the names and addresses of your shareholders, as well as the number and types of shares owned by each
- minutes of annual and special meetings of directors or shareholders, if any, and
- written consents.

If someone helped you incorporate, such as a lawyer, accountants, paralegal or financial planner, you probably received copies of these documents in a corporate records book, commonly called a "corporate kit." However, some lawyers attempt to hold on to corporate records in the hope that you will have them take care of all ongoing technicalities. If so, you will need to request a copy of all corporate documents in your client file.

If you can't locate a copy of your articles, write your Secretary of state's corporate filing office and request a certified or file-stamped copy of your articles. It's a good idea to call first so you can include the correct fee, which should be just a few dollars or so.

1. Articles of Incorporation

All business corporations must have the articles of incorporation. (While most states use the term "articles of incorporation" to refer to the basic document creating the corporation, some states, including Connecticut, Delaware, New York and Oklahoma, use the term "certificate of incorporation." Washington calls the document a "certificate of formation," and Tennessee calls it a "charter.") A corporation comes into existence when its articles of incorporation are filed with the state corporate filing office. The articles normally contain fundamental structural information, such as the name of the corporation, names and addresses of its directors, its registered agent and his or her office address and the corporation's capital stock structure.

For the majority of corporations, there is no other important information in this document. However, larger corporations sometimes adopt articles containing special provisions that impact future decision making processes of the corporation, such as additional classes of stock.

Prepare and file articles for a new corporation

If you have not yet formed your corporation, or if you are not comfortable doing it yourself, we can incorporate your business, online quickly and affordably, in all 50 states. Just go to our web site.

2. Bylaws

The bylaws of a corporation are a very important document. You do not file bylaws with the state - they are an internal document that contains rules for holding corporate meetings and other formalities according to state corporate laws.

Bylaws typically specify the frequency of regular meetings of directors and shareholders and the call, notice, quorum and voting rules for each type of meeting. They usually contain the rules for setting up and delegating authority to special committees of the board, the rights of directors and shareholders to inspect the corporate records and books, rights of directors and officers to insurance coverage or indemnification (reimbursement by the corporation for legal fees and judgments) in the event of lawsuits, plus a number of other standard legal provisions.

State law often gives corporations choice as to whether to place corporate operating rules and procedures in the articles of incorporation or bylaws. If you have a choice, it's always best to use the bylaws, because you can change them easily without the need for filing changes with the state. For example, many states allow you to place super-majority quorum or voting rules for directors' or shareholders' meetings in either document. If you use the bylaws for this purpose, since less stringent vote requirements normally apply to the amendment of bylaws, you can much more easily change these provisions. In contrast, if you change provisions in your articles later, a formal amendment to the articles must be filed with your state's corporate filing office.

Because the corporation laws of all states are subject to change, it's possible that bylaws that were valid when adopted will later go out of date. Fortunately, major changes to corporate laws happen only every decade or two, when states modernize their corporate statues. If your corporation has been in existence for a few years and you plan a major corporate decision such as the issuance of a new class of shares, declaration of a dividend or purchase of shares from a shareholder, it's wise to make sure your bylaw provisions are up to date by checking your state's current business corporation act.

If you haven't prepared bylaws

When businesses incorporate, they prepare minutes of the first meeting of the corporation's board of directors or of the incorporators (the person or persons who signed and filed the articles on behalf of the corporation). This meeting is usually referred to as the organizational meeting of the corporation. Minutes are simply a formal record of the proceedings of a meeting. The organizational meeting is usually held to approve standard items of business necessary for a new corporation to begin doing business.

Look through the minutes of your organizational meeting. These minutes are designed to document the essential organizational actions taken by the board or the incorporators. They typically show:

- the beginning tax elections made by the corporation - for example, the selection of the corporation's accounting period and tax year
- details of the corporation's first stock issuance
- approval of stock certificates and a corporate seal, and
- approval of other beginning business of the corporation, such as the opening of a corporate bank account.

If you don't have organizational minutes

Some corporations, especially those created in a rush, simply didn't prepare minutes of the first meeting of the board of directors or incorporators. If you don't have these minutes, don't worry about it. You'll normally do fine without them, or prepare them later or use out of the "kit."

3. Records Showing Stock Was Issued

A new corporation almost always issues stock to record the ownership interests of the persons who invest in the corporation. Corporations issue stock for cash, property or the performance of services that were rendered in forming the corporation. Many states prohibit the issuance of shares in return for a promise to pay for the shares later (in return for a promissory note) or for a promise to perform future services. If a small existing business is being incorporated, the business owners are normally issued shares in return for the transfer of business assets to the new corporation.

If you haven't issued stock or didn't keep written records showing who owns shares, you should do so. Stock certificates and stock transfer ledgers are available in most office supply stores.

Once you've organized your corporate records book, remember that while a corporate records book makes it easy for you to keep all key documents in one place, it won't work unless you consistently use it.

Minutes of Meetings and Written Consents

If your corporation has been in existence for some time, you may have records of annual and perhaps special corporate meetings. This especially likely if a lawyer helped you incorporate. Check your corporate records, or contact your attorney if you don't have copes.

STATE CORPORATE FILING OFFICES

Each state has a corporate filing office where you pay a fee and file paperwork for creating corporations, changing the corporate structure and dissolving corporations.

Different states use slightly different names for the office where corporate filings are mad. Most commonly, corporations are formed with and supervised by the Secretary of State or Department of Stat office. The department that handles corporate filings is commonly designated as the Corporations Division or Corporations Department.

Corporation filing offices are sometimes further divided into offices that oversee special areas of concern, such as corporate filings (for example, articles of incorporation or amendments to articles), corporate name availability, corporate fee information and corporate legal counsel. Don't be put off by this seeming structural complexity. If you need information, you'll normally find there is one phone number at the corporate filing office devoted to handling corporate inquiries from the public.

Contact Your Secretary of State on the Internet

Most Secretary of State Offices have a website where you can click a button to go to a page for the Corporations Division, to download corporate statutory forms (Amendment of Articles, Change of Registered Agent or Registered Office Address and the like). Many of these sites also contain links to your state's corporate tax office (for tax forms and information) and state employment, licensing and other agencies.

LOOKING UP THE LAW YOURSELF

The organization and operation of a corporation are tightly regulated by laws adopted by each state. The primary source of laws that apply to your corporation will be found in your state's corporation laws (statutes), often titled the "business Corporation Act" or designated with similar name.

Corporate statutes are organized by subject matter and are well indexed and cross-referenced. For the most part, the statutes themselves state a fairly simple rule or requirement that can be comprehended by the average reader.

Locate State Corporation Statutes

Many routine state legal rules, such as those for holding and voting at meetings, obtaining director or shareholder written consent to action without a meeting and conducting ongoing corporate business, are restated in your articles of incorporation and bylaws. Nevertheless, there may be times when you will want more detail on your stat's corporation statutes.

Once you locate your stat's corporate statutes, it usually only takes a minute or two to find a relevant corporate law requirement or procedure, or to satisfy your self that one does not exist.

Look Up Relevant Corporate Statutes

To start, you can browse through the table of contents at the beginning of your state's corporation act or the mini-table of contents often located at the beginning of each section heading in the act. Each heading covers major areas of corporate operation or procedure (for example, *Corporate Formation, Meetings, Stock Issuance, Corporate Officers, Records and Reports* and the like). Major headings are further broken down into sub-headings and sections that treat specific matters, such as *Articles of Incorporation, Bylaws and Director and Shareholder Meetings.*

You can usually do a search to find the statute you're interested in, by entering a few key terms.

4. Checking Other Laws

In addition to a state's Business Corporation Act, other state laws regulate special areas of corporate activity. These include:

Securities Act or Blue Sky Law. These laws contain each state's rules and procedures for offering, issuing, selling and transferring shares of corporate stock and other securities. (The term "blue sky law" was derived from the sometimes underhanded, and often colorful, practices of corporate con artists who, in return for a small investment in their latest get-rich-quick undertaking, would promise the "blue sky" to unsuspecting investors. The securities laws of each state attempt, through stock offering qualification and disclosure requirements, to tone down the picture painted by stock promoters to a more realistic hue.)

Tax or Revenue Code. If a state imposes a corporate income or franchise tax, the state's Tax or Revenue Code will typically contain these provisions.

Commercial Code. The state's Commercial Code contains the rules for entering into an enforcing commercial contracts, promissory notes and other standard commercial documents.

Other state and local laws. Various state laws may impact the activities and operations of all businesses, whether or not they are incorporated. For example, state and local building codes, professional and occupation licensing and other laws and regulations may apply to your business and its operations, so do a little extra research, especially if you business or profession may require particular licensing or registration.

BASIC FORMS

SEE SOME BASIC CORPORATE FORMS

MINUTES OF THE ANNUAL MEETING OF
SHAREHOLDERS OF

_____

An annual meeting of the shareholders of the corporation was held on
_____, 20   at   :_____.M., at
_____, state of_____, for
the purpose of electing the directors of the corporation and for the
transaction of any other business that may properly come before the
meeting: _____

_____

_____ acted as chairperson, and
_____ acted as secretary of the meeting.

The chairperson called the meeting to order.

The secretary announced that the meeting was called by
_____.

The secretary announced that the meeting was held pursuant to notice,
if and as required under the Bylaws of this corporation, or that notice
had been waived by all shareholders entitled to receive notice under
the Bylaws.

The secretary announced that an alphabetical list of the names and
numbers of shares held by all shareholders of the corporation was
available and open to inspection by any person in attendance at the
meeting.

The secretary announced that there were present, in person or by
proxy, representing a quorum of the shareholders, the following
shareholders, proxy holders and shares:

Name   Number of Shares

_____   _____

_____   _____

_____   _____

The secretary attached written proxy statements, executed by the appropriate shareholders, to these minutes for any shares listed above as held by a proxy holder.

The following persons were also present at the meeting:

Name   Title

_____   _____
_____   _____
_____   _____

The secretary announced that the minutes of the _____ meeting held on _____, 20___ were read at the meeting. After discussion, a vote was taken and the minutes of the meeting were approved by the shares in attendance.

The following annual and special reports were presented at the meeting by the following persons:

_____

_____

_____

The chairperson announced that the next item of business was the nomination and election of the board of directors for another _____ term of office. The following nominations were made and seconded:

Name(s) of Nominee(s)

_____

_____

_____

_____

_____

The secretary next took the votes of shareholders entitled to vote for the election of directors at the meeting, and, after counting the votes, announced that the following persons were elected to serve on the Board of Directors of this corporation for another term of office:

Names of Board Members

_____

_____

_____

_____

_____

On motion duly made and carried by the affirmative vote of _____ shareholders in attendance at the meeting, the following resolutions were adopted by shareholders entitled to vote at the meeting:_____

_____

_____

_____

_____

_____

_____

There being no further business to come before the meeting, it was adjourned on motion duly made and carried.

_____

_____, Secretary

NOTICE OF MEETING OF

_____

A_____ meeting of the stockholders
of _____ will be held at
_____, state
of _____, on _____, 20___ at ___ : ___ ___.M.

The purpose(s) of the meeting is/are as follows:

_____

_____

_____

_____

_____

_____

_____

If you are a shareholder and cannot attend the meeting and wish to designate another person to vote your shares for you, please deliver a signed proxy from to the secretary of the corporation before the meeting.

_____
Signature of Secretary

Name of Secretary: _____

Corporation: _____

Address: _____

Phone:_____Fax: _____

Sterling Cooper

MINUTES OF THE ANNUAL MEETING OF DIRECTORS OF

_____

An annual meeting of the directors of the corporation was held on
_____, 20   at   :   .M., at_____, state
of_____, for the purpose of reviewing the prior year's business
and discussing corporate operations for the upcoming year, and for the
transaction of any other business that may properly come before the
meeting:

_____

_____

_____

_____

_____   acted   as   chairperson,   and
_____ acted as secretary of the meeting.

The chairperson called the meeting to order.

The   secretary   announced   that   the   meeting   was   called   by
_____.

The secretary announced that the meeting was held pursuant to notice,
if and as required under the Bylaws of this corporation, or that notice
had been waived by all directors entitled to receive notice under the
Bylaws.

The secretary announced that the following directors were present at
the meeting:

Name of Director

_____

_____

_____

_____

_____

The above directors, having been elected to serve on the board for another_____term by the shareholders at an annual meeting of shareholders held on_____, 20 , accepted their positions on the board. The secretary then announced that the presence of these directors at the meeting represented a quorum of the board of directors as defined in the Bylaws of this corporation.

The following persons were also present at the meeting:

Name   Title

_____   _____

_____   _____

_____   _____

_____   _____

_____   _____

The secretary announced that the minutes of the _____ meeting held on _____, 20___ were read at the meeting. After discussion, a vote was taken and the minutes of the meeting were approved by the directors in attendance.

The following reports were presented at the meeting by the following persons:

_____

_____

_____

The chairperson announced that the next item of business was the appointment of the officers and of standing committee members of the corporation to another annual term of office. After discussion, the following persons were appointed to serve in the following capacities as officers or committee members or in other roles in the service of the corporation for the upcoming year.

Name   Title

_____   _____

_____   _____

_____   _____

_____   _____

PROXY

The undersigned shareholder of _____
_____
authorizes_____to act as his/her proxy
and to represent and vote his/her shares at a_____meeting
of shareholders to be held at_____, state of
_____, on_____, 20___at____:___.M.

Dated: _____

Signature of Shareholder: _____

Printed Name of Shareholder: _____

Please return proxy by_____, 20___to:

Name: _____

Title: _____

Corporation: _____

Address: _____

City, State, Zip: _____

Fax:_____Phone: _____

WAIVER OF NOTICE OF MEETING OF

_____

The undersigned _____ waive(s) notice of and
consent(s) to the holding of the _____ meeting of
the_____   of   _____
held   at   _____,   state   of
_____ , on _____ , 20___ at
___:___ , for the purpose (s) of: _____

_____

_____

_____

_____

_____

_____

_____

_____

Dated: _____

Signature   Printed Name

_____   _____

_____   _____

_____   _____

_____   _____

_____   _____

WRITTEN CONSENT TO ACTION WITHOUT MEETING

The undersigned_____of_____hereby
consent(s) as follows: _____

_____

_____

_____

_____

_____

_____

_____

_____

_____

_____

Dated: _____

Signature   Printed Name

_____   _____

_____   _____

_____   _____

_____   _____

_____   _____

_____   _____

S CORPORATION TAX ELECTION

The board of directors considered the advantages of electing S corporation tax status for the corporation under Section 1362 of the Internal Revenue Code. After discussion, it was agreed that the corporation shall elect S corporation tax status with the IRS.

It was further agreed that the treasurer of the corporation prepare and file IRS Form 2553 and any other required forms in a timely manner so that the S corporation tax election will be effective starting with the _____ tax year of the corporation. The treasurer was further instructed to have all shareholders and their spouses sign the shareholder consent portion of IRS From 2553.

Sterling Cooper

S CORPORATION SHAREHOLDERS' AGREEMENT

The undersigned shareholders and spouses of shareholders of _____ represent and agree as follows:

The board of directors has approved a resolution authorizing the corporation to elect S corporation tax status with the IRS under Section 1362 of the Internal Revenue Code, to be effective for the corporate tax year beginning_____.

To help preserve and maintain the effectiveness of this S corporation tax status, the undersigned agree that they shall not transfer, sell, assign, convey or otherwise dispose of their shares, or any interest in these shares, if such disposition would result in the corporation's no longer being eligible for S corporation tax status with the IRS.

The undersigned further agree to sign any consent forms or other documents necessary to elect and obtain S corporation tax status with the IRS in a timely matter as requested by the treasurer of the corporation.

The undersigned further agree that, even if a proposed transfer or other disposition of shares does not jeopardize the corporation's S corporation tax status, no such transfer or disposition shall take place until the proposed shareholder and the proposed shareholder's spouse consent to the corporation's S corporation tax status, and sign an agreement that contains substantially the same terms as this agreement.

This agreement may be terminated by the consent of a majority of the outstanding shareholders of this corporation. Any person who breaches this agreement shall be liable to the corporation, its officers, directors, shareholders, spouses of shareholders and any transferees of shareholders or their spouses, for all losses, claims, damages, taxes, fines, penalties and other liabilities resulting from the breach of this agreement.

This agreement shall bind all parties, their successors, assigns, legal representatives, heirs and successors in interest. The undersigned shall ensure that any such successors and representatives shall be given a copy of this agreement prior to, or at the same time as, the delivery of any share certificates to them. A conspicuous legend shall be placed on all share certificates of the corporation indicating that the shares are subject to restrictions on transferability.

Dated:

Signature   Printed Name

_____   _____

_____   _____

_____   _____

_____   _____

_____   _____

INDEMNIFICATION AND INSURANCE FOR DIRECTORS AND OFFICERS

The corporation shall indemnify its current directors and officers to the fullest extent permitted under the laws of this state. Such indemnification shall not be deemed to be exclusive of any other rights to which the indemnified person is entitled, consistent with law, under any provision of the Articles of Incorporation or Bylaws of the corporation, any general or specific action of the board of directors, the terms of any contract, or as may be permitted or required by common law.

The corporation may purchase and maintain insurance or provide another arrangement on behalf of any person who is a director or officer against any liability asserted against him or her and incurred by him or her in such a capacity or arising out of his or her status as a director or officer, whether or not the corporation would have the power to indemnify him or her against that liability under the laws of this state.

RESOLUTION APPROVING LOAN TO CORPORATION

It was resolved that it is in the best interests of the corporation to borrow the following amount(s) from the following individuals:

Amount   Name of Lender

$_____   _____

$_____   _____

$_____   _____

$_____   _____

$_____   _____

The terms of_____loan were included in a promissory note presented for approval at the meeting. The board determined that these terms were commercially reasonable. The board also determined that corporate earnings should be sufficient to pay back the loan(s) to the lender(s) according to the terms in the note(s), and that such repayment would not jeopardize the financial status of the corporation.

Therefore, the board approved the terms of_____note and directed the treasurer to sign_____note on behalf of the corporation. The secretary was directed to attach a copy of the note, signed by the treasurer, to this resolution and to place the resolution and attachment(s) in the corporate records book.

PROMISSORY NOTE:
INSTALLMENT PAYMENTS OF PRINCIPAL AND INTEREST
(AMORTIZED LOAN)

For Value Received,_____, the borrower, promises to pay to the order of_____the note holder, the principal amount of $_____, together with simple interest on the unpaid principal balance from the date of this note until the date this note is paid in full, at the annual rate of_____%. Payments shall be made at _____

_____.

Principal and interest shall be paid in equal installments $_____, beginning on _____, 20___ and continuing on _____until the principal and interest are paid in full. Each payment on this note shall be applied first to accrued but unpaid interest, and the remainder shall be applied to unpaid principal.

This note may be prepaid by the borrower in whole or in part at any time without penalty. This note is not assumable without the written consent of the note holder, which consent shall not be unreasonably withheld. This note is nontransferable by the note holder.

If any installment payment due under this note is not received by the note holder within _____ of its due date, the entire amount of unpaid principal and accrued but unpaid interest due under this note shall, at the option of the note holder, become immediately due and payable without prior notice from the note holder to the borrower. In the event of a default, the borrower shall be responsible for the costs of collection, including, in the event of a lawsuit to collect on this note, the note holder's reasonable attorney fees as determined by a court.

Date of Signing: _____

Name of Borrower: _____

Address of Borrower: _____

City or County and State Where Signed: _____

Signature of Borrower: _____

Treasurer on Behalf of _____

Sterling Cooper

REIMBURSEMENT OF ACTUAL TRAVEL AND ENTERTAINMENT EXPENSES TO EMPLOYEES UNDER ACCOUNTABLE REIMBURSEMENT PLAN

After discussion, it was agreed that the corporation shall adopt an accountable plan for the reimbursement of business-related travel and entertainment expenses paid by corporate employees while traveling away from home on business of the corporation. It was agreed that the treasurer of the corporation be instructed to reimburse the following corporate employees for their reasonable and necessary travel and entertainment expenses while performing services for the corporation on the terms noted below.

Name   Title

_____   _____

_____   _____

_____   _____

It was further agreed that, prior to any reimbursement, the employee be required to substantiate by receipts or other records, within a reasonable amount of time as set by the treasurer in accordance with IRS regulations, the date, type, amount and business purpose of each expense, and any other information required for the expenses to be deductible by the corporation under the Internal Revenue Code.

Upon providing proper substantiation, an employee shall be reimbursed for these expenses within_____. If the treasurer determines that an employee has been reimbursed for expenses that have not been properly substantiated, the treasurer shall see to it that the employee pays back the amount of unsubstantiated reimbursement within _____ of the treasurer's determination.

It was further agreed that reimbursement of the above expenses to the above employees shall be subject to the following additional terms:

_____

_____

_____

_____

AUTHORIZATION OF PER DIEM TRAVEL ALLOWANCE FOR EMPLOYEES

After discussion, the board agreed that the corporation shall pay its employees as per diem allowance of_____in addition to their regular salary and other compensation while traveling away from home on business for the corporation.

It was further agreed that any part of the allowance paid in excess of the allowable federal per diem rate for the locality where the employee stops or stays over would be required to be included in the employee's income for tax purposes.

APPROVAL OF THE ISSUANCE OF SHARES

After discussion, it was agreed that the corporation shall issue the following number of _____ shares _____ to the following persons in exchange for payment of the following:

Name	Number of Shares	Payment	Value
_____	_____	$_____	$_____
_____	_____	$_____	$_____
_____	_____	$_____	$_____
_____	_____	$_____	$_____
_____	_____	$_____	$_____
_____	_____	$_____	$_____
_____	_____	$_____	$_____
_____	_____	$_____	$_____
_____	_____	$_____	$_____
_____	_____	$_____	$_____
_____	_____	$_____	$_____
_____	_____	$_____	$_____

The president and treasurer are instructed to issue share certificates to each of the persons in accordance with the above terms upon receipt by the corporation of the payment for the shares and after preparing all papers necessary to complete and document the transfer fo the payment to the corporation.

Sterling Cooper

SALE AND ISSUANCE OF SHARES FOR PROPERTY

After discussion by the board of directors, it was

RESOLVED, that this corporation shall sell and issue shares of its stock_____to the following persons in consideration of property actually received, as follows:

Name	# of Shares	Des. of Property	Value
_____	_____	$_____	$_____
_____	_____	$_____	$_____
_____	_____	$_____	$_____
_____	_____	$_____	$_____
_____	_____	$_____	$_____
_____	_____	$_____	$_____
_____	_____	$_____	$_____
_____	_____	$_____	$_____
_____	_____	$_____	$_____
_____	_____	$_____	$_____

RESOLVED FURTHER, that the board of directors of this corporation, determines that the fair value of such property to this corporation in monetary terms is the value shown above.

RESOLVED FURTHER, that the appropriate officers of this corporation are directed to take such actions and execute such documents as are necessary to sell and issue the shares listed above.

APPENDIX 14.

ACQUISITION CALCULATION

BID/CASH FLOW CALCULATION (000 omitted)

DEAL NAME: _____

ASSETS	VALUE	LOAN VALUE
CASH	$_____	$_____
A/R	$_____	$_____
INVENTORY	$_____	$_____
_____	$_____	$_____
_____	$_____	$_____

NET WORTH OF COMPANY $_____

TOTAL VALUE/BID $_____

AMOUNT		REPAYMENT	TERM
$_____	REVOLVER LOAN	$_____/yr	_____
$_____	REV. INTEREST	$_____/yr	_____
$_____	SUB-DEBT PRINCIPAL	$_____/yr	_____
$_____	SUB-DEBT INTEREST	$_____/yr	_____
$_____	TERM DEBT	$_____/yr	_____
$_____	TERM DEBT INTEREST	$_____/yr	_____
$_____	TOTALS $_____/yr		

PRIOR YEAR EBITDA $_____EBITDA $_____
                    PLUS OFFICER'S COMPENSATION

APPENDIX 15

Brief Summary For Each State's
Formation Requirements

Alabama

Formation: Before filing its articles of incorporation, a domestic for profit corporation may reserve a name with the secretary of state's office. Articles of incorporation must include the following:

• The name of the corporation, which must include the word "corporation" or "incorporated" or an abbreviation of one of those words ("Inc." or "Corp.") The name may not contain language stating or implying that the corporation is organized for a purpose other than that permitted by its articles of incorporation. Except as provided below, a corporate name shall not be the same as, or deceptively similar to: (1) the corporate name of a corporation incorporated or authorized to transact business in Alabama; (2) a reserved or registered corporate name; or (3) the fictitious name adopted by a foreign corporation authorized to transact business in Alabama because its real name is unavailable. A corporation may apply to the secretary of state for authorization to use a name that is the same as, or deceptively similar to a name described above. The secretary of state shall authorize use of the name applied for if: (1) the other corporation consents to the use in writing and submits an undertaking in form satisfactory to the secretary of state to the name of the applying corporation; or (2) the applicant delivers to the secretary of state a certified copy of the final judgment of a court of competent jurisdiction establishing the applicant's right to use the name applied for in Alabama. A corporation may use the name (including the fictitious name) of another domestic or foreign corporation that is used in Alabama if the other corporation is incorporated or authorized to transact business in Alabama and the proposed user corporation: (1) has merged with the other corporation; (2) has been formed by reorganization of the other

corporation; or (3) has acquired all or substantially all of the assets, including the corporate name, of the other corporation.
- The duration or life of the corporation, if not perpetual;
- The purpose of organizing the corporation;
- The number of authorized shares the corporation may issue;
- The name of registered agent and address of resident office;
- The names and addresses of directors of the corporation; and
- The names and addresses of incorporators of the corporation.

You must file the original and two copies of the articles of incorporation and the certificate of name reservation in the county where the corporation's registered office is located.

Upon creation, the corporation may have a meeting of its board of directors to elect officers, adopt bylaws (which may contain any provision consistent with law and the articles of incorporation), and carry on any other business of the corporation. This meeting may be held inside or outside of Alabama.

Minimum Number of Incorporators: One.

Management Requirements: Directors must approve bylaws for the corporation, directors must be natural persons of at least 19 years of age, and there must be at least one director of the corporation.

State Tax Classification: Corporations are charged a state franchise tax

Contact Information: Corporations Division
Office of the Secretary of State
P. O. Box 5616
Montgomery, Alabama 36103-5616
Phone: (334) 242-5324
www.sos.state.al.us/business/corporations.cfm

Alaska

Formation: Before filing its articles of incorporation, a domestic for profit corporation must reserve a name with the secretary of state's office. Articles of incorporation must include the following:

- The name of the corporation, which must contain the words "Corporation," "Company," "Incorporated," "Limited," or an abbreviation of these words, but which cannot contain the words "city," "borough," or "village," or otherwise imply that the corporation is a municipality. The name of a city, borough, or village may be used in the corporate name;
- The purpose for which the corporation is being organized, which may be stated as any lawful business allowed by the Alaska Corporation Code and/or a more specific purpose. In addition, the Standard Industrial Classification Code(s) (SIC) which most closely describe the business activities of the corporation must be stated (see SIC code list); if the corporation is authorized to issue only one class of shares, the total number of shares that the corporation is authorized to issue must be stated;
- If the corporation is authorized to issue more than one class of shares or if a class of shares is to have two or more series, a statement reflecting one or more of the following conditions must be included: (1) the total number of shares of each class the corporation is authorized to issue, and the total number of shares of each series that the corporation is authorized to issue, or a statement that the board is authorized to fix the number of shares; (2) the designation of each class, and the designation of each series or a statement that the board may determine the designation of any series; (3) the rights, preferences, privileges, and restrictions granted to or imposed on the respective classes or series of shares or the holders of the shares, or that the board, within any limits and restrictions stated, may determine or alter the rights, preferences, privileges, and restrictions granted to or imposed on a wholly unissued class of shares or a wholly unissued series of any class of shares; and (4) if the number of shares of a series is authorized to be fixed by the board, the articles of incorporation may also authorize the board to increase or decrease, but not below the number of shares of the series then outstanding, the number of shares of a series after the issue of shares of that series;
- The physical address of its initial registered office and the name of its initial registered agent (a mailing address must also be given if different from the physical address);

- The name and address of each alien affiliate or a statement that there are no alien affiliates (alien means any person who is not a U.S. citizen or national of the U.S., or who is not lawfully admitted to the U.S. for permanent residence).

The existence of the corporation begins upon the issuance of a certificate of incorporation. Upon creation, the corporation must have a meeting of its board of directors to elect officers, adopt bylaws (which may contain any provision consistent with law and the articles of incorporation), and carrying on any other business of the corporation. This meeting may be held inside or outside of Alaska.

Minimum Number of Incorporators: One natural person, at least 18 years of age.

Management Requirements: Directors must approve bylaws for the corporation, directors must be at least 18 years of age, and there must be at least one director of the corporation. If, at the initial organizational meeting of the corporation, more than 162/3% of the then-current directors or incorporators refuse to adopt a motion to set the number of directors at less than five directors, there may not be fewer than five directors of the corporation.

State Tax Classification: Alaska corporations are charged a state income tax, at a variable rate, and a biennial corporation fee of $100,000.

Contact Information: The Division of Banking, Securities and Corporations
Department of Community and Economic
Development
P. O. Box 110808
Juneau, AK 99801-0808
Phone: (907) 465-2521
Facsimile: (907) 465-2549
www.dced.state.ak.us.bsc/corpdoc.htm

Arizona

Formation: Before filing its articles of incorporation, a domestic for-profit corporation may reserve a name with the secretary of state's office. Application and filing fees are associated with the reservation of a name. When filing its articles, you must include a cover sheet, a trade name certificate, or declaration of trade name assignee, or declaration of holder of trade name, and a certificate of disclosure. The articles of incorporation must include the following:

- The proposed name of the corporation, which must include the word "association," "bank," "company," "corporation," "limited," or "incorporated," but which shall not include the word "bank," "trust," "deposit," or "trust company" unless the corporation is or intends to become substantially involved in the banking or trust business;
- The initial business or affairs of the corporation;
- The fiscal year end date of the corporation;
- The number of shares of stock the corporation will be authorized to issue, series, class and preference, if any;
- The street address of the known place of business in Arizona. Maybe in care of the address of the statutory agent (if agent, cannot be a P. O. Box.);
- The name and address of the statutory agent (cannot be a P. O. Box);
- The name(s) and addressees) of the initial board of directors (minimum of one);
- The name(s) and addressees) of the incorporators (minimum of one);
- The signatures of all incorporators; and
- The signature of statutory agent (acknowledge acceptance).

Within sixty (60) days after filing with the commission, there must be published in a newspaper of general circulation in the county of the known place of business in Arizona, three (3) consecutive publications of a copy of the approved articles of incorporation or application for authority. Within 90 days after filing, an affidavit evidencing the publication must be filed with the commission.

The existence of the corporation begins upon the filing of the articles and related documents. Upon creation, the corporation must have a meeting of its board of directors to elect officers, adopt bylaws (which may contain any provision consistent with law and the articles of incorporation), and carry on any other business of the corporation. This meeting may be held inside or outside of Arizona.

Minimum Number of Incorporators: One.

Management Requirements: Directors must approve bylaws for the corporation, directors must be at least 18years of age, and there must be at least one director of the corporation.

State Tax Classification: Corporations are charged state income tax at the rate of 6.968%, and a transaction privilege tax at 5%.

Contact Information: Arizona Corporation Commission
Corporations Division
1300 West Washington
Phoenix, AZ 85007-2996
Phone: (602) 542-3026
www.cc.state.az.us/

Arkansas

Formation: Before filing its articles of incorporation, a domestic for profit corporation may reserve a name with the secretary of state's office. Articles of incorporation must include the following:

- Name of the corporation, which must include the word "Corporation" or "Incorporated" or an abbreviation of one of these words ("Inc." or "Corp."). The name must not be the same as or confusingly similar to the name of any domestic corporation or foreign corporation authorized to transact business in Arkansas;
- Duration or life of the corporation, if not perpetual;
- Purpose of organizing the corporation;
- Number of authorized shares the corporation may issue, classes and par value;
- Name of registered agent and address of resident office;
- Names, addresses, and number of directors of the corporation;
- Names and addresses of incorporators of the corporation;

The existence of the corporation begins immediately upon the filing of the articles of incorporation. Upon creation, the corporation may have a meeting of its board of directors to elect officers, adopt bylaws (which may contain any provision consistent with law and the articles of incorporation), and carryon any other business of the corporation. This meeting may be held inside or outside of Arkansas.

Minimum Number of Incorporators: One.

Management Requirements: Directors must approve bylaws for the corporation. Any two or more offices may be held by the same person, except the offices of president and secretary. When only one stockholder, all offices may be held by the same person.

State Tax Classification: Corporations are charged state franchise tax, assessed at the rate of .27% against the corporation's outstanding stock, and a variable corporate income tax.

Contact Information: Secretary of State
256 State Capital Building
Little Rock, AR 72201
Phone: (501) 682-1010
Facsimile: (501) 682-3510
www.sosweb.state.ar.us/

Formation: Before filing its articles of incorporation, a domestic for profit corporation may reserve a name with the secretary of state's office. Articles of incorporation must include the following:

• The name of the corporation; provided, however, that in order for the corporation to be subject to the provisions of this division applicable to a close corporation, the name of the corporation must contain the word "corporation," "incorporated," or "limited," or an abbreviation of one of such words. The name shall not include the word "bank," "trust," "trustee," or related words, unless a certificate of approval of the Commissioner of Financial Institutions is attached to the articles of incorporation. The name shall also not be likely to mislead the public or be the same as, or resemble so closely as to tend to deceive, the name of a domestic corporation, the name of a foreign corporation which is authorized to transact intrastate business or has registered its name, a name which a foreign corporation, a name which will become the record name of a domestic or foreign corporation upon the effective date of a filed corporate instrument where there is a delayed effective date, or a name which is under reservation for another corporation, except that a corporation may adopt a name that is substantially the same as an existing domestic corporation or foreign corporation which is authorized to transact intrastate business or has registered its name, upon proof of consent by such domestic or foreign corporation and a finding by the secretary of state that under the circumstances the public is not likely to be misled.

- The applicable one of the following statements: (1) the purpose of the corporation is to engage in any lawful act or activity for which a corporation may be organized under the General Corporation Law of California other than the banking business, the trust company business or the practice of a profession permitted to be incorporated by the California Corporations Code; or (2) the purpose of the corporation is to engage in the profession of (with the insertion of a profession permitted to be incorporated by the California Corporations Code) and any other lawful activities (other than the banking or trust company business) not prohibited to a corporation engaging in such profession by applicable laws and regulations.
- In case the corporation is a corporation subject to the Banking Law, the articles shall set forth a statement of purpose which is prescribed in the applicable provision of the Banking Law;
- In case the corporation is a corporation subject to the Insurance Code as an insurer, the articles shall additionally state that the business of the corporation is to be an insurer;
- If the corporation is intended to be a "professional corporation," the articles shall additionally contain the statement required by Section 13404 of the California Corporations Code;
- The articles shall not set forth any further or additional statement with respect to the purposes or powers of the corporation, except by way of limitation or except as expressly required by any law of California or any federal or other statute or regulation (including the Internal Revenue Code and regulations there under as a condition of acquiring or maintaining a particular status for tax purposes);
- The name and address in California of the corporation's initial agent for service of process; • If the corporation is authorized to issue only one class of shares, the total number of shares which the corporation is authorized to issue;

• If the corporation is authorized to issue more than one class of shares, or if any class of shares is to have two or more series: (1) the total number of shares of each class the corporation is authorized to issue, and the total number of shares of each series which the corporation is authorized to issue or that the board is authorized to fix the number of shares of any such series; (2) the designation of each class, and the designation of each series or that the board may determine the designation of any such series; and (3) the rights, preferences, privileges and restrictions granted to or imposed upon the respective classes or series of shares or the holders thereof, or that the board, within any limits and restrictions stated, may determine or alter the rights, preferences, privileges and restrictions granted to or imposed upon any wholly unissued class of shares or any wholly unissued series of any class of shares. As to any series the number of shares of which is authorized to be fixed by the board, the articles may also authorize the board, within the limits and restrictions stated therein or stated in any resolution or resolutions of the board originally fixing the number of shares constituting any series, to increase or decrease (but not below the number of shares of such series then outstanding) the number of shares of any such series subsequent to the issue of shares of that series. In case the number of shares of any series shall be so decreased, the shares constituting such decrease shall resume the status which they had prior to the adoption of the resolution originally fixing the number of shares of such series.

The corporate existence begins upon the filing of the articles of incorporation in the office of the secretary of state. Upon creation, the corporation may have a meeting of its board of directors to elect officers, adopt bylaws (which may contain any provision consistent with law and the articles of incorporation), and carryon any other business of the corporation. This meeting may be held inside or outside of California.

Minimum Number of Incorporators: One or more natural persons, partnerships, associations or corporations, domestic or foreign.

Management Requirements: Except for close corporations, the number or minimum number of directors shall not be less than three; provided, however, that (1) before shares are issued, the number may be one, (2) before shares are issued, the number may be two, (3) so long as the corporation has only one shareholder, the number may be one, (4) so long as the corporation has only one shareholder, the number may be two, and (5) so long as the corporation has only two shareholders, the number may be two. Directors may approve bylaws for the corporation, establishing the number of directors and other rules governing the corporation.

State Tax Classification: The state charges a minimum annual franchise tax of $800.00, assessed at the rate of 8.84% of net income. The State also assesses sales and use taxes, each at the rate of 5.75%.

Contact Information: Business Programs Division
1500 11th Street
Sacramento, CA95814
Phone: (916) 653-2318
www.ss.ca.gov;business/corp/corporate.htm

Colorado

Formation: Before filing its articles of incorporation, a domestic for profit corporation may reserve a name with the secretary of state's office. Articles of incorporation must include the following:

• Name of the corporation, which contains the term "corporation," "incorporated," "company," or "limited," or an abbreviation of such words. The name must not contain any term the inclusion of which would violate any statute of Colorado. The name must be distinguishable on the records of the secretary of state from every: (1) other entity name; (2) name that is reserved with the secretary of state under the laws of Colorado for another entity; (3) trade name that is registered with the secretary of state by another entity; and (4) trademark registered with the secretary of state by another entity. An entity name need not be in English if written in English letters or Arabic or Roman numerals.

- The classes of shares and the number of shares of each class that the corporation is authorized to issue. If more than one class of shares is authorized, the articles of incorporation shall prescribe a distinguishing designation for each class, and, before the issuance of shares of any class, the preferences, limitations, and relative rights of that class shall be described in the articles of incorporation. All shares of a class shall have preferences, limitations, and relative rights identical with those of other shares of the same class except to the extent otherwise permitted by section 7-106-102 of the Revised Colorado Statutes.
- The articles of incorporation shall authorize: (1) one or more classes of shares that together have unlimited voting rights; and (2) one or more classes of shares, which may be the same class or classes as those with voting rights, that together are entitled to receive the net assets of the corporation upon dissolution;
- The street address of the corporation's initial registered office and the name of its initial registered agent at that office;
- The address of the corporation's initial principal office;
- The name and address of each incorporator; and
- The written consent of the initial registered agent to the appointment unless such consent is provided in an accompanying document.

Upon creation, the corporation may have a meeting of its board of directors (or incorporators if board members have not yet been selected) to elect officers, adopt bylaws (which may contain any provision consistent with law and the articles of incorporation), and carryon any other business of the corporation. This meeting may be held inside or outside of Colorado.

Minimum Number of Incorporators: One or more natural persons of at least 18 years of age.

Management Requirements: Directors must approve bylaws for the corporation at the corporation's initial meeting. Any officers of the corporation must be at least one director. Any officers of the corporation must be at least 18 years of age.

State Tax Classification: The State assesses corporate income tax at the rate of 4.63%, charges a fee of $25.00 for a domestic biennial report, and a 2.9% sales and use tax.

Contact Information: Department of State
Business Services
1560 Broadway, Suite 200
Denver, CO 80202
Phone: (303) 894-2251
E-mail: sos.business@state.co.us
www.sos.state.co.us/pubs/business/main.htm

Connecticut

Formation: Before filing its certificate of incorporation, a domestic for profit corporation may reserve a name with the secretary of state's office. A certificate of incorporation must include the following:

• The name of the corporation, which must contain one of the following designations: "corporation," "incorporated," "company," "Societa per Azioni," or "limited," or the abbreviation "corp.," "inc.," "co.," "S.pA.," or "ltd.," or words or abbreviations of like import in another language. The name must not contain language stating or implying that the corporation is organized for a purpose other than that permitted by law and its certificate of incorporation. Except as provided below, a corporate name must be distinguishable upon the records of the secretary of the state from: (1) the corporate name of a corporation incorporated or authorized to transact business in Connecticut; (2) a reserved or registered corporate name; (3) the fictitious name adopted by a foreign corporation authorized to transact business in Connecticut; (4) the corporate name of a nonprofit corporation incorporated or authorized to transact business in Connecticut because its real name is unavailable; (5) the corporate name of any domestic or foreign nonstock corporation incorporated or authorized to transact business in Connecticut; (6) the name of any domestic or foreign limited partnership organized or authorized to transact business in Connecticut; (J) the name of any domestic or foreign limited liability company organized or authorized to transact business in Connecticut; and (8) the name of any domestic or foreign limited liability partnership organized or authorized to transact business in Connecticut. A corporation may apply to the secretary of state for authorization to use a name that is not distinguishable upon his records from one or more of the names described above. The secretary of state may authorize the use of the name applied for if:

(1) the other corporation, limited partnership, limited liability company, or limited liability partnership, as the case may be, consents to the use in writing and submits an undertaking in a form satisfactory to the secretary of state to change its name to a name that is distinguishable upon the records of the secretary of state from the name of the applying corporation; or (2) the applicant delivers to the secretary of state a certified copy of the final judgment of a court of competent jurisdiction establishing the applicant's right to use the name applied for in Connecticut. A corporation may use the name, including the fictitious name, of another domestic or foreign corporation that is used in Connecticut if the other corporation is incorporated or authorized to transact business in Connecticut and the corporation seeking to use the name: (1) has merged with the other corporation; (2) has been formed by reorganization of the other corporation; or (3) has acquired all or substantially all of the assets, including the corporate name, of the other corporation.

- The number of shares the corporation is authorized to issue;
- The classes of shares and the number of shares of each class that the corporation is authorized to issue. If more than one class of shares is authorized, the certificate of incorporation must prescribe a distinguishing designation for each class, and, prior to the issuance of shares of a class, the preferences, limitations and relative rights of that class must be described in the certificate of incorporation. All shares of a class shall have preferences, limitations and relative rights identical with those other shares of the same class.
- The certificate of incorporation shall authorized (1) one or more classes of shares that together have unlimited voting rights, and (2) one or more classes of shares, which may be the same class or classes as those with voting rights, that together are entitled to receive the net assets of the corporation upon dissolution;
- The street address of the corporation's initial registered office and the name of its initial registered agent at that office; and

- The name and address of each incorporator.

Upon creation, the corporation must have a meeting of its board of directors to elect officers, adopt bylaws (which may contain any provision consistent with law and the certificate of incorporation), and carryon any other business of the corporation. This meeting may be held inside or outside of Connecticut.

Minimum Number of Incorporators: One individual or entity.

Management Requirements: Directors must approve bylaws for the corporation. Directors must be at least 18 years of age, and there must be at least one director of the corporation.

State Tax Classification: The State assesses a 7.5% corporate business tax, charges a fee of $75.00 for biennial reports, and assesses both sales and use taxes at 6%.

Contact Information: Secretary of the State's Office
210 Capitol Ave., Suite 104
Hartford, CT 06106
Phone: (860) 509-6001
E-mail: crd@po.state.ct.us
www.sots.state.ct.us/

Delaware

Formation: Before filing its certificate of incorporation, a domestic for profit corporation must reserve a name with the department of state's office. The certificate of incorporation must include the following:

- The name of the corporation, which: (1) shall contain 1 of the words "association," "company," "corporation," "club," "foundation," "fund," "incorporated," "institute," "society," "union," "syndicate," or "limited," (or abbreviations thereof, with or without punctuation), or words (or abbreviations thereof, with or without punctuation) if like import of foreign countries or jurisdictions; provided, however that the division of corporations in the department of state may waive such requirement if such corporation executes, acknowledges and files with the department of state a certificate stating that its total assets are not less than $10,000,000; (2) shall be such as to distinguish it upon the records in the office of the division of corporations in the department of state from the names of other corporations or limited partnerships organized, reserved or registered as a foreign corporation or foreign limited partnership under the laws of Delaware, except with the written consent of such other foreign corporation or domestic or foreign limited partnership, executed, acknowledged and filed with the department of state; and, (3) shall not contain the word "bank," or any variation thereof, except for the name of a bank reporting to and under the supervision of the State Bank Commissioner or a subsidiary of a bank or savings association, or a corporation regulated under the Bank Holding Company Act of 1956, as amended, or the Home Owners' Loan Act, as amended; provided, however, this shall not be construed to prevent the use of the word "bank," or any variation thereof, in a context clearly not purporting to refer to a banking business or otherwise likely to mislead the public about the nature of the business of the corporation or to lead to a pattern and practice of abuse that might cause harm to the interests of the public or Delaware as determined by the division of corporations in the department of state;

- The address (which shall include the street, number, city and county) of the corporation's registered office in Delaware, and the name of its registered agent at such address;
- The nature of the business or purposes to be conducted or promoted. It shall be sufficient to state, either alone or with other businesses or purposes, that the purpose of the corporation is to engage in any lawful act or activity for which corporations may be organized under the General Corporation Law of Delaware, and by such statement all lawful acts and activities shall be within the purposes of the corporation, except for express limitations, if any;
- If the corporation is to be authorized to issue only 1 class of stock, the total number of shares of stock which the corporation shall have authority to issue and the par value of each of such shares, or a statement that all such shares are to be without par value. If the corporation is to be authorized to issue more than 1 class of stock, the certificate of incorporation shall set forth the total number of shares of all classes of stock which the corporation shall have

authority to issue and the number of shares of each class and shall specify each class the shares of which are to be without par value and each class the shares of which are to have par value and the par value of the shares of each such class. The certificate of incorporation shall also set forth a statement of the designations and the powers, preferences and rights, and the qualifications, limitations or restrictions thereof, which are permitted in respect of any class or classes of stock or any series of any class of stock of the corporation and the fixing of which by the certificate of incorporation is desired, and an express grant of such authority as it may then be desired to grant to the board of directors to fix by resolution or resolutions any thereof that may be desired but which shall not be fixed by the certificate of incorporation. The foregoing provisions do not apply to corporations which are not to have authority to issue capital stock. In the case of such corporations, the fact that they are not to have authority to issue capital stock shall be stated in the certificate of incorporation. The conditions of membership of such corporations shall likewise be stated in the certificate of incorporation or the certificate may provide that the conditions of membership shall be stated in the bylaws;

- The name and mailing address of the incorporator or incorporators;
- If the powers of the incorporator or incorporators are to terminate upon the filing of the certificate of incorporation, the names and mailing addresses of the persons who are to serve as directors until the first annual meeting of stockholders or until their successors are elected and qualify.

The existence of the corporation begins upon the filing of the certificate of incorporation with the division of corporations. Upon creation, the corporation may have a meeting of its board of directors to elect officers, adopt bylaws (which may contain any provision consistent with law and the certificate of incorporation), and carryon any other business of the corporation. This meeting may be held inside or outside of Delaware.

Minimum Number of Incorporators: Any person, partnership, association or corporation, singly or jointly with others, and without regard to such person's or entity's residence, domicile or state of incorporation, may incorporate or organize a corporation.

Management Requirements: Directors or original incorporators, depending upon the terms of the certificate of incorporation, may approve bylaws for the corporation. There must be at least one director on the corporation's board of directors.

State Tax Classification: The State assesses a variable franchise tax and a state corporation income tax at 8.7%.

Contact Information: State of Delaware
Division of Corporations
401 Federal Street, Suite 4
Dover, Delaware 19901
Phone: (302) 739-3073
Facsimile: (302) 739-3812
www.state.de.us/corp/index.htm

Florida

Formation: Before filing its articles of incorporation, a domestic for profit corporation may reserve a name with the division of corporations of the secretary of state. The articles of incorporation must include the following:

• The name of the corporation, which must contain the word "corporation," "company," or "incorporated," or the abbreviation "corp.," "Inc.," or "Co.," or words or abbreviations of like import in language, as will clearly indicate that it is a corporation instead of a natural person or partnership. The name may not contain language stating or implying that the corporation is organized for a purpose other than that permitted by statute or its articles of incorporation, and it may not contain language stating or implying that the corporation is connected with a state or federal government agency or a corporation chartered under the laws of the United States. The name must also be distinguishable from the names of all other entities or filings, except fictitious name registrations organized, registered, or reserved under the laws of Florida, which names are on file with the division of corporations.

- The street address of the initial principal office and, if different, the mailing address of the corporation;
- The number of shares the corporation is authorized to issue; if any preemptive rights are to be granted to shareholders, the provision therefore;
- The street address of the corporation's initial registered office and the name of its initial registered agent at that office together with a written acceptance; and
- The name and address of each incorporator.

The existence of the corporation begins upon the filing of the articles of incorporation with the secretary of state. Upon creation, the corporation may have a meeting of its board of directors to elect officers, adopt bylaws (which may contain any provision consistent with law and the articles of incorporation), and carryon any other business of the corporation. This meeting may be held inside or outside of Florida.

Minimum Number of Incorporators: One or more entities or natural persons.

Management Requirements: Directors or original incorporators, depending upon the terms of the certificate of incorporation, may approve bylaws for the corporation. There must be at least one director on the corporation's

State Tax Classification: The State assesses a corporate franchise (income) tax at the rate of 5.5%, documentary excise tax at $.35 per $100.00 of transfer, and sales and use tax assessed at 6%.

Contact Information: Division of Corporations
P. O. Box 6327
Tallahassee, FL32314
Phone: (850) 488-9000
www.dos.state.fl.us/doc/index.html

Georgia

Formation: Before filing its articles of incorporation, a domestic for profit corporation must reserve a name with the secretary of state's office. The articles of incorporation must include the following:

• The name of the corporation, which must contain the word "corporation," "incorporated," "company," or "limited," or the abbreviation "corp.," "inc.," "co.," or "ltd.," or words or abbreviations of like import in another language. The name may not contain language stating or implying that the corporation is organized for a purpose other than that permitted by law and its articles of incorporation. It may not contain anything which, in the reasonable judgment of the secretary of state, is obscene, and may not in any instance exceed 80 characters, including spaces and punctuation. Except as provided below, a corporate name must be distinguishable upon the records of the secretary of state from: (1) the corporate name of a corporation incorporated or authorized to transact business in Georgia; (2) a reserved or registered corporate name; (3) the fictitious name adopted by a foreign corporation authorized to transact business in Georgia because its real name is unavailable; (4) the corporate name of a nonprofit corporation incorporated or authorized to transact business in Georgia; (5) the name of a limited partnership or professional association filed with the secretary of state; and (6) the name of a limited liability company formed or authorized to transact business in Georgia. A corporation may apply to the secretary of state for authorization to use a name that is not distinguishable upon his records from one or more of the names described above. The secretary of state shall authorize use of the name applied for if the other corporation consents to the use in writing and files with the secretary of state articles of amendment to its articles of incorporation changing its name to a name that is distinguishable upon the records of the secretary of state from the name of the applying corporation. A corporation may use the name (including the fictitious name) of another domestic or foreign corporation that is used in Georgia if the other corporation is incorporated or authorized to transact business in Georgia and: (1) the proposed user corporation has merged with the other corporation; (2) the proposed user corporation has been formed by reorganization of the other corporation; or (3) the other domestic or foreign corporation has taken the steps required by law to change its name to a name that is distinguishable upon the records of the secretary of state from the name of the foreign corporation applying to use its former name.

- The number of shares the corporation is authorized to issue;
- The classes of shares and the number of shares of each class that the corporation is authorized to issue. If more than one class of shares is authorized, the articles of incorporation must prescribe a distinguishing designation for each class and, prior to the issuance of shares of a class, the preferences, limitations, and relative rights of that class must be described in the articles of incorporation.
- The articles of incorporation must authorize: (1) one or more classes of shares that together have unlimited voting rights; and (2) one or more classes of shares (which may be the same class or classes as those with voting rights) that together are entitled to receive the net assets of the corporation upon dissolution.
- The street address and county of the corporation's initial registered office and the name of its initial registered agent at that office;
- The name and address of each incorporator; and
- The mailing address of the initial principal office of the corporation, if different from the initial registered office.

The existence of the corporation begins upon the filing of the articles of incorporation with the secretary of state. Upon creation, the corporation may have a meeting of its board of directors to elect officers, adopt bylaws (which may contain any provision consistent with law and the articles of incorporation), and carryon any other business of the corporation. This meeting may be held inside or outside of Georgia.

Minimum Number of Incorporators: Any person, partnership, association or corporation, singly or jointly with others, and without regard to such person's or entity's residence, domicile or state of incorporation, may incorporate or organize a corporation.

Management Requirements: Directors or original incorporators, depending upon the terms of the certificate of incorporation, may approve bylaws for the corporation. There must be at least one director on the corporation's board of directors. Such director must be a natural person of at least 18 years of age.

State Tax Classification: The State assesses a graduated corporate franchise tax, charges $15.00 for corporate annual reports, assesses corporate income tax at the rate of 6%, and collects sales and use taxes at the rate of 4%.

Contact Information: Corporations Division
315 West Tower
2 Martin Luther King, Jr. Drive
Atlanta, Georgia 30334
Phone: (404) 656-2817
Facsimile: (404) 657-2248
www.sos.state.ga.us/corporations/

Hawaii

Formation: Before filing its articles of incorporation, a domestic for profit corporation may reserve a name with the director of the department of commerce and consumer affairs. The articles of incorporation must include the following:

• The name of the corporation, which: (1) shall contain the word "corporation," "incorporated," or "limited," or shall contain an abbreviation of one of the words; and (2) shall not be the same as, or substantially identical to, the name of any domestic corporation, partnership, limited liability company, or limited liability partnership existing or registered under the laws of Hawaii, or any foreign corporation, partnership, limited liability company, or limited liability partnership authorized to transact business in Hawaii, or any trade name, trademark, or service mark registered in Hawaii, or a name the exclusive right to which is, at the time, reserved in Hawaii, except that this shall not apply if the applicant files with the director either of the following: (a) the written consent from the entity or holder of a reserved or registered name to use the same or substantially identical name, and one or more words are added to make the name distinguishable from the other name; or (b) a certified copy of a final decree of a court of competent jurisdiction establishing the prior right of the applicant to the use of the name in Hawaii.

- The aggregate number of shares which the corporation shall have authority to issue, and, if the shares are to be divided into classes, the number of shares of each class;
- The mailing address of its initial or principal office and, if the corporation is required at the time of incorporation to have a registered office and registered agent in Hawaii, the street address of the corporation's initial registered office and the name of its initial registered agent at that office; provided that where no specific street address is available for the corporation's initial or principal office or for the corporation's registered office, the rural route post office number or post office box designated or made available by the United States Postal Service;
- The number of directors constituting the initial board of directors and the names and addresses of the individuals who are to serve as directors until the first annual meeting of shareholders or until their successors are elected and qualified; and
- The name, title, and address of each officer.

The existence of the corporation begins upon the delivery of the articles to the director of commerce and consumer affairs for filing. Upon creation, the corporation may have a meeting of its board members to elect officers, adopt bylaws (which may contain any provision consistent with law and the articles of incorporation), and carryon any other business of the corporation. This meeting may be held inside or outside of Hawaii.

Minimum Number of Incorporators: One or more individuals.
Management Requirements: Directors may approve bylaws for the corporation. If the corporation has only one shareholder, the corporation shall have one or more directors. If the corporation has two shareholders, the corporation shall have two or more directors. If the corporation has three or more shareholders, the corporation shall have three or more directors. The number of directors shall be fixed by, or in the manner provided in, the articles of incorporation or the bylaws, except as to the number constituting the initial board of directors, which number shall be fixed by the articles of incorporation.

The officers of a corporation shall consist of a president, one or more vice-presidents as may be prescribed by the bylaws, a secretary, and a treasurer, each of whom shall be elected or appointed by the board of directors at such time and in such manner as may be prescribed by the bylaws.

State Tax Classification: The state charges $25.00 for annual corporation reports and assesses a corporate income tax at a variable rate.

Contact Information: Department of Commerce and Consumer Affairs
Business Registration Division
P. O. Box 40
Honolulu, Hawaii 96810
Phone: (808) 586-2744
Facsimile: (808) 586-2733
www.businessregistrations.com/index.html

Idaho

Before filing its certificate of incorporation, a domestic for profit corporation may reserve a name with the secretary of state's office. The certificate of incorporation must include the following:

• The name of the corporation, which must contain the word "corporation" "incorporation," "company," or "limited." or the abbreviation "corp.," "inc.," "co.," or "ltd.," or words or abbreviations of like import in another language; provided however, that if the word "company" or its abbreviation is used it shall not be immediately preceded by the word "and" or by an abbreviation of or symbol representing the word "and." The name may not contain language stating or implying that the corporation is organized for any unlawful purpose or any purpose inconsistent with its articles of incorporation. Except as provided below, a corporate name must be distinguishable upon the records of the secretary of state from: (1) the corporate name of a corporation incorporated or authorized to transact business in Idaho; (2) a name reserved or registered under Idaho Code; (3) the fictitious name adopted by a foreign corporation authorized to transact business in Idaho because its real name is unavailable; (4) the corporate name of a nonprofit corporation incorporated or authorized to transact business in Idaho; and (5) the name of any limited partnership, limited liability partnership or limited liability company which is organized under the laws of Idaho or registered to do business in Idaho. A corporation may apply to the secretary of state for authorization to use a name that is not distinguishable on his records from one or more of the names described above. The secretary of state shall authorize use of the name applied for if (1) the other corporation, holder of a reserved or registered name, limited partnership, limited liability partnership or limited liability company consents to the use in writing and submits an undertaking in a form satisfactory to the secretary of state to change its name to a name that is distinguishable upon the records of the secretary of state from the name of the applying corporation; or (2) the applicant delivers to the secretary of state a certified copy of the final judgment of a court of competent jurisdiction establishing the applicant's right to use the name applied for in Idaho. A corporation may use the name, including the fictitious name, of another domestic or foreign corporation or limited liability company that is used in Idaho if the other corporation or limited liability company is organized or authorized to transact business in Idaho and the proposed user corporation: (1) has merged with the other corporation or limited liability company; (2) has been formed by reorganization of the other corporation or limited liability company; or (3) has acquired all or substantially all of the assets, including the name, of the other corporation or limited liability company.

- The number of shares the corporation is authorized to issue;
- The street address of the corporation's initial registered office and the name of its initial registered agent at that office; and
- The name and address of each incorporator.

The existence of the corporation begins upon the filing of the certificate of corporation with the secretary of state. Upon creation, the corporation has a meeting of its incorporators or initial board members to elect directors, officers, adopt bylaws (which may contain any provision consistent law and the articles of incorporation), and carryon any other business of corporation. This meeting may be held inside or outside of Idaho.

Minimum Number of Incorporators: Any individual or entity may incorporate or organize a corporation.

Management Requirements: Directors or original incorporators, depending upon the terms of the articles of incorporation, may approve bylaws for the corporation. There must be at least one director on the corporation's board of directors.

State Tax Classification: Idaho assesses a corporate income tax at 8% a use tax at 5%.

Contact Information: Office of the Secretary of State
700WJefferson, Room 203
P. O. Box 83720
Boise, ID 83720-0080
Telephone (208) 334-2300
Facsimile (208) 334-2282
www.idsos.state.id.us/

Illinois

Formation: Before filing its articles of incorporation, a domestic for-profit corporation may reserve a name with the secretary of state's office. The articles of incorporation must include the following:

- The name of the corporation, which must contain, separate and apart from any other word or abbreviation in such name, the word "corporation," company," "incorporated," or "limited," or an abbreviation of one of such words, and if the name of a foreign corporation does not contain, separate and apart from any other word or abbreviation, one of such words or abbreviations, the corporation shall add at the end of its name, as a separate word abbreviation, one of such words or an abbreviation of one of such words. The name must not contain any word or phrase which indicates or implies that the corporation: (1) is authorized or empowered to conduct the business of insurance, assurance, indemnity, or the acceptance of savings deposits; (2) is authorized or empowered to conduct the business of banking less otherwise permitted by the Commissioner of Banks and Real Estate pursuant to Section 46 of the Illinois Banking Act; or (3) is authorized or empowered to be in the business of a corporate fiduciary unless otherwise permitted by the Commissioner of Banks and Real Estate. The word "trust," trustee," or "fiduciary," may be used by a corporation only if it has first compiled Corporate Fiduciary Act. The word "bank," "banker," or "banking," may only be used by a corporation if it has first complied with the Illinois Banking Act. The name must be distinguishable upon the records in the office of the secretary of state from the corporate name or assumed corporate name of any domestic corporation, whether profit or not for profit, existing under any act of Illinois or of any foreign corporation, whether profit or not for profit, authorized to transact business in Illinois, or a name the exclusive right to which is, at the time, reserved or registered, except that, subject to the discretion of the secretary of state, a foreign corporation that has a name otherwise prohibited may be issued a certificate of authority to transact business in Illinois, if the foreign corporation: (1) elects to adopt an assumed corporate name or names in accordance with Illinois statutes; and (2) agrees in its application for a certificate of authority to transact business in Illinois only under such assumed corporate name or names. Furthermore, the name must contain the word "trust," if it be a domestic corporation organized for the purpose of accepting and executing trusts, shall contain the word "pawners," if it be a domestic corporation organized as a pawners' society, and shall contain the word "cooperative," if it be a domestic corporation organized as a cooperative association for pecuniary profit. The name must not contain a word or phrase, or an abbreviation or derivation thereof, the use of which is prohibited or restricted by any statute of Illinois unless such restriction has been complied with. The name must consist of letters of the English alphabet, Arabic or Roman numerals, or symbols capable of being readily reproduced by the office of the secretary of state. It must be the name under which the corporation shall transact business in Illinois unless the corporation shall also elect to adopt an assumed corporate name or names; provided, however, that the corporation may use any divisional designation or trade name without complying with the requirements listed above, provided the corporation also clearly discloses its corporate name. For the purposes of the foregoing, the secretary of state shall determine whether a name is "distinguishable" from another name. Without excluding other names which may not constitute distinguishable names in Illinois, a name is not considered distinguishable solely because it contains one or more of the following: (1) the word "corporation," "company," "incorporated," or "limited," or an abbreviation of one of such words; (2) articles, conjunctions, contractions, abbreviations, different tenses or number of the same word.

- The purpose or purposes for which the corporation is organized, which may be stated to be, or to include, the transaction of any or all lawful businesses for which corporations may be incorporated under Illinois statutes;
- The address of the corporation's initial registered office and the name of its initial registered agent at that office;
- The name and address of each incorporator;
- The number of shares of each class the corporation is authorized to issue;
- The number and class of shares which the corporation proposes to issue without further report to the secretary of state, and the consideration to be received, less expenses, including commissions, paid or incurred in connection with the issuance of shares, by the corporation.
- If shares of more than one class are to be issued, the consideration for shares of each class shall be separately stated;
- If the shares are divided into classes, the designation of each class and a statement of the designations, preferences, qualifications, limitations, restrictions, and special or relative rights with respect to the shares of each class: and
- If the corporation may issue the shares of any preferred or special class in series, then the designation of each series and a statement of the variations in the relative rights and preferences of the different series, if the same are fixed in the articles of incorporation, or a statement of the authority vested in the board of directors to establish

series and determine the variations in the relative rights and preferences of the different series.

The existence of the corporation begins upon issuance of a certificate of incorporation by the secretary of state. Upon creation, the corporation may have a meeting of its incorporators or initial board members to elect directors, officers, adopt bylaws (which may contain any provision consistent with law and the articles of incorporation), and carryon any other business of the corporation. This meeting may be held inside or outside of Illinois.

Minimum Number of Incorporators: Anyone individual over the age of 18 or anyone foreign or domestic corporation.

Management Requirements: Directors or original incorporators, depending upon the terms of the articles of incorporation, may approve bylaws for the corporation. There must be at least one director on the corporation's board of directors.

State Tax Classification: Illinois assesses a corporate income tax at 4.8%, sales and use taxes at 1.25% and a franchise tax. The franchise tax is initially assessed at the rate of 0.15% of paid-in capital, but decreases to 0.1% after the first year of corporate existence.

Contact Information: Secretary of State
Department of Business Services
Springfield, IL62756
Phone: (217) 782-6961
www.sos.state.il.us

Indiana

Formation: Before filing its articles of incorporation, a domestic for-profit corporation may reserve a name with the secretary of state's office. The articles of incorporation must include the following:

• The name of the corporation, which must contain the word "corporation," "incorporated," "company," or "limited," or the abbreviation "corp.," "inc.," "co.," or "ltd.," or words or abbreviations of like import in another language. The name may not contain language stating or implying that the corporation is organized for a purpose other than that permitted by statute and its articles of incorporation. Except as discussed below, a corporate name must be distinguishable upon the records of the secretary of state from: (1) the corporate name of a corporation incorporated or authorized to transact business Indiana; (2) a reserved or registered corporate name; and (3) the corporate name of a not-for-profit corporation incorporated or authorized to transact business in Indiana. A corporation may apply to the secretary of state for authorization to use a name that is not distinguishable upon the secretary of state's records from one or more of the names described above the secretary of state shall authorize use of the name applied for if: (1) the other corporation files its written consent to the use, signed by any current officer of the corporation; or (2) the applicant delivers to the secretary of state a certified copy of the final judgment of a court of competent jurisdiction establishing the applicant's right to use the name applied for in Indiana. A corporation may use the name, including the fictitious name, of another domestic or foreign corporation that is used in Indiana if the other corporation is incorporated or authorized to transact business in Indiana and the aid user corporation: (1) has merged with the other corporation; (2) has been formed by reorganization of the other corporation; or (3) has acquired all or substantially all of the assets, including the corporate name, of the other corporation.

- The number of shares the corporation is authorized to issue;
- The street address of the corporation's initial registered office in Indiana the name of its initial registered agent at that office; and
- The name and address of each incorporator.

The existence of the corporation begins upon the filing of the articles of incorporation with the secretary of state. Upon creation, the corporation may have a meeting of its incorporators or initial board members to elect directors, officers, adopt bylaws (which may contain any provision consistent with law and the articles of incorporation), and carry on any other business he corporation. This meeting may be held inside or outside of Indiana.

Minimum Number of Incorporators: Any individual or entity may incorporate or organize a corporation.

Management Requirements: Directors or original incorporators, depending upon the terms of the articles of incorporation, may approve bylaws for the corporation. If there are fewer than 50 stockholders in the corporation, the corporation may operate without a board of directors, provided it set forth in its articles of incorporation who will perform management functions for the corporations. A corporation must, however, have at least one officer.

State Tax Classification: The State charges $30.00 for corporate biennial reports, assesses a corporate income tax against gross income at the rate of 3.4%, and a supplemental net income tax at the rate of 4.5%. The State also assesses sales and use taxes at the rate of 5%.

Contact Information:

Indiana Secretary of State
Business Services
302 W Washington
Room E-018
Indianapolis, IN 46204
Phone: (317) 232-6576
Facsimile: (317) 233-3387
www.ai.org/sos/bus_service/

Iowa

Formation: Before filing its certificate of incorporation, a domestic for-profit corporation may reserve a name with the secretary of state's office. The certificate of incorporation must include the following:

• The name of the corporation, which must contain the word "corporation," "incorporated," "company," or "limited," or the abbreviation "corp., " inc.," "co.," or "ltd.," or words or abbreviations of like import in another language. The name must not contain language stating or implying that the corporation is organized for a purpose other than that permitted by law and its articles of incorporation. Except as provided below, a corporate name must be distinguishable upon the records of the secretary of state from all of the following: (1) the corporate name of a corporation incorporated or authorized transact business in Iowa; (2) a reserved or registered corporate name; (3) the fictitious name adopted by a foreign corporation or a not-for-profit foreign corporation authorized to transact business in Iowa because its real name is unavailable; and (4) the corporate name of a not-for-profit corporation incorporated or authorized to transact business in Iowa. A corporation may apply to the secretary of state for authorization to use a name that is not distinguishable upon the secretary's records from one or more of the names described above. The secretary of state shall authorize use of the name applied for if one of the following conditions applies: (1) the other corporation consents to the use in writing and submits an undertaking in form satisfactory to the secretary of state to change its name to a name that is distinguishable upon the records of the secretary of state from the name of the applying corporation; (2) the applicant delivers to the secretary of state a certified copy of the final judgment of a court of competent jurisdiction establishing the applicant's right to use the name applied for in Iowa. A corporation may use the name, including the fictitious name, of another domestic or foreign corporation that is used in Iowa if the other corporation is incorporated or authorized to transact business in Iowa and the proposed user corporation submits documentation to the satisfaction of the secretary of state establishing one of the following conditions: (1) it has merged with the other corporation; (2) it has been formed by reorganization of the other corporation; or (3) it has acquired all or substantially all of the assets, including the corporate name, of the other corporation.

- The number of shares the corporation is authorized to issue;
- The street address of the corporation's initial registered office and the and the name of its initial registered agent at that office; and
- The name and address of each incorporator.

The existence of the corporation begins upon the filing of the certificate of incorporation with the secretary of state. Upon creation, the corporation may have a meeting of its incorporators or initial board members to elect directors, officers, adopt bylaws (which may contain any provision consistent with law and the articles of incorporation), and carryon any other business of the corporation. This meeting may be held inside or outside of Iowa.

Minimum Number of Incorporators: Any individual or entity may incorporate or organize a corporation.

Management Requirements: Directors or original incorporators, depending upon the terms of the articles of incorporation, may approve bylaws for the corporation. There must be at least one director on the corporation's board of directors.

State Tax Classification: The State charges $30.00 for corporate annual reports, assesses a variable rate corporate income tax, and assesses sales and use taxes at the rate of 5%.

Contact Information: Business Services Division
Office of the Secretary of State
1305 E. Walnut
2nd Floor Hoover Bldg.
Des Moines, Iowa 50319
Phone: (515) 281-5204
www.sos.state.ia.uslbusiness/services.html

Kansas

Formation: Before filling its articles of incorporation, a domestic for-profit corporation may reserve a name with the secretary of state's office. The articles of incorporation must include the following:

- The name of the corporation, which, except for banks, must contain one of the words "association," "church," "college," "company," "corporation," "club," "foundation," "fund," "incorporated," "institute," "society," "union," "syndicate," or "limited," or one of the abbreviations "co.," "corp.," "inc.," "ltd.," or words or abbreviations of like import in other languages if they are written in Roman characters or letters. The name must be such as to distinguish it upon the records of the office of the secretary of state from the names of other corporations, limited liability companies and limited partnerships organized, reserved or registered under the laws of Kansas, unless there shall be obtained the written consent of such other corporations, limited liability company or limited partnership executed, acknowledged and with the secretary of state.
- The address, which shall include the street, number, city and county of the corporation's registered office in Kansas, and the name of its resident agent at such address;
- The nature of the business or purposes to be conducted or promoted. It is sufficient to state, either alone or with other businesses or proposes, that the purpose of the corporation is to engage in any lawful act or activity for which corporations may be organized under the Kansas general corporations code, and by such statement all lawful acts and activities shall be within the purposes of the corporation, except for express limitations, if any;
- If the corporation is to be authorized to issue only one class of stock, the total number of shares of stock which the corporation shall have authority to issue and the par value of such shares, or a statement that all such shares are to be without par value. If the corporation is to be authorized to issue more than one class of stock, the articles of incorporation must set forth the total number of shares of all classes of stock which the corporation will have authority to issue and the

numbers of shares of each class, and shall classify each class the shares of which are to be without par value, and each class the shares of which are to have a par value and the par value of the shares of such class. The articles of incorporation must also set forth a statement of the designations and the powers, preferences and rights, and the qualifications, limitations or restrictions on each class of stock, and an express grant of such authority as it may then be desired to grant to the board of directors to fix by resolution or resolutions any of the foregoing which are fixed by the articles of incorporation.

• The name and mailing address of the incorporator or incorporators; and

• If the powers of the incorporator or incorporators are to terminate upon the filing of the articles of incorporation, the names and mailing addresses of the persons who are to serve as directors until the first annual meeting of the stockholders or until their successors are elected and qualify.

The existence of the corporation begins upon the filing of the articles of incorporation with the secretary of state. Upon creation, the corporation may have a meeting of its incorporators or initial board members to elect directors, officers, adopt bylaws (which may contain any provision consistent with law and the articles of incorporation), and carryon any other business of the corporation. This meeting may be held inside or outside of Kansas.

Minimum Number of Incorporators: Any individual or entity may incorporate or organize a corporation.

Management Requirements: Directors or original incorporators, depending upon the terms of the articles of incorporation, may approve bylaws for the corporation. There must be at least one director on the corporation's board of directors.

State Tax Classification: The State assesses a corporate franchise tax at the rate of $1.00 per $1,000 of the corporation's shareholders' equity, with a minimum tax of $20.00 and a maximum tax of $2,500. The State also assesses a corporate income tax of 4%, with a surtax of

3.35% imposed on taxable income in excess of $50,000, and sales and use taxes assessed at the rate of 4.9%.

Contact Information: Kansas Secretary of State
Corporations Division
120 SW10th Ave., Room 100
Topeka, KS66612-1240
Phone: (785) 296-4564
Facsimile: (785) 296-4570
www.kssos.orglcorpwelc.html

Kentucky

Formation: Before filing its articles of incorporation, a domestic for-profit corporation may reserve a name with the secretary of state's office. The articles of incorporation must include the following:

• The name of the corporation, which must contain the word "corporation," "incorporated," "company," or "limited," or the abbreviation "corp.," "inc.," "co.," or "ltd.," or words or abbreviations of like import in another lane. The name shall not contain language stating or implying that the corporation is organized for a purpose other than that permitted by Kentucky law and its articles of incorporation. Except as provided below, a corporate name must be distinguishable upon the records of the Secretary of State from: (1) the corporate name of a corporation incorporated or authorized to transact business in Kentucky; (2) a reserved or registered corporate name; (3) fictitious name adopted by a foreign corporation authorized to transact business in Kentucky because its real name is unavailable; (4) the corporate name of a not-for-profit corporation incorporated or authorized to transact business in Kentucky; and (5) a name filed with the secretary of state. A corporation may apply to the secretary of state for authorization to use a name that is not distinguishable upon his records from one or more of the names described above. The secretary of state shall authorize use of the name applied for if: (1) the other corporation consents to the use in writing and submits an undertaking in form satisfactory to the secretary of state to change its name to a name that is distinguishable upon the records of the secretary of state from the name of the applying corporation; or (2) the applicant delivers to the secretary of state a certified copy of the final judgment of a court of competent jurisdiction establishing the applicant's right to use the name applied for in Kentucky. A corporation may use the name (including the fictitious name) of another domestic or foreign corporation that is used in Kentucky if the other corporation is incorporated or authorized to transact business in Kentucky and the proposed user corporation: (1) has merged with the other corporation; (2) has been formed by reorganization of the other corporation; or (3) has acquired all or substantially all of the assets including the corporate name, of the other corporation.

- The number of shares the corporation is authorized to issue;
- The street address of the corporation's initial registered office and the names of its initial registered agent at that office;
- The mailing address of the corporation's principal office; and
- The name and mailing address of each incorporator.

The existence of the corporation begins upon the filing of the certificate of incorporation with the secretary of state. Upon creation, the corporation may have a meeting of its incorporators or initial board members to elect directors, officers, adopt bylaws (which may contain any provision consistent with law and the articles of incorporation), and carryon any other business of the corporation. This meeting may be held inside or outside of Kentucky.

Minimum Number of Incorporators: Anyone individual or entity may incorporate or organize a corporation.

Management Requirements: Directors or original incorporators, depending upon the terms of the articles of incorporation, may approve bylaws for the corporation. There must be at least one director on the corporation's board of directors.

State Tax Classification: The State assesses a corporate franchise tax at the rate of $2.10 per $1,000 of total capital employed in the corporation in the State. Kentucky also assesses a variable rate corporate organizational tax, corporate income tax, and sales and use taxes at the rate of 6%.

Contact Information: Kentucky Secretary of State
700 Capital Avenue
Suite 152, State Capitol
Frankfort, KY40601
Phone: (502) 564-3490
Facsimile: (502) 564-5687
www.sos.state.ky.us/

Louisiana

Formation: Before filing its articles of incorporation, a domestic for-profit corporation may reserve a name with the secretary of state's office. The articles of incorporation must include the following:

- The name of the corporation, which must contain the word "corporation," "incorporated," or "limited," or the abbreviation of any of those words, or may contain instead the word "company" or the abbreviation "co." if the latter word or abbreviation is not immediately preceded by the word "and" or the symbol "&." No corporate name may contain the phrase "doing business as" or the abbreviation "d/b/a." The corporate name must not imply that the corporation is an administrative agency of any parish or of Louisiana or of the United States. Except as provided below, the corporate name must be distinguishable from any reserved name, the name of any other corporation, limited liability company, or trade name registered with the secretary of state. The applying corporation may use a name which is not distinguishable upon the records of the secretary of state from any of the names mentioned above if: (1) the other corporation is about to change its name, or to cease doing business, or is being liquidated, or, if a foreign corporation, is about to withdraw from doing business in Louisiana, and the written consent of the other corporation to the adoption of its name or a undistinguishable name has been given and is filed with the articles of incorporation; (2) the other corporation has previously been authorized to do business in Louisiana for more than two years and has never actively engaged in business in Louisiana; (3) the other corporation has failed to pay the corporate franchise tax or taxes due by it to the state for the preceding five years; or (4) the other corporation, if a foreign corporation, is not authorized to do business in Louisiana and has not filed a Louisiana corporate franchise tax return for two consecutive years.

- In general terms, the purpose or purposes for which the corporation is to be formed, or that its purpose is to engage in any lawful activity for which corporations may be formed under law;
- The duration of the corporation, if other than perpetual;
- The aggregate number of shares which the corporation shall have the authority to issue;
- If the shares are to consist of one class only, the par value of each share or a statement that all of the shares are without par value;
- If the shares are to be divided into classes, the number of shares of each class; the par value of the shares of each class or a statement that such shares are without par value; the designation of each class and, insofar as fixed in the articles, each series of each preferred or special class; a statement of the preferences, limitations and relative rights of the shares of each class and the variations in relative rights and preferences as between series, insofar as the same are fixed in the articles; and a statement of any authority vested in the board of directors to amend the articles to fix the preferences, limitations and relative rights of the shares of any class, and to establish, and fix variations in relative rights as between any series of any preferred or special class;
- The full name and post office address of each incorporator; and
- The taxpayer identification number of the corporation.

The existence of the corporation begins upon the filing of the articles of incorporation with the secretary of state. Upon creation, the corporation may have a meeting of its incorporators or initial board members to elect directors, officers, adopt bylaws (which may contain any provision consistent with law and the articles of incorporation), and carryon any other business of the corporation. This meeting may be held inside or outside of Louisiana.

Minimum Number of Incorporators: Any individual or entity may incorporate or organize a corporation.

Management Requirements: Directors or original incorporators, depending upon the terms of the articles of incorporation, may approve bylaws for the corporation. There must be at least one director on the corporation's board of directors.

State Tax Classification: The State charges $25.00 for corporate annual reports, assesses a corporate franchise tax at the rate of $3.00 per $1,000 of capital stock, surplus, undivided profits, and borrowed capital, and a variable rate corporate income tax. Louisiana also assesses sales and use taxes at the rate of 4%.

    Contact Information: Louisiana Secretary of State
Commercial Division
P. O. Box 94125
Baton Rouge, LA 70804
Phone: (225) 925-4704
E-mail: commercial@sec.state.1a.us
www.sec.state.la.us/comm/comm-index.htm

Maine

Formation: Before filing its articles of incorporation, a domestic for-profit corporation may reserve a name with the secretary of state's office. The articles of incorporation must include the following:

• The name of the corporation, which must not contain any word or phrase which indicates or implies that it is organized for any purpose for which a corporation may not be organized under Maine law. The name may not be the same as, or deceptively similar to, the name of any domestic entity, any foreign entity authorized to transact business or to carryon activities in Maine, or a name the exclusive right to which is, at the time, reserved, or the name of an entity that has in effect a registration of its name, or the assumed name of a entity, unless: (1) the other entity executes and files with the secretary of state proof of a resolution of its board of directors, members or management, authorizing the use of a similar name by the corporation seeking to use the similar name; or (2) a foreign corporation seeking to file under a similar or identical name executes and files with the secretary of state proof of a resolution of its board of directors that it will not do business under that similar or identical name, but instead will do business under an assumed name. The name may not be the same as, or deceptively similar to, any registered mark, unless: (1) the owner or holder of the mark executes and files with the secretary of state proof of authorization of the use of a similar name by the corporation seeking to use the similar name; (2) a foreign corporation seeking to file under a similar or identical name executes and files with the secretary of state proof of a resolution of its board of directors that it will not do business under that similar or identical name, but instead will do business under an assumed name; or (3) the registered owner or holder of the mark is the same person or entity as the corporation seeking to use the same or similar name and files proof of ownership with the secretary of state.

- The municipality or other place in Maine where the corporation is located;
- The address of the initial registered office and the name of the initial clerk;
- Either: (1) the number of directors constituting the initial board of directors and, if they have been selected and the powers of the incorporator or incorporators are to terminate upon filing of the articles, the names and addresses of the persons who are to serve as directors until the first annual meeting of shareholders or until their successors be elected and qualify; or (2) the following statement: "There shall be no director initially; the shares of the corporation will not be sold to more than 20 persons; the business of the corporation will be managed by the shareholders."
- The relevant information regarding the shares, including classes and series of shares, which the corporation shall be authorized to issue.
- If the shares of a corporation are to consist of one class only, the articles shall state: (1) the total number of such shares which the corporation shall have authority to issue; and (2) the par value of each of such shares or a statement that all of such shares are to be without par value.
- If the shares of a corporation are divided into two or more classes, the articles of incorporation: (1) shall designate each class of shares;

(2) as to each class, shall specify the total number of such shares which the corporation shall have authority to issue, and the par value, if any, or a statement that the shares are to be without par value; and (3) shall specify the relative rights, preferences and limitations of the shares of each class.

- If shares of any preferred or special class are to be issued in series, the articles of incorporation shall state whether the shares have par value or are without par value; and shall either (1) designate each series within any class of shares, and specify the relative rights, preferences and limitations as among such series, to the extent that such is to be specified in the articles, or (2) set forth any authority of the board of directors to establish and designate series within any class of shares and determine the relative rights, preferences and limitations as among such series.
- In addition, by way of summary, the articles shall state (1) the aggregate par value of all shares having par value which the corporation shall have authority to issue, and (2) the total number of shares without par value which the corporation shall have authority to issue.
- The articles of incorporation shall be signed by each incorporator, with his name and residence address legibly printed or typed beneath or opposite his signature; if an incorporator is a corporation, the title of the person signing for it shall be stated, and the address of its principal place of business shall be stated.

The existence of the corporation begins upon the filing of the articles of corporation with the secretary of state. Upon creation, the corporation may have a meeting of its incorporators or initial board members to elect directors, officers, adopt bylaws (which may contain any provision consistent with law and the articles of incorporation), and carryon any other business of the corporation. This meeting may be held inside or outside of Maine.

Minimum Number of Incorporators: Any individual or entity may incorporate or organize a corporation.

Management Requirements: Directors or original incorporators, depending upon the terms of the articles of incorporation, may approve bylaws for the corporation. Unless there are fewer than 20 shareholders of the corporation, there must be at least three directors on the corporation's board of directors.

State Tax Classification: The State charges $60.00 for the corporate annual report, assesses a variable rate corporate income tax, and assesses sales and use taxes at the rate of 5%.

Contact Information: Maine Department of the Secretary of State
Bureau of Corporations, Elections and Commissions
101 State House Station
Augusta, ME04333-0101
Reporting and Information Section: (207) 287-4190
Examining Section: (207) 287-4195
Facsimile: (207) 287-5874
www.state.me.us/sos/cec/corp/corp.htm

Maryland

Before filing its articles of incorporation, a domestic for-profit corporation may reserve a name with the secretary of state's office. The articles of incorporation must include the following:

• The corporate name, which must contain the word "Corporation," Incorporated," "Limited," "Inc.," "Corp.," or "Ltd." The name must be distinguishable from all other entities on record in Maryland. You may call (410) 67-1330 for a non-binding check for name availability. Acceptance of a name guarantees only that the corporation will have that name. It does not mean you cannot be sued for trade name or trademark infringement.
• The name and address of the individuals who are incorporating. The address should be one where mail can be received. It can be anywhere, even a foreign country.
• A statement certifying that the incorporator is 18 years old or older, and that the incorporator(s) are forming a corporation under the general laws of Maryland;
• The description of the business of the corporation.

- The address of the principal place of business. It must be a specific address in Maryland and must include street, city and zip code. It cannot be a post office box.
- The name and address of an agent designated to accept service of process if the corporation is summoned to court for any reason. The agent must be either an adult citizen of Maryland or another existing Maryland corporation. The address must include the street, city and zip code. The address must be in Maryland and cannot be a post office box. A corporation cannot act as its own resident agent. That person must also sign the articles of incorporation.
- The number of shares of stock the corporation will have the authority to issue as well as the par value of each share. If the aggregate par value (number of shares multiplied by the par value) exceeds $100,000, or if over 5,000 shares of stock without par value is used, the filing fee will increase beyond $40.00 minimum. If stock without par value is used, insert "$0" as the par value per share.
- The number of directors and the names of those adult individuals who will be directors. These individuals do not have to be residents of Maryland.
- The incorporators must sign the articles of incorporation.

The existence of the corporation begins upon the filing of the certificate corporation with the secretary of state. Upon creation, the corporation may have a meeting of its incorporators or initial board members to elect directors, officers, adopt bylaws (which may contain any provision consistent with law and the articles of incorporation), and carryon any other business the corporation. This meeting may be held inside or outside of Maryland.

Minimum Number of Incorporators: Any individual over the age of 18 may form a corporation.

Management Requirements: Directors or original incorporators, depending upon the terms of the articles of incorporation, may approve bylaws for the corporation. There must be at least three directors on the corporation's board of directors, unless there is no outstanding stock or fewer than three shareholders. In such event, the number of directors shall not be less than the number of shareholders, unless there are greater than three shareholders. The corporation must have a president, secretary and treasurer.

State Tax Classification: The State charges $100 for corporate annual reports, assesses a corporate income tax at 7%, and sales and use taxes at the rate of 5%.

    Contact Information: Corporate Records
        301 W Preston Street
        Room 801
        Baltimore, Maryland 21201-2395
        Phone: (410) 767-1340
        Toll-free in Maryland: (888) 246-5941
        www.dat.state.md.us/sdatweb/charter.html

Massachusetts

Formation: Before filing its articles of organization, a domestic for-profit corporation may reserve a name with the secretary of the commonwealth's office. The articles of organization must include the following:

- The name of the corporation, which must also include some indication that the business is incorporated. The secretary of the commonwealth has determined that the words "corporation", "incorporated", "limited", or any abbreviation thereof are sufficient to indicate corporate status. Further, the corporations division will not allow the use of symbols as part of a corporate name. For example, one cannot use $ensible $ales as a corporate name. Such symbols may be protected by filing a trademark or service mark. A corporation cannot assume the name or trade name of another corporation, firm, association or person carrying on business in Massachusetts at the present time or within three years prior thereto, or assume a name which is under reservation in Massachusetts, or assume a name so similar to any of the forgoing as to be likely to be mistaken for it, except with the written consent of said corporation, firm, association, or person. The standard of similarity is that which would mislead a person of average intelligence taking into account all of the facts and circumstances.

- The purposes for which the corporation is formed;
- The total number of shares and the par value, if any, of each class of stock which the corporation is authorized to issue;
- If more than one class of stock is authorized, a distinguishing designation for each class and prior to the issuance of any shares of a class if shares of any other class are outstanding a description of the preferences, voting powers, qualifications and special or relative rights or privileges of that class and of each other class of which shares are outstanding, and of each series then established within any class;
- A statement in which the incorporators, state their names and post office addresses, and in which they associate themselves with the intention of forming a corporation.

The existence of the corporation begins upon the filing of the articles of organization with the secretary of the commonwealth. Upon creation, the corporation may have a meeting of its incorporators or initial board members to elect directors, officers, adopt bylaws (which may contain any provision consistent with law and the articles of organization), and carryon any other business of the corporation. This meeting may be held inside or outside of Massachusetts.

Minimum Number of Incorporators: Any individual over the age of 18 or any entity may incorporate or organize a corporation.

Management Requirements: Directors or original incorporators, depending upon the terms of the articles of incorporation, may approve bylaws for the corporation. The number of directors shall be fixed or determined in the manner provided in the by-laws but shall not be less than three, except where there are less than three stockholders. If there are two stockholders, the number of directors shall not be less than two. If there is only one stockholder or prior to the issue of any stock, there need only be one director.

State Tax Classification: The State charges $85.00 for corporate annual reports, assesses a corporate excise tax at the rate of $2.60 per $1,000 of value of Massachusetts tangible property, plus 9.5% of corporate net income. The state assesses a corporate franchise tax, and also assesses sales and use taxes at the rate of 5%.

Contact Information: The Corporations Division of the
Secretary of the Commonwealth's Office
One Ashburton Place
Boston, MA 02108-1512
Phone: (617) 727-9640
www.state.ma.us/sec/cor/coridx.htm

Michigan

Formation: Before filing its certificate of incorporation, a domestic for-profit corporation may reserve a name with the department of commerce.

The articles of incorporation must include the following:

• The name of the corporation, which must contain the word "corporation," "company," "incorporated," or "limited," or. any of the following abbreviations, corp., co., inc., or ltd. The name shall not contain a word or phrase, or abbreviation or derivative of a word or phrase, which indicates or implies that the corporation is formed for a purpose other than the purposes permitted by its articles of incorporation. The name shall distinguish the corporate name upon the records of the department of commerce from all of the following: (1) the corporate name of any other domestic corporation or foreign corporation authorized to transact business in Michigan; (2) the corporate name of any corporation subject to the nonprofit corporation act, or any corporation authorized to conduct affairs in Michigan under that act; (3) a corporate name currently reserved, registered, or assumed; (4) the name of any domestic limited partnership or foreign limited partnership as filed or registered under the Michigan revised uniform limited partnership act, or any name currently reserved or assumed under that act; (5) the name of any domestic limited liability company or foreign limited liability company as filed or registered under the Michigan limited liability company act, or any name currently reserved or assumed under that act. The name of a corporation shall not contain a word or phrase, an abbreviation, or derivative of a word or phrase, the use of which is prohibited or restricted by any other statute of Michigan, unless in compliance with that restriction. Furthermore, unless the corporation is engaged in such businesses, the corporate name shall not imply that the corporation is a banking corporation, an insurance or surety company, or a trust company, and the corporation shall not use the word "bank," "industrial bank," "deposit," "surety," "security," "trust," or "trust company" in its corporate name, or use a combination of the letters or words with other letters or words in its corporate name to indicate or convey the idea of a bank or banking or industrial banking activity or security unless from the other words constituting the name, it is clear that the business conducted does not include the business of banking.

- The purposes for which the corporation is formed. It is a sufficient to state that the corporation may engage in any activity within the purposes for which corporations may be formed under the business corporation act. Any corporation which proposes to conduct educational purposes shall state the purposes and shall comply with all requirements of the Public Acts of 1931.
- The aggregate number of shares that the corporation has the authority to issue.
- If the shares are, or are to be, divided into classes, or into classes and series, the designation of each class and series, the number of shares in each class and series, and a statement of the relative rights, preferences and limitations of the shares of each class and series, to the extent that the designations, numbers, relative rights, preferences, and limitations have been determined.
- If any class of shares is to be divided into series, a statement of any authority vested in the board to divide the class of shares into series, and to determine or change for any series its designation, number of shares, relative rights, preferences and limitations.
- The street address, and the mailing address if different from the street address, of the corporation's initial registered office and the name of the corporation's initial resident agent at that address.
- The names and addresses of the incorporators.
- The duration of the corporation, if other than perpetual.

The existence of the corporation begins upon the filing of the certificate of incorporation with the department of commerce. Upon creation, the corporation may have a meeting of its incorporators or initial board members to elect directors, officers, adopt bylaws (which may contain any provision consistent with law and the articles of incorporation), and carry on any other business of the corporation. This meeting may be held inside or outside of Michigan.

Minimum Number of Incorporators: Any individual or entity may incorporate or organize a corporation.

Management Requirements: Directors or original incorporators, depending upon the terms of the articles of incorporation, may approve bylaws for the corporation. There must be at least one director on the corporation's board of directors. The officers of a corporation shall consist of a president, secretary, treasurer, and, if desired, a chairman of the board, one or more vice-presidents, and such other officers as may be prescribed by the bylaws or determined by the board of directors.

State Tax Classification: The State charges $15.00 for corporate annual reports, along with a privilege fee, assesses a business tax at the rate of 2%, and assesses sales and use taxes at the rate of 6%.

    Contact Information: Bureau of Commercial Services
Corporation Division
P.O. Box 30054
Lansing, MI 48909
Phone: (517) 241-6470
Fax Filing Service: (517) 334-8048
E-mail: bcsinfo@cis.state.mi.us
www.cis.state.mi.us/corp/

Minnesota

Formation: Before filing its articles of incorporation, a domestic for-profit corporation may reserve a name with the secretary of state's office. The articles of incorporation must include the following:

• The name of the corporation, which must contain the word "corporation," "incorporated," or "limited," or shall contain an abbreviation of one or more of these words, or the word "company," or the abbreviation "co." if that word or abbreviation is not immediately preceded by the word "and" or the character "&." The name must be in the English language or in any other language expressed in English letters or characters, and it must not contain a word or phrase that indicates or implies that it is incorporated for a purpose other than a legal business purpose. Furthermore, the name must be distinguishable upon the records in the office of the secretary of state from the name of each entity authorized or registered to do business in Minnesota, whether profit or nonprofit, and each name the right to which is, at the time of incorporation, reserved, unless there is filed with the articles one of the following: (1) the written consent of the entity authorized or registered to do business in Minnesota or the holder of a reserved name or a name filed by or registered with the secretary of state having a name that is not distinguishable; (2) a certified copy of a final decree of a court in Minnesota establishing the prior right of the applicant to the use of the name in Minnesota; or (3) the applicant's affidavit that the entity with the name that is not distinguishable has been incorporated or on file in Minnesota for at least three years prior to the affidavit, if it is a domestic entity, or has been authorized or registered to do business in Minnesota for at least three years prior to the affidavit, if it is a foreign entity, or that the holder of a name filed or registered with the secretary of state, filed or registered that name at least three years prior to the affidavit; that the entity or holder has not during the three-year period before the affidavit filed any document with the secretary of state; that the applicant has mailed written notice to the entity or the holder of a name filed or registered with the secretary of state, by certified mail, return receipt requested, properly addressed to the registered office of the entity or in care of the agent of the entity, or the address of the holder of a name filed or registered with the secretary of state, shown in the records of the secretary of state, stating that the applicant intends to use a name that is not distinguishable and the notice has been returned to the applicant as undeliverable to the addressee entity, or holder of a name filed or registered with the secretary of state; that the applicant, after diligent inquiry, has been unable to find any telephone listing for the entity with the name that is not distinguishable in the county in which is located the registered office of the entity shown in the records of the secretary of state or has been unable to find any telephone listing for the holder of a name filed or registered with the secretary of state in the county in which is located the address of the holder shown in the records of the secretary of state; and that the applicant has no knowledge that the entity or holder of a name filed or registered with the secretary of state is currently engaged in business in Minnesota.

- The address of the registered office of the corporation and the name of its registered agent, if any, at that address;
- The aggregate number of shares that the corporation has authority to issue; and
- The name and address of each incorporator.

The existence of the corporation begins upon the filing of the articles of incorporation with the secretary of state. Upon creation, the corporation may have a meeting of its incorporators or initial board members to elect directors, officers, adopt bylaws (which may contain any provision consistent with law and the articles of incorporation), and carryon any other business of the corporation. This meeting may be held inside or outside of Minnesota.

Minimum Number of Incorporators: One or more natural persons of at least 18 years of age.

Management Requirements: Directors or original incorporators, depending upon the terms of the articles of incorporation, may approve bylaws for the corporation. There must be at least one director on the corporation's board of directors. A corporation must have one or more natural persons exercising the functions of the offices of chief executive officer and chief financial officer.

State Tax Classification: The State charges $20.00 for corporate annual reports, assesses a corporate income tax at the basic rate of9.8%, with additional tax on property, payrolls, and sales and receipts and the type of corporation. The State also assesses sales and use taxes at the rate of 6.5%.

Contact Information: Business Services Director
            Minnesota Secretary of State
            180 State Office Building
            100 Constitution Avenue

Saint Paul, MN55155-1299
Phone: (651) 296-2803
Toll free Phone: 1-877-551-6S0S (6767)
Facsimile: (651) 215-0683
E-mail: business.services@state.mn.us
www.sos.state.mn.uslbusiness/index.html

Mississippi

Before filing its articles of incorporation, a domestic for-profit corporation may reserve a name with the secretary of state's office. The articles of incorporation must include the following:

• The name of the corporation, which must contain the word "corporation," "incorporated," "company," or "limited," or the abbreviation "corp.," "inc.," "co.," or "ltd.," or words or abbreviations of like import in another language. The name may not contain language stating or implying that the corporation is organized for a purpose other than that permitted by law and its articles of incorporation. Except as provided below, a corporate name must be distinguishable upon the records of the secretary of state from: (1) the corporate name of a corporation incorporated or authorized to transact business in Mississippi; (2) a reserved or registered corporate name; (3) the fictitious name adopted by a foreign corporation authorized to transact business in Mississippi because its real name is unavailable; and (4) the corporate name of a not-for-profit corporation incorporated or authorized to transact business in Mississippi. A corporation may apply to the secretary of state for authorization to use a name that is not distinguishable upon his records from one or more of the names described above. The secretary of state shall authorize use of the name applied for if: (1) the other corporation consents to the use in writing and submits an undertaking in form satisfactory to the secretary of state to change its name to a name that is distinguishable upon the records of the secretary of state from the name of the applying corporation; or (2) the applicant delivers to the secretary of state a certified copy of the final judgment of a court of competent jurisdiction establishing the applicant's right to use the name applied for in Mississippi. A corporation may use the name (including the fictitious name) of another domestic or foreign corporation that is used in Mississippi if the other corporation is incorporated or authorized to transact business in Mississippi and the proposed user corporation; (1) has merged with the other corporation; (2) has been formed by reorganization of the other corporation; or (3) has acquired all or substantially all of the assets, including the corporate name, of the other corporation.

- The number of shares the corporation is authorized to issue and the classes of shares and the number of shares of each class that the corporation is authorized to issue. If more than one class of shares is authorized, the articles of incorporation must prescribe a distinguishing designation for each class, and prior to the issuance of shares of a class the preferences, limitations and relative rights of that class must be described in the articles of incorporation. All shares of a class must have preferences, limitations and relative rights identical with those of other shares of the same class except to the extent otherwise permitted by law. The articles of incorporation must authorize one or more classes of shares that together have unlimited voting rights, and one or more classes of shares (which may be the same class or classes as those with voting rights) that together are entitled to receive the net assets of the corporation upon dissolution.
- The street address of the corporation's initial registered office and the name of its initial registered agent at that office; and
- The name and address of each incorporator.

The existence of the corporation begins upon the filing of the articles of incorporation with the secretary of state. Upon creation, the corporation may have a meeting of its incorporators or initial board members to elect directors, officers, adopt bylaws (which may contain any provision consistent with law and the articles of incorporation), and carryon any other business of the corporation. This meeting may be held inside or outside of Mississippi.

Minimum Number of Incorporators: Any individual or entity may incorporate or organize a corporation.

Management Requirements: Directors or original incorporators, depending upon the terms of the articles of incorporation, may approve bylaws for the corporation. There must be at least one director on the corporation's board of directors. Said director must be an individual.

State Tax Classification: The State charges $25.00 for annual corporate reports, assesses a corporate franchise tax at the rate of $2.50 per $1,000 or fraction thereof of the value of capital used, invested, or employed by the corporation, and assesses a variable rate corporate income tax. The State also assesses sales and use taxes at the rate of 7%.

Contact Information:

Business Services Division
Mississippi Secretary of State
P.O. Box 136
Jackson, MS39205
Phone: (601) 359-1633
Toll free: (800) 256-3494
Facsimile: (601) 359-1499
www.sos.state.ms.usibusserv
/corp/corporations.html

Missouri

Formation: Before filing its articles of incorporation, a domestic for-profit corporation may reserve a name with the secretary of state's office. The articles of incorporation must include the following:

• The name of the corporation, which must contain the word "corporation," "company," "incorporated," or "limited," or shall end with an abbreviation of one of said words. The name may not contain any word or phrase which indicates or implies that it is any governmental agency or organized for any purpose other than a purpose for which corporations may be organized under this Missouri law. It must be distinguishable from the name of any domestic corporation existing under any law of Missouri or any foreign corporation authorized to transact business in Missouri, or any limited partnership or limited liability company existing or transacting business in Missouri, or a name the exclusive right to which is, at the time, reserved. If the name is the same, a word shall be added to make such name distinguishable from the name of such other corporation, limited liability company or limited partnership.

- The address, including street and number, if any, of its initial registered office in Missouri, and the name of its initial registered agent at such address;
- The aggregate number of shares which the corporation shall have the authority to issue, and the number of shares of each class, if any, that are to have a par value and the par value of each share of each such class, and the number of shares of each class, if any, that are to be without par value and also a statement of the preferences, qualifications, limitations, restrictions, and the special or relative rights including convertible rights, if any, in respect of the shares of each class;
- The extent, if any, to which the preemptive right of a shareholder to acquire additional shares is limited or denied;
- The name and place of residence of each incorporator;
- The number of years the corporation is to continue, which may be any number or perpetual;
- The purposes for which the corporation is formed;
- If the incorporators, the directors or the shareholders choose to do I so, a provision eliminating or limiting the personal liability of a director to the corporation or its shareholders for monetary damages for breach of fiduciary duty as a director, provided that such provision shall not eliminate or limit the liability of a director (1) for any breach of the director's duty of loyalty to the corporation or its shareholders, (2) for acts or omissions not in subjective good faith or which involve intentional misconduct or a knowing violation of law, or (3) for any transaction from which the director derived an improper personal benefit. No such provision shall eliminate or limit the liability of a director for any act or omission occurring prior to the date when such provision becomes effective;
- Either (1) the number of directors to constitute the first board of directors and a statement to the effect that thereafter the number of

directors shall be fixed by, or in the manner provided in, the bylaws of the corporation, and that any changes shall be reported to the secretary of state within thirty calendar days of such change, or (2) the number of directors to constitute the board of directors, except that the number of directors to constitute the board of directors must be stated in the articles of incorporation if the corporation is to have less than three directors.

• Any other provisions, not inconsistent with law, which the incorporators, the directors or the shareholders may choose to insert.

The existence of the corporation begins upon the filing of the articles of incorporation with the secretary of state. Upon creation, the corporation may have a meeting of its incorporators or initial board members to elect directors, officers, adopt bylaws (which may contain any provision consistent with law and the articles of incorporation), and carryon any other business of the corporation. This meeting may be held inside or outside of Missouri.

Minimum Number of Incorporators: Any natural person over the age of 18 may incorporate or organize a corporation.

Management Requirements: Directors or original incorporators, depending upon the terms of the articles of incorporation, may approve bylaws for the corporation. A corporation shall have three or more directors, except that a corporation may have one or two directors provided the number of directors to constitute the board of directors is stated in the articles of incorporation. Every corporation must have a president and a secretary, who shall be chosen by the directors.

State Tax Classification: The State charges an annual registration fee of $40.00, assesses a corporate franchise tax at the rate of .05% of the par value of outstanding shares and surplus in excess of $200,000 (par value set at $5.00 or greater). The State also assesses a corporate income tax at the rate of 6.25% and sales and use taxes at the rate of 4.225%.

Contact Information:　　Corporations Division
James C. Kirkpatrick State Information Center
P.O. Box 778
Jefferson City, Missouri 65102
Phone: (573) 751-4153
www.mosl.sos.state.mo.us;bus-ser/soscor.html

Montana

Formation: Before filing its articles of incorporation, a domestic for-profit corporation may reserve a name with the secretary of state's office. The articles of incorporation must include the following:

• The name of the corporation, which must contain the word "corporation," "incorporated," "company," or "limited"; the abbreviation "corp.," "inc.," "co.," or "ltd."; or words or abbreviations of similar meaning in another language. The name may not contain language that states or implies that the corporation is organized for a purpose or purposes other than those permitted by law and its articles of incorporation. Except as set forth below, a corporate name must be distinguishable in the records of the secretary of state from: (1) the corporate name of another corporation incorporated or authorized to transact business in Montana; (2) a reserved or registered corporate name; (3) the fictitious name adopted by a foreign corporation authorized to transact business in Montana because its real name is unavailable; (4) the corporate name of a not-for-profit corporation incorporated or authorized to transact business in Montana; (5) the corporate name of a domestic corporation that has dissolved, but only distinguishable for a period of 120 days after the effective date of its dissolution; and. (6) any assumed business name, limited partnership name, limited liability company name, trademark, or service mark registered or reserved with the secretary of state. A corporation may apply to the secretary of state for authorization to use a name that is not distinguishable in the secretary of state's records from one or more of the names described in above. The secretary of state shall authorize use of the name applied for if: (1) the other corporation consents to the use in writing and submits an undertaking in a form satisfactory to the secretary of state to change its name to a name that is distinguishable in the records of the secretary of state from the name of the applying corporation; or (2) the applicant delivers to the secretary of state a certified copy of the final judgment of a court of competent jurisdiction establishing the applicant's right to use the name applied for in Montana. A corporation, limited liability company, or limited partnership may use the name, including the fictitious name, of another domestic or foreign corporation, limited liability company, or limited partnership that is used in Montana if the other corporation, limited liability company, or limited partnership is incorporated or authorized to transact business in Montana and the proposed user corporation, limited liability company, or limited partnership: (1) has merged with the other corporation, limited liability company, or limited partnership; (2) has been formed by reorganization of the other corporation, limited liability company, or limited partnership; (3) has acquired all or substantially all of the assets, including the corporate name, of the other corporation, limited liability company, or limited partnership; or (4) has obtained written permission from the other corporation, limited liability company, or limited partnership for use of the name and has filed a copy of the grant of permission with the secretary of state.

- The number of shares the corporation is authorized to issue;
- The street address of the corporation's initial registered office and, if different, the mailing address;
- The name of its initial registered agent at that office;
- The name and address of each incorporator.

The existence of the corporation begins upon the filing of the articles of incorporation with the secretary of state. Upon creation, the corporation may have a meeting of its incorporators or initial board members to elect directors, officers, adopt bylaws (which may contain any provision consistent with law and the articles of incorporation), and carryon any other business of the corporation. This meeting may be held inside or outside of Montana.

Minimum Number of Incorporators: Any individual or entity may incorporate or organize a corporation.

Management Requirements: Directors or original incorporators, depending upon the terms of the articles of incorporation, may approve bylaws for the corporation. There must be at least one director on the corporation's board of directors. Such director must be an individual.

State Tax Classification: The State charges $10.00 for corporate annual reports, and a corporate income tax at 6.75% ("S" corporations exempt).

Contact Information: Business Services Bureau
Secretary of State
State Capitol, Room 260
P. O. Box 202801
Helena, Montana 59620-2801
Phone: (406) 444-3665
Facsimile: (406) 444-3976
www.state.mt. us/sos/index.htm

Nebraska

Formation: Before filing its articles of incorporation, a domestic for-profit corporation may reserve a name with the secretary of state's office. The articles of incorporation must include the following:

• The name of the corporation, which must contain the word corporation, incorporated, company, or limited, or the abbreviation corp., inc., co., or ltd., or words or abbreviations of like import in another language, except that a corporation organized to conduct a banking business may use a name which includes the word bank without using any such words or abbreviations. The name may not contain language stating or implying that the corporation is organized for a purpose other than that permitted by law and its articles of incorporation. Except as provided below, a corporate name shall be distinguishable upon the records of the secretary of state from: (1) the corporate name of a corporation incorporated or authorized to transact business in Nebraska; (2) a reserved or registered corporate name; (3) the fictitious name adopted by a foreign corporation authorized to transact business in Nebraska because its real name is unavailable; (4) the corporate name of a not-for-profit corporation incorporated or authorized to transact business in Nebraska; and (5) a trade name registered in Nebraska. A corporation may apply to the secretary of state for authorization to use a name that is not distinguishable upon his or her records from one or more of the names described above. The secretary of state shall authorize use of the name applied for if: (1) the other corporation consents to the use in writing and submits an undertaking in a form satisfactory to the secretary of state to change its name to a name that is distinguishable upon the records of the secretary of state from the name of the applying corporation; or (2) the applicant delivers to the secretary of state a certified copy of the final judgment of a court of competent jurisdiction establishing the applicant's right to use the name applied for in Nebraska. A corporation may use the name, including the fictitious name, of another domestic or foreign corporation that is used in Nebraska if the other corporation is incorporated or authorized to transact business in Nebraska and the proposed user corporation has: (1) merged with the other corporation; (2) been formed by reorganization of the other corporation; or (3) acquired all or substantially all of the assets, including the corporate name, of the other corporation.

- The number of shares the corporation is authorized to issue and, if such shares are to consist of one class only, the par value of each of such shares or, if such shares are to be divided into classes, the number of shares of each class and a statement of the par value of the shares of each such class;
- The street address of the corporation's initial registered office and the name of its initial registered agent at that office;
- The name and street address of each incorporator; and
- Any provision limiting or eliminating the requirement to hold an annual meeting of the shareholders if the corporation is registered or intends to register as an investment company under the federal Investment Company Act of 1940. The provision shall not be effective if such corporation does not become or ceases to be so registered.

The existence of the corporation begins upon the filing of the articles of incorporation with the secretary of state. Upon creation, the corporation may have a meeting of its incorporators or initial board members to elect directors, officers, adopt bylaws (which may contain any provision consistent with law and the articles of incorporation), and carry on any other business of the corporation. This meeting may be held inside or outside of Nebraska.

Minimum Number of Incorporators: Any individual or entity may incorporate or organize a corporation.

Management Requirements: Directors or original incorporators, depending upon the terms of the articles of incorporation, may approve bylaws for the corporation. There must be at least one director on the corporation's board of directors. Such director must be an individual.

State Tax Classification: The State assesses a graduated corporate franchise tax, a graduated corporate income tax, and sales and use taxes at the rate of 5%.

Contact Information:	Nebraska Secretary of State, Corporate Division
	State Capitol, Room 1301
	Lincoln, Nebraska 68509
	Phone: 402-471-4079
	www.nol.org;business.html

Nevada

The Best State To Incorporate In.

Formation: Before filing its articles of incorporation, a domestic for-profit corporation may reserve a name with the secretary of state's office. The articles of incorporation must include the following:

• The name of the corporation. A name appearing to be that of a natural person and containing a given name or initials must not be used as a corporate name except with an additional word or words such as "Incorporated," "Limited," "Inc.," "Ltd.," "Company," "Co.," "Corporation," "Corp.," or other word which identifies it as not being a natural person. The name proposed for a corporation must be distinguishable on the records of the secretary of state from the names of all other artificial persons formed, organized, registered or qualified that are on file in the office of the secretary of state and all names that are reserved in the office of the secretary of state. If a proposed name is not so distinguishable, the secretary of state shall return the articles of incorporation containing the proposed name to the incorporator, unless the written, acknowledged consent of the holder of the name on file or reserved name to use the same name or the requested similar name accompanies the articles of incorporation. A proposed name is not distinguishable from a name on file or reserved name solely because one or the other contains distinctive lettering, a distinctive mark, a trademark or a trade name, or any combination of these. The name of a corporation whose charter has been revoked, which has merged and is not the surviving entity or whose existence has otherwise terminated is available for use by any other artificial person.

- The name of the person designated as the corporation's resident agent, the street address of the resident agent where process may be served upon the corporation, and the mailing address of the resident agent if different from the street address.
- The number of shares the corporation is authorized to issue and, if more than one class or series of stock is authorized, the classes, the series and the number of shares of each class or series which the corporation is authorized to issue, unless the articles authorize the board of directors to fix and determine in a resolution the classes, series and numbers of each class or series.
- The number, names and post office box or street addresses, either residence or business, of the first board of directors or trustees, together with any desired provisions relative to the right to change the number of directors.
- The name and post office box or street address, either residence or business of each of the incorporators executing the articles of incorporation.

The existence of the corporation begins upon the filing of the certificate incorporation with the Secretary of State. Upon creation, the corporation may have a meeting of its incorporators or initial board members to elect directors, officers, adopt bylaws (which may contain any provision consistent with law and the articles of incorporation), and carry on any other business of the corporation. This meeting may be held inside or outside of Nevada.

Minimum Number of Incorporators: Any person may incorporate or organize a corporation.

Management Requirements: Directors or original incorporators, depending upon the terms of the articles of incorporation, may approve bylaws for the corporation. There must be at least one director on the corporation's board of directors. Such director must be a natural person of at least 18 years of age. Every corporation must have a president, a secretary and a treasurer.

State Tax Classification: The State charges $85.00 for corporate annual reports, a business privilege tax at $25.00 per employee, and sales and use taxes vary by county but are generally 7.5%.

Contact Information: Corporate Recordings/Corporate Information
Secretary of State-Annex Office
202 N. Carson Street
Carson City, NV 89701-4271
Phone: (775) 684-5708
Facsimile: (775) 684-5725
E-mail: sosmail@govmail.state.nv.us
www.os.state.nv. us/

New Hampshire

Formation: Before filing its articles of incorporation, a domestic for-profit corporation may reserve a name with the secretary of state's office. The articles of incorporation must include the following:

• The name of the corporation, which must contain the word "corporation," "incorporated," or "limited," or the abbreviation "corp.," "inc.," or "ltd.," or words or abbreviations of like import in another language. The name may not contain language stating or implying that the corporation is organized for a purpose other than that permitted by RSA293-A:3.01 and its articles of incorporation. Except as provided below, a corporate name shall not be the same as, or deceptively similar to: (1) the corporate name of a corporation incorporated or authorized to transact business in New Hampshire; (2) a reserved or registered name; (3) the fictitious name of another foreign corporation authorized to transact business in New

Hampshire; (4) the corporate name of a not-for-profit corporation incorporated or authorized to transact business in New Hampshire; (5) the name of an agency or instrumentality of the United States or New Hampshire or a subdivision thereof; (6) the name of any recognized political party, unless written consent is obtained from the authorized representative of the respective political organization; (7) the name of a registered foreign partnership; and (8) the name of a New Hampshire investment trust. A corporation may apply to the secretary of state for authorization to use a name that is the same as, or deceptively similar to, one or more of the names described above. The secretary of state shall authorize the use of the name applied for if: (1) the holder or holders of the name as described above gives written consent to use the same or deceptively similar name; and if the name is the same, one or more words are added to the name to make the new name distinguishable from the other name; or (2) the corporation consents to the use in writing and submits an undertaking in form satisfactory to the secretary of state to change its name to a name that is not the same as, or deceptively similar to, the name of the applying corporation; or (3) the applicant delivers to the secretary of state a certified copy of the final judgment of a court of competent jurisdiction establishing the applicant's right to use the' name applied for in New Hampshire. A corporation may use the name (including the fictitious name) of another domestic or foreign corporation that is used in New Hampshire if the other corporation is incorporated or authorized to transact business in New Hampshire and the proposed user corporation: (1) has merged with the other corporation; (2) has been formed by reorganization of the other corporation; or (3) has acquired all or substantially all of the assets, including the corporate name, of the other corporation.

- The number of shares the corporation is authorized to issue;
- The street address of the corporation's initial registered office and the name of its initial registered agent at that office;
- The name and address of each incorporator.

The existence of the corporation begins upon the filing of the articles of incorporation with the Secretary of State. Upon creation, the corporation may have a meeting of its incorporators or initial board members to elect directors, officers, adopt bylaws (which may contain any provision consistent with law and the articles of incorporation), and carryon any other business of the corporation. This meeting may be held inside or outside of New Hampshire.

Minimum Number of Incorporators: Any individual or entity may incorporate or organize a corporation.

Management Requirements: Directors or original incorporators, depending upon the terms of the articles of incorporation, may approve bylaws for the corporation. There must be at least one director on the corporation's board of directors.

State Tax Classification: The State charges $100.00 for corporate annual reports, assesses a business profits tax at the rate of 8%, and a business enterprise tax at the rate of 0.25%.

Contact Information:

New Hampshire Secretary of State
Corporate Division
25 Capitol Street Floor 3
Concord, NH 03301-6312
Phone: (603) 271-3244
Corporation Information Phone:(603) 271-3246
www.webster.state.nh. us/sos/corporate/

New Jersey

Formation: Before filing its certificate of incorporation, a domestic for-profit corporation may reserve a name with the secretary of state's office. The certificate of incorporation must include the following:

- The name of the corporation, which must not contain any word or phrase, or abbreviation or derivative thereof, which indicates or implies that it is organized for any purpose other than one or more of the purposes permitted by its certificate of incorporation. The name shall be such as to distinguish it upon the records in the office of the secretary of state from the names of other for profit and nonprofit domestic corporations and for profit and nonprofit foreign corporations qualified to do business in New Jersey and from the names of domestic limited partnerships and foreign limited partnerships and from names subject to a current name reservation or a current name registration, unless there is filed a certified copy of a final judgment of a court of competent jurisdiction establishing the prior right of the corporation to the use of such name in New Jersey. The name must not contain any word or phrase, or any abbreviation or derivative thereof, the use of which is prohibited or restricted by any statute of New Jersey, unless any such restrictions have been complied with. Furthermore, the name must contain the word "corporation," "company," "incorporated," or shall contain an abbreviation of one of those words, or shall include the abbreviation "Ltd." or shall contain words or abbreviations of like import in other languages, except that a foreign corporation which does not have those words or an abbreviation thereof in its name shall add at the end of its name one of those words or an abbreviation thereof for use in New Jersey.

- The purpose or purposes for which the corporation is organized. It shall be sufficient to state, alone or with specifically enumerated purposes, that the corporation may engage in any activity within the purposes for which corporations may be organized under this law, and all such activities shall by such statement be deemed within the purposes of the corporation, subject to express limitations, if any;
- The aggregate number of shares which the corporation shall have authority to issue;
- If the shares are, or are to be, divided into classes, or into classes and series, the designation of each class and series, the number of shares in each class and series, and a statement of the relative rights, preferences and limitations of the shares of each class and series, to the extent that such designations, numbers, relative rights, preferences and limitations have been determined;
- If the shares are, or are to be, divided into classes, or into classes and series, a statement of any authority vested in the board to divide the shares into classes or series or both, and to determine or change for any class or series its designation, number of shares, relative rights, preferences and limitations;

- Any provision not inconsistent with law which the incorporators elect to set forth for the management of the business and the conduct of the affairs of the corporation, or creating, defining, limiting or regulating the powers of the corporation, its directors and shareholders or any class of shareholders, including any provision which is required or permitted to be set forth in the bylaws;
- The address of the corporation's initial registered office, and the name of the corporation's initial registered agent at such address. The address of the registered office as shown on the certificate of incorporation shall be a complete address, including the number and street location of the registered office and, if applicable, the post office box number;
- The number of directors constituting the first board and the names and addresses of the persons who are to serve as such directors;
- The names and addresses of the incorporators;
- The duration of the corporation if other than perpetual; and
- If the certificate of incorporation is to be effective on a date subsequent to the date of filing, the effective date of the certificate.

The existence of the corporation begins upon the filing of the certificate of incorporation with the secretary of state, or upon the date specified therein. Upon creation, the corporation may have a meeting of its incorporators or initial board members to elect directors, officers, adopt bylaws (which may contain any provision consistent with law and the articles of incorporation), and carryon any other business of the corporation. This meeting may be held inside or outside of New Jersey.

Minimum Number of Incorporators: Any individual of at least 18 years of age or any entity may incorporate or organize a corporation.

Management Requirements: Directors or original incorporators, depending upon the terms of the articles of incorporation, may approve bylaws for the corporation. There must be at least one director on the corporation's board of directors. The officers of a corporation shall consist of a president, a secretary, a treasurer, and, if desired, a chairman of the board, one or more vice presidents, and such other officers as may be prescribed by the by-laws.

State Tax Classification: The State charges $40.00 for corporate annual reports, assesses a variable rate corporate franchise tax, a corporate income tax at the rate of 7.25%, and sales and use taxes at the rate of 6%.

Contact Information: Division of Revenue
P. O. Box 308
Trenton, NJ 08625
Phone: (609) 292-9292
www.state.nj.us/treasury/revenue/dcr/dcrpg
1.html

New Mexico

Formation: Before filing its articles of incorporation, a domestic for-profit corporation may reserve a name with the secretary of state's office. The articles of incorporation must include the following:

• The name of the corporation, which must contain the word "corporation," "company," "incorporated," or shall contain an abbreviation of one of those words, or shall include the abbreviation Ltd. or shall contain words or abbreviations of like import in other languages. The name must not contain any word or phrase, or abbreviation or derivative thereof, which indicates or implies that it is organized for any purpose other than one or more of the purposes permitted by law or its certificate of incorporation. The name shall be such as to distinguish it upon the records in the office of the secretary of state from the names of other for profit and nonprofit domestic corporations and for profit and nonprofit foreign corporations qualified to do business in New Mexico and from the names of domestic limited partnerships and foreign limited partnerships and from names subject to a current name reservation or a current name registration, unless there is filed a certified copy of a final judgment of a court of competent jurisdiction establishing the prior right of the corporation to the use of such name in New Mexico. The name must not contain any word or phrase, or any abbreviation or derivative thereof, the use of which is prohibited or restricted by any statute of New Mexico, unless any such restrictions have been complied with.

- The period of duration, if other than perpetual;
- The purpose or purposes for which the corporation is organized, which may include the transaction of any lawful business for which corporations may be incorporated under the Business Corporation Act;
- The aggregate number of shares which the corporation shall have authority to issue and, if the shares are to be divided into classes, the number of shares of each class;
- If the shares are to be divided into classes, the designation of each class;
- If the corporation is to issue the shares of any preferred or special class in series, then the designation of each series and a statement of the variations in the relative rights and preferences as between series insofar as they are to be fixed in the articles of incorporation, and a statement of any authority to be vested in the board of directors to establish series and fix and determine the variations in the relative rights and preferences as between series;
- Any provisions limiting or denying to shareholders the preemptive right to acquire unissued shares of securities convertible into such shares or carrying a right to subscribe to or acquire shares;
- The address of its initial registered office, and the name of its initial registered agent at the address;
- The number of directors constituting the initial board of directors and the names and addresses of the persons who are to serve as directors until the first annual meeting of shareholders or until their successors are elected and qualify; and
- The name and address of each incorporator.

The existence of the corporation begins upon the filing of the articles of incorporation with the secretary of state. Upon creation, the corporation may have a meeting of its incorporators or initial board members to elect directors, officers, adopt bylaws (which may contain any provision consistent with law and the Articles of Incorporation), and carryon any other business of the corporation. This meeting may be held inside or outside of New Mexico.

Minimum Number of Incorporators: Any individual or entity may incorporate or organize a corporation.

Management Requirements: Directors or original incorporators, depending upon the terms of the articles of incorporation, may approve bylaws for the corporation. There must be at least one director on the corporation's board of directors.

State Tax Classification: The State charges $25.00 for corporate biennial reports, and a franchise tax of $50.00, and also assesses a variable rate corporate income tax.

Contact Information: State Corporation Commission
Corporation Department
P.O. Box 1269
Sante Fe, New Mexico 87504-1269
Phone: (50S) 827-4511

New York

Formation: Before filing its certificate of incorporation, a domestic for-profit corporation may reserve a name with the department of state. The certificate of incorporation must include the following:

• The name of the corporation, which must contain the word "corporation," "incorporated," or "limited," or an abbreviation of one of such words; or, in the case of a foreign corporation, it shall, for use in this state, add at the end of its name one of such words or an abbreviation thereof. The name must be such as to distinguish it from the names of corporations of any type or kind, or a fictitious name of an authorized foreign corporation, as such names appear on the index of names of existing domestic and authorized foreign corporations of any type or kind, including fictitious names of authorized foreign in the department of state, division of corporations, or a name the right to which is reserved. The name may not contain any word or phrase, or any abbreviation or derivative thereof, the use of which is prohibited or restricted by any other statute of New York, unless in the latter case the restrictions have been complied with. The name may not contain any word or phrase, or any abbreviation or derivative thereof, in a context which indicates or implies that the corporation, if domestic, is formed or, if foreign, is authorized for any purpose or is possessed in this state of any power other than a purpose for which, or a power with which, the domestic corporation may be and is formed or the foreign corporation is authorized. Specifically, a corporate name may not contain any of the following phrases, or any abbreviation or derivative thereof: board of trade; state police; urban development; chamber of commerce; state trooper; urban relocation; community renewal; or tenant relocation. A corporate name may not contain any of the following words or any abbreviation or derivative thereof: acceptance; endowment; loan; annuity; fidelity; mortgage; assurance; finance; savings; bank; guaranty; surety; benefit; indemnity; title; bond; insurance; trust; casualty; investment; underwriter; doctor; or lawyer; unless written approval from the appropriate authorities or regulatory bodies is included in the certificate of incorporation. The name must not, unless the approval of the state board of standards and appeals is attached to the certificate of incorporation, or application for authority or amendment thereof, contain any of the following words or phrases, or any abbreviation or derivative thereof: union, labor, council, industrial organization, in a context which indicates or implies that the domestic corporation is formed or the foreign corporation authorized as an organization of working men or women or wage earners or for the performance, rendition or sale of services as labor or management consultant, adviser or specialist, or as negotiator or arbitrator in labor-management disputes. The name must not, unless the approval of the state department of social services is attached to the certificate of incorporation, or application for authority or amendment thereof, contain the word "blind" or "handicapped." Such approval may be granted by the state department of social services, if in its opinion the word "blind" or "handicapped" as used in the corporate name proposed will not tend to mislead or confuse the public into believing that the corporation is organized for charitable or non-profit purposes related to the blind or the handicapped. The name must not contain any words or phrases, or any abbreviation or derivation thereof in a context which will tend to mislead the public into believing that the corporation is an agency or instrumentality of the United States or the state of New York or a subdivision thereof or is a public corporation. The name must not contain any word or phrase, or any abbreviation or derivation thereof, which, separately, or in context, shall be indecent or obscene, or shall ridicule or degrade any person, group, belief, business or agency of government, or indicate or imply any unlawful activity. A corporate name must not, unless the approval of the attorney general is attached to the certificate of incorporation, or application for authority or amendment thereof, contain the word "exchange" or any abbreviation or derivative thereof. Such approval shall not be granted by the attorney general, if in his opinion the use of the word "exchange" in the proposed corporate name would falsely imply that the corporation conducts its business at a place where trade is carried on in securities or commodities by brokers, dealers, or merchants.

- The purpose or purposes for which it is formed, it being sufficient to state, either alone or with other purposes, that the purpose of the corporation is to engage in any lawful act or activity for which corporations may be organized under the laws of New York, provided that it also state that it is not formed to engage in any act or activity requiring the consent or approval of any state official, department, board, agency or other body without such consent or approval first being obtained. By such statement all lawful acts and activities will be within the purposes of the corporation, except for express limitations therein or in law, if any.
- The county within New York in which the office of the corporation is to be located;
- The aggregate number of shares which the corporation shall have the authority to issue; if such shares are to consist of one class only, the par value of the shares or a statement that the shares are without par value; or, if the shares are to be divided into classes, the number of shares of each class and the par value of the shares having par value and a statement as to which shares, if any, are without par value.

- If the shares are to be divided into classes, the designation of each class and a statement of the relative rights, preferences and limitations of the shares of each class.
- If the shares of any preferred class are to be issued in series, the designation of each series and a statement of the variations in the relative rights, preferences and limitations as between series insofar as the same are to be fixed in the certificate of incorporation, a statement of any authority to be vested in the board to establish and designate series and to fix the variations in the relative rights, preferences and limitations as between series and a statement of any limit on the authority of the board of directors to change the number of shares of any series of preferred shares;
- A designation of the secretary of state as agent of the corporation upon whom process against it may be served and the post office address within or without this state to which the secretary of state shall mail a copy of any process against it served upon him;
- If the corporation is to have a registered agent, his name and address within New York and a statement that the registered agent is to be the agent of the corporation upon whom process against it may be served; and
- The duration of the corporation, if other than perpetual.

The existence of the corporation begins upon the filing of the certificate of incorporation, once per week for six successive weeks, in two newspapers of the county in which the office of the corporations is located, to be designated by the county clerk, one of which newspapers must be a newspaper published in the city or town in which the office is intended to be located, if there is a newspaper such city or town; or, if no newspaper is published there, in the newspaper nearest to such city or town. An affidavit of the printer or publisher of each of such newspapers is sufficient proof of such publication and must be filed with the department of state. Upon creation, the corporation may have a meeting of its incorporators or initial board members to elect directors, officers, adopt bylaws (which may contain any provision consistent with law and the certificate of incorporation), and carryon any other business of the corporation. This meeting may be held inside or outside of New York.

Minimum Number of Incorporators: Any individual of at least 18 years of age may incorporate or organize a corporation.

Management Requirements: Directors or original incorporators, depending upon the terms of the articles of incorporation, may approve bylaws for the corporation. There must be at least one director on the corporation's board of directors. The board may elect or appoint a president, one or more vice-presidents, a secretary and a treasurer, and such other officers as it may determine, or as may be provided in the bylaws.

State Tax Classification: The State assesses a variable rate corporate franchise tax. New York also assesses a stock transfer tax at the rate of *2½ ¢* per share on transfers other than by sale, and a variable stock transfer tax when shares are sold. The State also assesses sales and use taxes at the rate of 4%.

Contact Information: New York State Department of State
Division of Corporations, State Records, and Uniform Commercial Code
41 State Street
Albany, NY 12231-0001
Phone: (518) 473-2492
Facsimile: (518) 474-1418
E-mail: corporations@dos.state.ny.us
www.dos.state.ny.us/corp/corpwww.html

North Carolina

Formation: Before filing its articles of incorporation, a domestic for-profit corporation may reserve a name with the secretary of state's office. The articles of incorporation must contain the following:

• The name of the corporation, which must contain the word "corporation," "incorporated," "company," or "limited," or the abbreviation "corp.," "inc.," "co.," or "ltd." The name must not contain language stating or implying that the corporation is organized for a purpose other than that permitted by law and its articles of incorporation. Except as provided below, a corporate name must be distinguishable upon the records of the secretary of state from: (1) the corporate name of a corporation incorporated or authorized to transact business in North Carolina; (2) a reserved or registered corporate name; (3) the fictitious name adopted by a foreign corporation authorized to transact business in North Carolina because its real name is unavailable; (4) the corporate name of a nonprofit corporation incorporated or authorized to transact business in North Carolina; and (5) the name used, reserved, or registered by a limited liability company or by a limited partnership. A person may apply to the secretary of state for authorization to use a name that is not distinguishable upon his records from one or more of the names described above. The secretary of state shall authorize use of the name applied for if: (1) the other corporation consents to the use in writing and submits an undertaking in form satisfactory to the secretary of state to change its name to a name that is distinguishable upon the records of the secretary of state from the name of the applicant; or (2) the applicant delivers to the secretary of state a certified copy of the final judgment of a court of competent jurisdiction establishing the applicant's right to use the name applied for in North Carolina.

• The number of shares the corporation is authorized to issue;
• The classes of shares and the number of shares of each class that the corporation is authorized to issue. If more than one class of shares is authorized, the articles of incorporation must prescribe a distinguishing designation for each class, and, prior to the issuance of shares of a class, the preferences, limitations, and relative rights of that class must be described in the articles of incorporation. All shares of a class must have preferences, limitations, and relative rights identical with those of other shares of the same class unless the articles of incorporation divide a class into series. If a class is divided into series, all the shares of anyone series must have preferences, limitations, and relative rights identical with those of other shares of the same series.
• The articles of incorporation must authorize: (1) one or more classes of shares that together have unlimited voting rights, and (2) one or

more classes of shares (which may be the same class or classes as those with voting rights) that together are entitled to receive the net assets of the corporation upon dissolution.

- The street address, and the mailing address if different from the street address, of the corporation's initial registered office, the county in which the initial registered office is located, and the name of the corporation's initial registered agent at that address; and
- The name and address of each incorporator.

The existence of the corporation begins upon the filing of the articles of incorporation with the secretary of state. Upon creation, the corporation may have a meeting of its incorporators or initial board members to elect directors, officers, adopt bylaws (which may contain any provision consistent with law and the articles of incorporation), and carryon any other business of the corporation. This meeting may be held inside or outside of North Carolina.

Minimum Number of Incorporators: Any individual or entity may incorporate or organize a corporation.

Management Requirements: Directors or original incorporators, depending upon the terms of the articles of incorporation, may approve bylaws or the corporation. There must be at least one director on the corporation's board of directors.

State Tax Classification: The State assesses a corporate franchise tax at the rate of $1.50 per $1,000 of whichever yields the highest tax: (a) capital stock, surplus and undivided profits allocable to North Carolina; (b) investments in North Carolina tangible property; or (c) 55% of the appraised tangible personal property plus all intangible property in the State. North Carolina also assesses a corporate income tax at the rate of 6.9% and sales and use taxes at the rate of 4%.

Contact Information: Corporations Division
P. O. Box 29622
Raleigh, NC 27626-0622
Phone: (919) 807-2225
Facsimile: (919) 807-2039
www.secretary.state.nc.us/corporations/

North Dakota

Formation: Before filing its articles of incorporation, a domestic for-profit corporation may reserve a name with the secretary of state's office. The articles of incorporation must include the following:

- The name of the corporation, which must contain the word "corporation," "incorporated," "company," or "limited," or the abbreviation "corp.," "inc.," "co.," or "ltd.," or words or abbreviations of like import in another language. The name may not contain language stating or implying that the corporation is organized for any unlawful purpose. Except as provided below, a corporate name must not be the same as, or deceptively similar to, the name of a domestic or foreign corporation, limited liability company, or limited partnership, whether profit or nonprofit, authorized to do business in North Dakota, or a name the right to which is, at the time of incorporation, reserved, or is a fictitious name registered with the office of the secretary of state, or is a trade name registered with the office of the secretary of state. The secretary of state may authorize a corporation to use a name that is not distinguishable on its records from one or more of the names described above. The secretary of state shall authorize use of the name applied for if: (1) the other corporation, holder of a reserved or registered name, limited partnership, limited liability partnership or limited liability company consents to the use in writing and submits an undertaking in a form satisfactory to the secretary of state to change its name to a name that is distinguishable upon the records of the secretary of state from the name of the applying corporation; or (2) the applicant delivers to the secretary of state a certified copy of the final judgment of a court in North Dakota establishing the applicant's right to use the name applied for in North Dakota.
- The address of the registered office of the corporation and the name of its registered agent at that address;
- The aggregate number of shares that a corporation has authorized to issue;
- The name and address of each incorporator; and

- The effective date of incorporation if a later date that than on which the certificate of incorporation is issued by the secretary of state.

The existence of the corporation begins upon the issuance of the certificate of incorporation by the secretary of state. Upon creation, the corporation may have a meeting of its incorporators or initial board members to elect directors, officers, adopt bylaws (which may contain any provision consistent with law and the Articles of Incorporation), and carryon any other business of the corporation. This meeting may be held inside or outside of North Dakota.

Minimum Number of Incorporators: Any individual or entity may incorporate or organize a corporation.

Management Requirements: Directors or original incorporators, depending upon the terms of the articles of incorporation, may approve bylaws for the corporation. There must be at least one director on the corporation's board of directors. The corporation must have the officers of president, one or more vice presidents, secretary, and treasurer.

State Tax Classification: The State charges $25.00 for annual corporate reports, assesses a variable rate corporate income tax, and sales and use taxes at the rate of 5%.

Contact Information: Secretary of State
600 E. Boulevard Ave. Dept. 108
Bismarck, NO 58505-0500
Phone: (701) 328-4284
Toll Free: (800) 352-0867 ext. 8-4284
Facsimile: (701) 328-2992
E-mail: sosbir@state.nd.us

Ohio

Formation: Before filing its articles of incorporation, a domestic for-profit corporation may reserve a name with the secretary of state's office. The articles of incorporation must include the following:

- The name of the corporation, which must end with or include the word or abbreviation "company," "co.," "corporation," "corp.," "incorporated," or "inc." The name must be distinguishable upon the records of the secretary of state from all of the following: (1) the name of any other corporation, whether nonprofit or for profit and whether that of a domestic or of a foreign corporation authorized to do business in Ohio; (2) the name of any limited liability company registered in the office of the secretary of state, whether domestic or foreign; (3) the name of any limited liability partnership registered in the office of the secretary of state, whether domestic or foreign; (4) the name of any limited partnership registered in the office of the secretary of state, whether domestic or foreign; (5) any trade name the exclusive right to which is at the time in question registered in the office of the secretary of state. The name must not contain any language that indicates or implies that the corporation is connected with a government agency of Ohio, another state, or the United States.

- The place in Ohio where the principal office of the corporation is to be located;
- The authorized number and the par value per share of shares with par value, and the authorized number of shares without par value, except that the articles of a banking, safe deposit, trust, or insurance corporation shall not authorize shares without par value;
- The express terms, if any, of the shares; and, if the shares are classified, the designation of each class, the authorized number and par value per share, if any, of the shares of each class, and the express terms of the shares of each class;
- If the corporation is to have an initial stated capital, the amount of that stated capital.

The existence of the corporation begins upon the filing of the certificate of incorporation with the secretary of state. Upon creation, the corporation may have a meeting of its incorporators or initial board members to elect directors, officers, adopt bylaws (which may contain any provision consistent with law and the articles of incorporation), and carryon any other business of the corporation. This meeting may be held inside or outside of Ohio.

Minimum Number of Incorporators: Any individual or entity may incorporate or organize a corporation.

Management Requirements: Directors or original incorporators, depending upon the terms of the articles of incorporation, may approve bylaws for the corporation. The number of directors shall be not less than three or, if not so fixed, shall be three. If all of the shares of a corporation are owned by one or two shareholders, the number of directors may be less than three, but not less than the number of shareholders. The officers of a corporation shall consist of a president, a secretary, a treasurer, and, if desired, a chairman of the board, one or more vice presidents, and such other officers and assistant officers as may be deemed necessary.

State Tax Classification: The State assesses a variable rate corporate franchise tax and sales and use taxes at the rate of 5%.

Contact Information: Ohio Secretary of State
Business Services Division
180 E. Broad St., 16th Floor
Columbus, Ohio 43215
Phone: (614) 466-3910
Toll Free: 1-877-SOS-FILE (1-877-767-3453)
Facsimile: (614) 466-3899
www.state.oh.us/sos/

Oklahoma

State Corporation Statute: Ok. Statutes §§ 18.1001 through 18.1144.

Formation: Before filing its certificate of incorporation, a domestic for-profit corporation may reserve a name with the secretary of state's office. The certificate of incorporation must include the following:

• The name of the corporation, which must contain the word "association," "company," "corporation," "club," "foundation," "fund," "incorporated," "institute," "society," "union," "syndicate," or "limited," or the abbreviation "corp.," "inc.," "co.," or "ltd.," or words or abbreviations of like import in another language; provided that such abbreviations are written in Roman characters or letter. A corporate name must be distinguishable upon the records of the secretary of state from (1) names of other corporations organized under the laws of Oklahoma then existing or which existed at any time during the preceding three years; (2) names of foreign corporations registered in accordance with the laws of Oklahoma then existing or which existed at any time during the preceding three years; (3) names of then existing limited partnerships whether organized pursuant to the laws of Oklahoma or registered as foreign limited partnerships in Oklahoma: (4) trade names or fictitious names filed with the secretary of state; (5) corporate, limited liability company or limited partnership names registered with the secretary of state; or (6) names of then existing limited liability companies, whether organized pursuant to the laws of Oklahoma or registered as foreign limited liability companies in Oklahoma.

- The address, including the street, number, city and county, of the corporation's registered office in Oklahoma, and the name of the corporation's registered agent at such address;
- The nature of the business or purposes to be conducted or promoted. It shall be sufficient to state, either alone or with other business purposes, that the purpose of the corporation is to engage in any lawful act or activity for which corporations may be organized under the general corporation law of Oklahoma, and by such statement, all lawful acts and activities shall be within the purposes of the corporation, except for express limitations, if any.
- If the corporation is to be authorized to issue only one class of stock, the total number of shares of stock which the corporation shall have authority to issue and the par value of each of such shares, or a statement that all such shares are to be without par value. If the corporation is to be authorized to issue more than one class of stock, the certificate of incorporation must set forth the total number of shares of all classes of stock which the corporation shall have authority to issue and the number of shares of each class, and shall specify each class the shares of which are to have par value and the par value of shares of each such class.

- The name and mailing address of the incorporator or incorporators; and
- If the powers of the incorporator or incorporators are to terminate upon the filing of the certificate of incorporation, the names and mailing addresses of the persons who are to serve as directors until the first annual meeting of shareholders or until their successors are elected and qualify. You must file the certificate of incorporation with the secretary of state. As of January 2001, the filing fee was based upon the authorized capital stock of the corporation. The filing fees were assessed at the rate of 0.1% of the authorized capital stock for such corporation; provided that the minimum fee for any such service was $50.00.

The existence of the corporation begins upon the filing of the certificate of incorporation with the Secretary of State. Upon creation, the corporation may have a meeting of its incorporators or initial board members to elect directors, officers, adopt bylaws (which may contain any provision consistent with law and the Articles of Incorporation), and carryon any other business of the corporation. This meeting may be held inside or outside of Oklahoma.

Minimum Number of Incorporators: Any individual or entity may incorporate or organize a corporation.

Management Requirements: Directors or original incorporators, depending upon the terms of the articles of incorporation, may approve bylaws for the corporation The stock, property and affairs, of such corporation shall be managed by the board of directors, which shall consist of 5 members, all of whom must be stockholders, and who shall be elected at the annual meeting of the stockholders. At the first meeting of the stockholders, there shall be elected 5 directors, one of whom shall serve one year, two of whom shall serve two years, and the remaining two of whom shall serve three years.

State Tax Classification: The State assesses a corporate franchise tax at the rate of $1.25 per $1,000 or fraction thereof used, invested or employed in Oklahoma. Oklahoma also assesses a corporate income tax at the rate of 6% and sales and use taxes at the rate of 4.5%.

Contact Information: Business Records Department
2300 N. Lincoln Blvd., Room 101
Oklahoma City, OK 73105-4897
Phone: (900) 555-2424 (A flat fee of $5.00)
Facsimile: (405) 521-3771
www.sos.state.ok.us/

Oregon

Formation: Before filing its articles of incorporation, a domestic for-profit corporation may reserve a name with the secretary of state's office. The articles of incorporation must include the following:

• The name of the corporation, which must contain one or more of the words "corporation," "incorporated," "company," or "limited," or an abbreviation of one or more of those words. A corporate name must not contain the word "cooperative." The name must be written in the alphabet used to write the English language and may include Arabic and Roman numerals and incidental punctuation. Except as provided below, it must be distinguishable upon the records of the secretary of state from any other corporate name, professional corporate name, nonprofit corporate name, cooperative name, limited partnership name, business trust name, reserved name, registered corporate name or assumed business name of active record with the secretary of state. The corporate name need not satisfy the requirement mentioned above if the applicant delivers to the secretary of state a certified copy of a final judgment of a court of competent jurisdiction that finds that the applicant has a prior or concurrent right to use the corporate name in Oregon. Corporations are not prohibited from transacting business under an assumed business name.
• The number of shares the corporation is authorized to issue;
• The address, including street and number, and mailing address, if different, of the corporation's initial registered office and the name of its initial registered agent at that office;
• The name and address of each incorporator; and

- A mailing address to which notices may be mailed until an address has been designated by the corporation in its annual report.

The existence of the corporation begins upon the filing of the articles of incorporation with the secretary of state. Upon creation, the corporation may have a meeting of its incorporators or initial board members to elect directors, officers, adopt bylaws (which may contain any provision consistent with law and the articles of incorporation), and carryon any other business of the corporation. This meeting may be held inside or outside of Oregon.

Minimum Number of Incorporators: Any individual of at least 18 years of age or any entity may incorporate or organize a corporation.

Management Requirements: Directors or original incorporators, depending upon the terms of the articles of incorporation, may approve bylaws for the corporation. There must be at least one director on the corporation's board of directors. Such director must be an individual of at least 18 years of age. The corporation must have both a president and secretary as officers.

State Tax Classification: The State charges $30 for corporate annual reports, assesses a corporate excise tax at the rate of 6.6%, and a corporate income tax at the rate of 6.6%.

Contact Information: Janet Sullivan, Director
Corporations Division
Public Service Building
255 Capitol St. NE, Suite 151
Salem, OR 97310-1327
Phone: (503) 986-2200
E-mail: business-info.sos.bic@state.or.us
www.sos.state.or.us/corporation/bic;bic.htm

Pennsylvania

Formation: Before filing its articles of incorporation, a domestic for-profit corporation may reserve a name with the department of state. The articles of incorporation must include the following:

- The name of the corporation, which must contain one of the following corporate designators: Corporation, Corp., Company, Co.,

Incorporated, Inc., Limited, Ltd., Association, Fund, Syndicate, or other such words or abbreviations of like import in languages other than English. The words "Company" or "Co." may be immediately preceded by "and" or "&" whether or not they are immediately followed by one of the words "Incorporated," "Inc.," "Limited," or "Ltd." For example, John Doe & Co. The corporate name shall be distinguishable upon the records of the department from: (1) the name of any other domestic corporation for profit or not-for-profit which is either in existence or for which articles of incorporation have been filed but have not yet become effective, or of any foreign corporation for profit or not for profit which is either authorized to do business in Pennsylvania or for which an application for a certificate of authority has been filed but has not yet become effective, or the name of any registered association. A name the exclusive right to which is at the time reserved by any other person whatsoever in the manner provided by statute.

- The address, including street and number, if any, of its initial registered office in Pennsylvania;
- A statement that the corporation is incorporated under the provisions of the Business Corporation Law of 1988.
- A statement that the corporation is to be organized upon a non-stock basis, or if it is to be organized on a stock basis: (1) the aggregate number of shares that the corporation shall have authority to issue (it shall not be necessary to set forth in the articles the designations of the classes of shares of the corporation, or the maximum number of shares of each class that may be issued); (2) a statement of the voting rights, designations, preferences, limitations and special rights in respect of the shares of any class or any series of any class, to the extent that they have been determined; (3) a statement of any authority vested in the board of directors to divide the authorized and unissued shares into classes or series, or both, and to determine for any such class or series its voting rights, designations, preferences, limitations and special rights.
- The name and address, including street and number, if any, of each of the incorporators.
- The term for which the corporation is to exist, if not perpetual.

- If the articles are to be effective on a specified date, the hour, if any, and the month, day and year of the effective date.
- Any other provisions that the incorporators may choose to insert.

The existence of the corporation begins upon the filing of the articles of incorporation with the department of state. Upon creation, the corporation may have a meeting of its incorporators or initial board members to elect directors, officers, adopt bylaws (which may contain any provision consistent with law and the articles of incorporation), and carryon any other business of the corporation. This meeting may be held inside or outside of Pennsylvania.

Minimum Number of Incorporators: Any individual of at least 18 years of age or any entity may incorporate or organize a corporation.

Management Requirements: Directors or original incorporators, depending upon the terms of the articles of incorporation, may approve bylaws for the corporation. There must be at least one director on the corporation's board of directors. Such director must be at least 18 years of age. Every business corporation shall have a president, a secretary and a treasurer, or persons who shall act as such, regardless of the name or title by which they may be designated, elected or appointed.

State Tax Classification: The State assesses a corporate income tax at the rate of9.99%, a capital stock tax at the rate of7.49 mills per dollar of capital stock value, and sales and use taxes at the rate of 6%.

Contact Information: Department of State
Corporation Bureau
P. O. Box 8722
Harrisburg, PA17105-8722
Phone: (717) 787-1057
www.dos.state.pa.us/corp/index.htm

Rhode Island

Formation: Before filing its articles of incorporation, a domestic for-profit corporation may reserve a name with the secretary of state's office. The articles of incorporation must include the following:

• The name of the corporation, which must contain the word "corporation," "company," "incorporated," or "limited," or shall contain an abbreviation of one of the words. The name must not contain any word or phrase which indicates or implies that it is organized for any purpose other than one or more of the purposes contained in its articles of incorporation. Except as provided below, the name must not be the same as, or deceptively similar to, the name of any domestic corporation, whether for profit or not for profit, or limited partnership existing under the laws of Rhode Island or any foreign corporation, whether for profit or not for profit, or limited partnership authorized to transact business in Rhode Island, or domestic or foreign limited liability company or a name the exclusive right to which is, at the time filed, reserved or registered, or the name of a corporation or a limited partnership which has in effect a registration of its corporate or limited partnership. The foregoing does not apply if the applicant files with the secretary of state either of the following: (1) the written consent of the other corporation, limited partnership, limited liability company or holder of a filed, reserved or registered name to use that name or deceptively similar name, and one or more words are added to make the name distinguishable from the other name; or (2) a certified copy of a final decree of a court of competent jurisdiction establishing the prior right of the applicant to the use of the name in Rhode Island. Furthermore, the name may be the same as, or deceptively similar to, the name of a corporation or other association the certificate of incorporation or organization of which has been revoked by the secretary of state as permitted by law and the revocation has not been withdrawn within one year from the date of the revocation. A corporation with which another corporation, domestic or foreign, is merged, or which is formed by the reorganization or consolidation of one or more domestic or foreign corporations or upon a sale, lease, or other disposition to, or exchange with, a domestic corporation of all or substantially all the assets of another corporation, domestic or foreign, including its name, may have the same name as that used in Rhode Island by any of the corporations if at the time the other corporation was organized under the laws of, or is authorized to transact business in, Rhode Island.

- The period of duration, which may be perpetual.
- The specific purpose or purposes for which the corporation is organized and which may include the transaction of any or all lawful business for which corporations may be incorporated.
- If the corporation is to be authorized to issue only one class of stock, the total number of shares of stock which the corporation has authority to issue; and: (1) the par value of each of the shares; or (2) a statement that all the shares are to be without par value;
- If the corporation is to be authorized to issue more than one class of stock, the total number of shares of all classes of stock which the corporation has authority to issue and: (1) the number of the shares of each class of stock that are to have a par value and the par value of each share of each class; and/or (2) the number of the shares that are to be without par value; and (3) a statement of all or any of the designations and the powers, preferences, and rights, including voting rights, and the qualifications, limitations, or restrictions of them, which are permitted by Rhode Island law in respect of any class or classes of stock of the corporation and the fixing of which by the articles of association is desired, and an express grant of the authority as it may then be desired to grant to the board of directors to fix by vote or votes any of them that may be desired but which is not fixed by the articles.
- Any provisions dealing with the preemptive right of shareholders.
- Any provision, not inconsistent with law, which the incorporators elect to set forth in the articles of incorporation for the regulation of the internal affairs of the corporation, including, but not limited to, a provision eliminating or limiting the personal liability of a director to the corporation or to its stockholders for monetary damages for breach of the director's duty as a director; provided that the provision does not eliminate or limit the liability of a director for: (1) any breach of the director's duty of loyalty to the corporation or its stockholders; (2) acts or omissions not in good faith or which involve intentional misconduct or a knowing violation of law; (3) liability imposed pursuant to the provisions of § 7-1.1-43 of the

Rhode Island Code; or (4) any transaction from which the director derived an improper personal benefit; and also including; (5) any provision which is required or permitted to be set forth in the bylaws. No provision eliminating or limiting the personal liability of a director will be effective with respect to causes of action arising prior to the inclusion of the provision in the articles of incorporation of the corporation.

- The address of its initial registered office, and the name of its initial registered agent at the address.
- The number of directors, if any, constituting the initial board of directors, or, if none, the titles of the initial officers of the corporation and the names and addresses of the persons who are to serve as directors or officers until the first annual meeting of shareholders or until their successors are elected and qualify.
- The name and address of each incorporator.
- If the corporate existence is to begin at a time subsequent to the issuance of the certificate of incorporation by the secretary of state, the date when corporate existence begins.

The existence of the corporation begins upon the filing of the certificate of incorporation with the secretary of state, or upon a later date specified therein. Upon creation, the corporation may have a meeting of its incorporators or initial board members to elect directors, officers, adopt bylaws (which may contain any provision consistent with law and the articles of incorporation), and carryon any other business of the corporation. This meeting may be held inside or outside of Rhode Island.

Minimum Number of Incorporators: Any individual or entity may incorporate or organize a corporation.

Management Requirements: Directors or original incorporators, depending upon the terms of the articles of incorporation, may approve bylaws for the corporation. There must be at least one director on the corporation's board of directors. The officers of a corporation consist of a chairperson of the board of directors, if prescribed by the bylaws, a president, one or more vice presidents, if prescribed by the bylaws, a secretary, and a treasurer.

State Tax Classification: The State charges $50.00 for corporate annual reports, assesses a variable rate corporate franchise tax, and assesses sales and use taxes at the rate of 7%.

Contact Information: First Stop Business Center
100 North Main Street, 2nd Floor
Providence, RI02903-1335
Phone: (401) 222-2185
Facsimile: (401) 222-3890
E-mail: firststop@sec.state.rLus
www.sec.state.ri. us!bus/frststp.htm

South Carolina

Formation: Before filing its articles of incorporation, a domestic for-profit corporation may reserve a name with the secretary of state's office. The articles of incorporation must include the following:

• The name of the corporation, which must contain the word "corporation," "incorporated," "company," or "limited," the abbreviation "corp.," "inc.," "co.," or "ltd.," or words or abbreviations of like import in another language. The name may not contain language stating or implying that the corporation is organized for a purpose other than that permitted by law and its articles of incorporation. Except as provided below, a corporate name must be distinguishable upon the records of the secretary of state from: (1) the corporate name of a corporation incorporated or authorized to transact business in South Carolina; (2) a reserved or registered corporate name; (3) the fictitious name adopted by a foreign corporation authorized to transact business in South Carolina because its real name is unavailable; (4) the corporate name of a not-for-profit corporation incorporated or authorized to transact business in South Carolina; (5) the name of a limited partnership authorized to transact business in South Carolina. A corporation may apply to the secretary of state for authorization to use a name that is not distinguishable upon his records from one or more of the names described above. The secretary of state shall authorize use of the name applied for if: (1) the other corporation consents to the use in writing and submits an undertaking in form satisfactory to the secretary of state to change its name to a name that is distinguishable upon the records of the secretary of state from the name of the applying corporation; or (2) the applicant delivers to the secretary of state a certified copy of the final judgment of a court of competent jurisdiction establishing the applicant's right to use the name applied for in South Carolina. A corporation may use the name (including the fictitious name) of another domestic or foreign corporation that is used in South Carolina if the other corporation is incorporated or authorized to transact business in South Carolina and the proposed user corporation: (1) has merged with the other corporation; (2) has been formed by reorganization of the other corporation; or (3) has acquired all or substantially all of the assets, including the corporate name, of the other corporation.

- The number of shares the corporation is authorized to issue, itemized by classes;
- The street address of the corporation's initial registered office and the, name of its initial registered agent at that office;
- The name and address of each incorporator;
- The signature of each incorporator; and
- A certificate, signed by an attorney licensed to practice in South Carolina, that all of the requirements of South Carolina law governing corporate formation have been compiled with.

The existence of the corporation begins upon the filing of the articles of incorporation with the secretary of state. Upon creation, the corporation may have a meeting of its incorporators or initial board members to elect directors, officers, adopt bylaws (which may contain any provision consistent with law and the articles of incorporation), and carryon any other business of the corporation. This meeting may be held inside or outside of South Carolina.

Minimum Number of Incorporators: Any individual or entity may incorporate or organize a corporation.

Management Requirements: Directors or original incorporators, depending upon the terms of the articles of incorporation, may approve bylaws for the corporation. There must be at least one director on the corporation's board of directors.

State Tax Classification: The State assesses a corporate franchise tax at the rate of $15.00 plus 1 mill per $1.00 paid to capital stock and surplus, a corporate income tax at the rate of 5%, and sales and use taxes at the rate of 4%.

Contact Information: South Carolina Secretary of State
Business Filings
P. O. Box 11350
Columbia, SC 29211
Customer Services: (803) 734-2158
www.scsos.com/

South Dakota

Formation: Before filing its articles of incorporation, a domestic for-profit corporation may reserve a name with the secretary of state's office. The articles of incorporation must include the following:

• The name of the corporation, which must contain the word "corporation," "company," "incorporated," or "limited," or shall contain an abbreviation of one of such words. The name must not contain any word or phrase which indicates or implies that it is organized for any purpose other than one or more of the purposes stated in its articles of incorporation. The name must be distinguishable upon the records of the secretary of state from the name of any other corporation, whether for profit or not for profit, organized under the laws of South Dakota; the name of any foreign corporation, whether for profit or not for profit, authorized to engage in any business in South Dakota; or any corporate name reserved or registered as permitted by the laws of South Dakota; or the name of any limited partnership certified or registered in South Dakota; or the name of any limited liability company. Corporate names or limited partnership names already in use, with generic, proper, geographical or descriptive terms which have acquired a secondary meaning shall be protected. The foregoing does not apply if the applicant files with the secretary of state either: (1) the written consent signed by the president or a vice president and by the secretary or an assistant secretary of the other corporation; by a holder of a reserved or registered name; or by a general partner of a limited partnership to use the same or a distinguishable name; (2) a certified copy of a final decree of a court of competent jurisdiction establishing the prior right of the applicant to the use of such name in South Dakota; or (3) in the case of a foreign corporation, if the corporate name is not available for use, a resolution of its board of directors adopting an assumed name for use in transacting business in South Dakota, which assumed name is not distinguishable from the name of any domestic corporation, any foreign corporation authorized to engage in any business in South Dakota, or any corporate name reserved or registered as permitted by the laws of South Dakota, or the name of any limited partnership certified or registered in South Dakota or any other assumed name filed with the secretary of state by a foreign corporation authorized to transact business in South Dakota. The name must be transliterated into letters of the English alphabet, if it is not in English. A corporation with which another corporation, domestic or foreign, is merged, or which is formed by the reorganization or consolidation of one or more domestic or foreign corporations or upon a sale, lease or other disposition to or exchange with, a domestic corporation of all or substantially all the assets of another corporation, domestic or foreign, including its name, may have the same name as that used in South Dakota by any of such corporations if the other corporation was organized under the laws of, or is authorized to transact business in South Dakota.

- The period of duration, which may be perpetual;
- The purpose or purposes for which the corporation is organized;
- The aggregate number of shares which the corporation shall have authority to issue; if such shares are to consist of one class only, the par value of each of such shares, or a statement that all of such shares are without par value; or, if such shares are to be divided into classes, the number of shares of each class, and a statement of the par value of the shares of each such class, or that such shares are to be without par value;
- If the shares are to be divided into classes, the designation of each class and a statement of the preferences, limitations and relative rights in respect of the shares of each class;

- If the corporation is to issue the shares of any preferred or special class in series, then the designation of each series and a statement of the variations in the relative rights and preferences as between series insofar as the same are to be fixed in the articles of incorporation, and a statement of any authority to be vested in the board of directors to establish series and fix and determine the variations in the relative rights and preferences as between series;
- A statement that the corporation will not commence business until consideration of the value of at least one thousand dollars has been received for the issuance of shares;
- Any provision limiting or denying to shareholders the preemptive right to acquire additional or treasury shares of the corporation;
- Any provision, not inconsistent with law, which the incorporators elect to set forth in the articles of incorporation for the regulation of the internal affairs of the corporation, including any provision restricting the transfer of shares and any provision which is required or permitted to be set forth in the bylaws;
- The street address, or a statement that there is no street address, of the registered office, the name of its registered agent at such address and his written consent to the appointment;
- The number of directors constituting the initial board of directors and the names and addresses of the persons who are to serve as directors until the first annual meeting of shareholders or until their successors be elected and qualify;
- The name and address of each incorporator.

The existence of the corporation begins upon the issuance of the certificate of existence by the secretary of state. Upon creation, the corporation may have a meeting of its incorporators or initial board members to elect directors, officers, adopt bylaws (which may contain any provision consistent with law and the articles of incorporation), and carryon any other business of the corporation. This meeting may be held inside or outside of South Dakota.

Minimum Number of Incorporators: Any natural person of at least 18 years of age may incorporate or organize a corporation.

Management Requirements: Directors or original incorporators, depending upon the terms of the articles of incorporation, may approve bylaws for the corporation. There must be at least one director on the corporation's board of directors.

State Tax Classification: The State charges $90.00 for the original corporate report, $50.00 for annual corporate reports, and assesses sales and use taxes at the rate of 4%.

    Contact Information: Secretary of State
Capitol Building
500 East Capitol Avenue Ste 204
Pierre, SD 57501-5070
Phone: (605) 773-4845
Facsimile: (605) 773-4550
E-mail: mary.heidelberger@state.sd.us
www.state.sd.us/sos/sos.htm

Tennessee

Formation: Before filing its corporate charter, a domestic for-profit corporation may reserve a name with the secretary of state's office. The corporate charter must include the following:

- The name of the corporation, which must contain the word "corporation," "incorporated," "company," or the abbreviation "corp.," "inc.," "co.," or words or abbreviations of like import in another language (provided they are written in roman characters or letters); provided, that if such corporation is formed for the purpose of an insurance or banking business, the name of such corporation need not contain any of the aforementioned words or abbreviations. The name may not contain language stating or implying that the corporation: (1) transacts or has power to transact any business for which authorization in whatever form and however denominated is required under the laws of Tennessee, unless the appropriate commission or officer has granted such authorization and certifies that fact in writing; (2) is organized as, affiliated with, or sponsored by, any fraternal, veterans', service, religious, charitable, or professional organization, unless that fact is certified in writing by the organization with which affiliation or sponsorship is claimed; (3) is an agency or instrumentality of, affiliated with or sponsored by the United States or the state of Tennessee or a subdivision or agency thereof, unless such fact is certified in writing by the appropriate official of the United States or the state of Tennessee or subdivision or agency thereof; or (4) is organized for a purpose other than that permitted by law and its charter. Except as provided below, a corporate name must be distinguishable upon the records of the secretary of state from: (1) the corporate name or assumed corporate name of a corporation incorporated or authorized to transact business in Tennessee; (2) an assumed, reserved or registered corporate name; (3) the corporate name of a not-for-profit corporation incorporated or authorized to transact business in Tennessee; (4) a limited partnership name reserved or organized under the laws of Tennessee or registered as a foreign limited partnership in Tennessee; and (5) the name of a limited liability company authorized to do business as a foreign limited liability company in Tennessee. A corporation may apply to the secretary of state for authorization to use a name that is not distinguishable upon the secretary of state's records from one or more of the names described above. The secretary of state shall authorize use of the name applied for if: (1) the other corporation, limited partnership or foreign limited liability company consents to the use in writing and submits an undertaking in form satisfactory to the secretary of state to change its name to a name that is distinguishable upon the records of the secretary of state from the name of the applying corporation; or (2) the applicant delivers to the secretary of state a certified copy of the final judgment of a court of competent jurisdiction establishing the applicant's right to use the name applied for in Tennessee. A domestic corporation or a foreign corporation authorized to transact business or applying for a certificate of authority to transact business may elect to adopt an assumed corporate name.

- The number of shares the corporation is authorized to issue;
- The street address and zip code of the corporation's initial registered office, the county in which the office is located, and the name of its initial registered agent at that office;

- The name and address and zip code of each incorporator;
- The street address and zip code of the initial principal office of the corporation;
- The number of shares of each class that the corporation is authorized to issue. If more than one class of shares is authorized, the charter must prescribe a distinguishing designation for each class, and prior to the issuance of shares of a class, the preferences, limitations, and relative rights of that class must be described in the charter. All shares of a class must have preferences, limitations, and relative rights identical with those of other shares of the same class, except to the extent that the board of directors may be authorized in the charter to determine such rights; and
- A statement that the corporation is for profit.

The existence of the corporation begins upon the filing of the corporate charter with the secretary of state. Upon creation, the corporation may have a meeting of its incorporators or initial board members to elect directors, officers, adopt bylaws (which may contain any provision consistent with law and the corporate charter), and carryon any other business of the corporation. This meeting may be held inside or outside of Tennessee.

Minimum Number of Incorporators: Any individual of at least 18 years of age may incorporate or organize a corporation.

Management Requirements: Directors or original incorporators, depending upon the terms of the articles of incorporation, may approve bylaws for the corporation. There must be at least one director on the corporation's board of directors. Such director must be an individual. There must be a president and secretary of the corporation.

State Tax Classification: The State charges $20.00 for annual corporate reports, assesses annual franchise taxes at the rate of $.25 per $100.00 of net worth, assesses an excise tax at the rate of 6%, and sales and use taxes at the rate of 6%.

Contact Information: Division of Business Services
312 Eighth Avenue North
6th Floor, William R. Snodgrass Tower
Nashville, TN 37243
Corporate Certification Phone:

2222

(615) 741-6488
Corporate Information Phone:
(615) 741-2286
E-mail: services@mail.state.tn.us
www.state. tn.us/sos/service.htm

Texas

Formation: Before filing its articles of incorporation, a domestic for-profit corporation may reserve a name with the secretary of state's office. The articles of incorporation must include the following:

• The name of the corporation, which must contain the word "corporation," "company," or "incorporated," or shall contain an abbreviation of one of such words, and shall contain such additional words as may be required by law. It must not contain any word or phrase which indicates or implies that it is organized for any purpose other than one or more of the purposes contained in its articles of incorporation. A corporate name may not contain the word "lottery." It may not be the same as, or deceptively similar to, the name of any domestic corporation, limited partnership, or limited liability company existing under the laws of Texas, or the name of any foreign corporation, non-profit corporation, limited partnership, or limited liability company authorized to transact business in Texas, or a name the exclusive right to which is, at the time, reserved or registered. A name may be similar if written consent is obtained from the existing corporation, limited partnership, or limited liability company having the name deemed to be similar or the person for whom the name deemed to be similar is reserved in the office of the secretary of state. Any domestic or foreign corporation having authority to transact business in Texas may do so under an assumed name by filing an assumed name certificate.
• The period of duration, which may be perpetual;
• The purpose or purposes for which the corporation is organized which may be stated to be, or to include, the transaction of any or all lawful business for which corporations may be incorporated;

- The aggregate number of shares which the corporation shall have authority to issue; if such shares are to consist of one class only, the par value of each of such shares, or a statement that all of such shares are without par value; or, if such shares are to be divided into classes, the number of shares of each class, and a statement of the par value of the shares of each class or that such shares are to be without par value;
- If the shares are to be divided into classes, the designation of each class and statement of the preferences, limitations, and relative rights in respect of the shares of each class;
- If the corporation is to issue the shares of any class in series, then the designation of each series and a statement of the variations in the preferences, limitations and relative rights as between series insofar as the same are to be fixed in the articles of incorporation, and a statement of any authority to be vested in the board of directors to establish series and fix and determine the preferences, limitations and relative rights of each series;
- A statement that the corporation will not commence business until it has received for the issuance of shares consideration of the value of a stated sum which shall be at least $1,000;
- Any provision limiting or denying to shareholders the preemptive right to acquire additional or treasury shares of the corporation;
- If a corporation elects to become a close corporation, any provision (1) required or permitted to be stated in the articles of incorporation of a close corporation, but not in the articles of incorporation of an ordinary corporation, (2) contained or permitted to be contained in a shareholders' agreement which the incorporators elect to set forth in articles of incorporation, or (3) that makes a shareholders' agreement part of the articles of incorporation of a close corporation, but any such provision shall be preceded by a statement that the provision shall be subject to the corporation remaining a close corporation;
- Any provision, not inconsistent with law providing for the regulation of the internal affairs of the corporation;
- The street address of its initial registered office and the name of its initial registered agent at such address;

- The number of directors constituting the initial board of directors and the names and addresses of the person or persons who are to serve as directors until the first annual meeting of shareholders or until their successors be elected and qualify, or, in the case of a close corporation that, is to be managed in some other manner pursuant to a shareholders' agreement by the shareholders or by the persons empowered by the agreement to manage its business and affairs, the names and addresses of the person or persons who, pursuant to the shareholders' agreement, will perform the functions of the initial board of directors;
- The name and address of each incorporator, unless the corporation is being incorporated pursuant to a plan of conversion or a plan of merger, in which case the articles need not include such information; and
- If the corporation is being incorporated pursuant to a plan of conversion or a plan of merger, a statement to that effect, and in the case of a plan of conversion, the name, address, date of formation, and prior form of organization and jurisdiction of incorporation or organization of the converting entity.

The existence of the corporation begins upon the filing of the articles of incorporation with the secretary of state. Upon creation, and subsequent to its receipt of at least $1,000 as consideration for shares of stock, the corporation may have a meeting of its incorporators or initial board members to elect directors, officers, adopt bylaws (which may contain any provision consistent with law and the articles of incorporation), and carryon any other business of the corporation. This meeting may be held inside or outside of Texas.

Minimum Number of Incorporators: Any individual of at least 18 years of age may incorporate or organize a corporation.

Management Requirements: Directors or original incorporators, depending upon the terms of the articles of incorporation, may approve bylaws for the corporation. There must be at least one director on the corporation's board of directors. There also must be a president and secretary of the corporation.

State Tax Classification: The State assesses a corporate franchise tax at the rate of .25% per year of net taxable capital and 4.5% of net taxable earned surplus, and sales and use taxes at the rate of 6.25%.

Contact Information: Corporations Section
Secretary of State
P. O. Box 13697
Austin, Texas 78711
Phone: (512) 463-5583
E-mail: corphelp@sos.state.tx.us
www.sos.state.tx.us/corp/index.shtml

Utah

Formation: Before filing its articles of incorporation, a domestic for-profit corporation may reserve a name with the department of commerce. The articles of incorporation must include the following:

• The name of the corporation, which must contain the word "corporation," "incorporated," or "company," the abbreviation "corp.," "inc.," or "co.," or words or abbreviations of like import to the words or abbreviations listed above in another language. The name may not contain language stating or implying that the corporation is organized for a purpose other than that permitted by law and the corporation's articles of incorporation. Without the written consent of the United States Olympic Committee, the name may not contain the words "Olympic," "Olympiad," or "Citius Altius Fortius." Without the written consent of the State Board of Regents, may not contain the words "university," "college," or "institute." Except as provided below, the name of a corporation must be distinguishable upon the records of the corporations division from the following: (1) the name of any domestic corporation incorporated in or foreign corporation authorized to transact business in Utah; (2) the name of any domestic or foreign nonprofit corporation incorporated or authorized to transact business in Utah; (3) the name of any domestic or foreign limited liability company. formed or authorized to transact business in Utah; (4) the name of any limited partnership formed or authorized to transact business in

Utah; (5) any name reserved or registered with the corporations division for a corporation, limited liability company, or general or limited partnership, under the laws of Utah; and (6) any business name, fictitious name, assumed name, trademark, or service mark registered by the division. A corporation may apply to the division for authorization to file its articles of incorporation under, or to register or reserve, a name that is not distinguishable upon its records from one or more of the names described above. The division shall approve the application if: (1) the other person whose name is not distinguishable from the name under which the applicant desires to file, or which the applicant desires to register or reserve: (A) consents to the filing, registration, or reservation in writing; and (B) submits an undertaking in a form satisfactory to the division to change its name to a name that is distinguishable from the name of the applicant; or (2) the applicant delivers to the division a certified copy of the final judgment of a court of competent jurisdiction establishing the applicant's right to make the requested filing in Utah under the name applied for. A corporation may make a filing under the name, including the fictitious name, of another domestic or foreign corporation that is used or registered in Utah if: (1) the other corporation is incorporated or authorized to transact business in this state; and (2) the filing corporation: (a) has merged with the other corporation; or (b) has been formed by reorganization of the other corporation.

- The purpose or purposes for which the corporation is organized;
- The number of shares the corporation is authorized to issue;
- With respect to each class of shares the corporation is authorized to issue, the classes of shares and the number of shares of each class that the corporation is authorized to issue. If more than one class of shares is authorized, the articles of incorporation must prescribe a distinguishing designation for each class, and prior to the issuance of shares of a class the preferences, limitations, and relative rights of that class must be described in the articles of incorporation. All shares of a class must have preferences, limitations, and relative rights identical with those of other shares of the same class except to

the extent otherwise permitted by Sections 16-1Oa-601 and 602 of the Utah Code.

• The street address of the corporation's initial registered office and the name and signature of its initial registered agent at that office; and

• The name and address of each incorporator.

The existence of the corporation begins upon the filing of the articles of incorporation with the department of commerce. Upon creation, the corporation may have a meeting of its incorporators or initial board members to elect directors, officers, adopt bylaws (which may contain any provision consistent with law and the articles of incorporation), and carryon any other business of the corporation. This meeting may be held inside or outside of Utah.

Minimum Number of Incorporators: Any individual or entity may incorporate or organize a corporation.

Management Requirements: Directors or original incorporators, depending upon the terms of the articles of incorporation, may approve bylaws for the corporation. Prior to the issuance of shares of stock, there must be at least one director on the corporation's board of directors. Once the corporation has issued shares of stock, there must be two directors if there are two shareholders, or at least three directors if there are at least three shareholders. Directors must be natural persons.

State Tax Classification: The State charges $10.00 for corporate annual reports, assesses a corporate franchise tax at the rate of 5% of Utah taxable income, a corporate income tax of 5%, and sales and use taxes at the rate of 4.75%.

Contact Information: Utah Department of Commerce
Division of Corporations and
Commercial Code
160 E. 300th Street
Salt Lake City, UT 84111
Phone: (801) 530-4849
www.commerce.state.ut.us/corporat/corpcoc.htm

Vermont

Formation: Before filing its certificate of incorporation, a domestic for-profit corporation may reserve a name with the secretary of state's office. The certificate of incorporation must include the following:

• The name of the corporation, which must contain the word "corporation," "incorporated," "company," or "limited," or the abbreviation "corp.," "inc.," "co.," or "ltd.," or words or abbreviations of like import in another language. The name may not contain language stating or implying that the corporation is organized for a purpose other than that permitted by law and its articles of incorporation. A corporate name must not have the word "cooperative" or any abbreviation thereof as part of its name unless the corporation is a worker cooperative corporation or the articles of incorporation contain all of the provisions required of a corporation organized-as a cooperative association. The name must not include any word not otherwise authorized by law. Except as provided below, a corporate name, based upon the records of the secretary of state, must be distinguishable from, and not the same as, deceptively similar to, or likely to be confused with or mistaken for any name granted, registered, or reserved under this chapter, or the name of any other entity, whether domestic or foreign, that is reserved, registered, or granted by or with the secretary of state. A corporation may apply to the secretary of state for authorization to use a name that is not distinguishable from, or is the same as, deceptively similar to, or likely to be confused with or mistaken for one or more of the names described above, as determined from review of the records of the secretary of state. The secretary of state shall authorize use of the name applied for if: (1) the other corporation or business consents to the use in writing and submits an undertaking in form satisfactory to the secretary of state to change its name to a name that is distinguishable from, and not the same as, deceptively similar to, or likely to be confused with or mistaken for the name of the applying corporation; or (2) the applicant delivers to the secretary of state a certified copy of the final judgment of a court of competent jurisdiction establishing the applicant's right to use the name applied for in Vermont. A corporation may use the name (including the fictitious name) of another domestic or foreign corporation that is used in Vermont if the other corporation is incorporated or authorized to transact business in Vermont and the proposed user corporation: (1) has merged with the other corporation; (2) has been formed by reorganization of the other corporation; or (3) has acquired all or substantially all of the assets, including the corporate name, of the other corporation.

- The classes of shares, if any, and the number of shares in each class that the corporation is authorized to issue;
- The number of shares the corporation is authorized to issue;
- The street address of the corporation's initial registered office and the name of its initial registered agent at that office;
- The name and address of each incorporator;
- One or more classes of shares must have unlimited voting rights; and
- One or more classes of shares (which may be the same class or classes as those with voting rights) must be entitled to receive the net assets of the corporation upon dissolution.

The existence of the corporation begins upon the filing of the articles of incorporation with the secretary of state. Upon creation, the corporation may have a meeting of its incorporators or initial board members to elect directors, officers, adopt bylaws (which may contain any provision consistent with law and the articles of incorporation), and carryon any other business of the corporation. This meeting may be held inside or outside of Vermont.

Minimum Number of Incorporators: Any individual of at least 18 years of age may incorporate or organize a corporation.

Management Requirements: Directors or original incorporators, depending upon the terms of the articles of incorporation, may approve bylaws for the corporation. A board of directors of a corporation, which is not a close corporation, must consist of three or more individuals, with the number specified in or fixed in accordance with the articles of incorporation or bylaws. If the number of shareholders in any corporation is less than three, the number of directors may be as few as the number of shareholders. A corporation must have a president and a secretary.

State Tax Classification: The State charges $15.00 for annual corporation reports, assesses a variable rate corporate income tax, and assesses sales and use taxes at the rate of 5%.

Contact Information: Vermont Secretary of State
Corporations Division
81 River Street, Drawer 09
Montpelier, VT 05609-1104
Phone: (802) 828-2386
Facsimile: (802) 828-2853
www.sec.state.vt.us/corps/corpindex.htm

Virginia

Formation: Before filing its certificate of incorporation, a domestic for-profit corporation may reserve a name with the state corporation commission. The certificate of incorporation must include the following:

• The name of the corporation, which must contain the word "corporation," "incorporated," "company," or "limited," or the abbreviation "corp.," "inc.," "co.," or "ltd." Such words and their corresponding abbreviations may be used interchangeably for all purposes. A corporate name shall not contain: (1) any language stating or implying that it will transact one of the special kinds of businesses listed in Section 13.1-620of the Virginia Code, unless it proposes in fact to engage in such special kind of business; or (2) any word or phrase that is prohibited by law for such corporation. Except as provided below, a corporate name shall be distinguishable upon the records of the commission from: (1) the corporate name of a domestic corporation or a foreign corporation authorized to transact business in Virginia; (2) a reserved or registered corporate name; (3) the designated name adopted by a foreign corporation, whether issuing or not issuing shares, because its real name is unavailable; and (4) the corporate name of a non-stock corporation incorporated or authorized to transact business in Virginia. A domestic corporation may apply to the commission for authorization to use a name that is not distinguishable upon its records from one or more of the names described above. The commission shall authorize use of the name applied for if: (1) the other entity consents to the use in writing and submits an undertaking in form satisfactory to the commission to change its name to a name that is distinguishable upon the records of the commission from the name of the applying corporation.

- The number of shares the corporation is authorized to issue;
- If more than one class of shares is authorized, the number of authorized shares of each class and a distinguishing designation for each class;
- The address of the corporation's initial registered office (including both (1) the post-office address with street and number, if any and (2) the name of the city or county in which it is.-located), and the name of its initial registered agent at that office;
- A statement which declares that the agent is either (1) a resident of Virginia and either a director of the corporation or a member of the Virginia State Bar or (2) a professional corporation, professional limited liability company, or registered limited liability partnership registered with the Virginia State Bar.

The existence of the corporation begins upon the issuance of a certificate of incorporation by the state corporation commission. Upon creation, the corporation may have a meeting of its incorporators or initial board members to elect directors, officers, adopt bylaws (which may contain any provision consistent with law and the articles of incorporation), and carryon any other business of the corporation. This meeting may be held inside or
outside of Virginia.

Minimum Number of Incorporators: Any individual or entity may incorporate or organize a corporation.

Management Requirements: Directors or original incorporators, depending upon the terms of the articles of incorporation, may approve bylaws for the corporation. There must be at least one director on the corporation's board of directors.

State Tax Classification: The State charges $50.00 on the first 5,000 authorized share, and $15.00 for each additional 5,000 shares, as an annual registration fee. Virginia also assesses a corporate income tax at the rate of 6% and sales and use taxes at the rate of 3.5%.

Contact Information: Office of the Clerk
Virginia State Corporation Division
P.O. Box 1197
Richmond, Virginia 23218
Phone: (804) 371-9733
www.state.va.us/scc/division/clk/index.htm

Washington

Formation: Before filing its certificate of incorporation, a domestic for-profit corporation may reserve a name with the secretary of state's office. The certificate of incorporation must include the following:

• The name of the corporation, which must contain the word "corporation," "incorporated," "company," or "limited," or the abbreviation "corp.," "inc.," "co.," or "ltd." The name must not contain language stating or implying that the corporation is organized for a purpose other than those permitted by law and its articles of incorporation. It must not contain any of the following words or phrases: "Bank," "banking," "banker," "trust," "cooperative," or any combination of the words "industrial" and "loan," or any combination of any two or more of the words "building," "savings," "loan," "home," "association," and "society," or any other words or phrases prohibited by any statute of Washington. Except provided below, the name must be distinguishable upon the records of the secretary of state from: (1) the corporate name of a corporation incorporated or authorized to transact business in Washington; (2) a reserved or registered corporate name; (3) the fictitious name adopted by a foreign corporation authorized to transact business in Washington because its real name is unavailable; (4) the corporate name or reserved name of a not-for-profit corporation incorporated or authorized to conduct affairs in Washington; (5) the name or reserved name of a mutual corporation or miscellaneous corporation incorporated or authorized to do business in Washington; (6) the name or reserved name of a foreign or domestic limited partnership formed or registered under the laws of Washington; (7) the name or reserved name of a limited liability company organized or registered under the laws of Washington; and (8) the name or reserved name of a limited liability partnership registered under Washington law. A corporation may apply to the secretary of state for authorization to use a name that is not distinguishable upon the records from one or more of the names described above. The secretary of state shall authorize use of the name applied for if: (1) the other corporation, company, holder, limited liability partnership, or limited partnership consents to the use in writing and files with the secretary of state documents necessary to change its name or the name reserved or registered to a name that is distinguishable upon the records of the secretary of state from the name of the applying corporation; or (2) the applicant delivers to the secretary of state a certified copy of the final judgment of a court of competent jurisdiction establishing the applicant's right to use the name applied for in Washington. A corporation may use the name, including the fictitious name, of another domestic or foreign corporation, limited liability company, limited partnership, or limited liability partnership, that is used in Washington if the other entity is formed or authorized to transact business in Washington, and the proposed user corporation: (1) has merged with the other corporation, limited liability company, or limited partnership; or (2) has been formed by reorganization of the other corporation.

- The number of shares the corporation is authorized to issue;
- The street address of the corporation's initial registered office and the name of its initial registered agent at that office;
- The name and address of each incorporator; and
- The articles of incorporation or bylaws must either specify the number of directors or specify the process by which the number of

directors will be fixed, unless the articles of incorporation dispense with a board of directors.

Washington

Formation: Before filing its certificate of incorporation, a domestic for-profit corporation may reserve a name with the secretary of state's office. The certificate of incorporation must include the following:

• The name of the corporation, which must contain the word "corporation," "incorporated," "company," or "limited," or the abbreviation "corp.," "inc.," "co.," or "ltd." The name must not contain language stating or implying that the corporation is organized for a purpose other than those permitted by law and its articles of incorporation. It must not contain any of the following words or phrases: "Bank," "banking," "banker," "trust," "cooperative," or any combination of the words "industrial" and "loan," or any combination of any two or more of the words "building," "savings," "loan," "home," "association," and "society," or any other words or phrases prohibited by any statute of Washington. Except provided below, the name must be distinguishable upon the records of the secretary of state from: (1) the corporate name of a corporation incorporated or authorized to transact business in Washington; (2) a reserved or registered corporate name; (3) the fictitious name adopted by a foreign corporation authorized to transact business in Washington because its real name is unavailable; (4) the corporate name or reserved name of a not-for-profit corporation incorporated or authorized to conduct affairs in Washington; (5) the name or reserved name of a mutual corporation or miscellaneous corporation incorporated or authorized to do business in Washington; (6) the name or reserved name of a foreign or domestic limited partnership formed or registered under the laws of Washington; (7) the name or reserved name of a limited liability company organized or registered under the laws of Washington; and (8) the name or reserved name of a limited liability partnership registered under Washington law. A corporation may apply to the secretary of state for authorization to use a name that is not distinguishable upon the records from one or more of the names described above. The secretary of state shall authorize use of the name applied for if: (1) the other corporation, company, holder, limited liability partnership, or limited partnership consents to the use in writing and files with the secretary of state documents necessary to change its name or the name reserved or registered to a name that is distinguishable upon the records of the secretary of state.

State Tax Classification: The State charges $50.00 as an annual license fee, and assesses a retail sales tax at the rate of 6.5%.

Contact Information: Corporations Division
          801 Capitol Way S.
          P. O. Box 40234
          Olympia, WA98504-0234
          Phone: (360) 753-7115
          E-mail: corps@secstate.wa.gov
          www.secstate.wa.gov/corps/default.htm

West Virginia

Formation: Before filing its certificate of incorporation, a domestic for-profit corporation may reserve a name with the secretary of state's office. The articles of incorporation must include the following:

• The name of the corporation, which must contain the word "corporation," "company," "incorporated," or "limited," or shall contain an abbreviation of one of such words. The name must not contain any word or phrase which indicates or implies that it is organized for any purpose other than one or more of the purposes contained in its articles of incorporation. The name must be transliterated into letters of the English alphabet, if it is not in English. No corporation may be chartered in West Virginia under any name which includes the word "engineer," "engineers," "engineering" or any combination of the same unless the purpose of the corporation is to practice professional engineering, and one or more of the incorporators is a registered professional engineer. The name must not be the same as, and shall be distinguishable from: (1) the name of any domestic corporation, domestic limited partnership, domestic limited liability partnership, or domestic limited liability company existing under the laws of West Virginia; (2) the name of any foreign corporation, foreign limited partnership, foreign limited liability partnership, foreign limited liability company, or any other foreign business entity authorized to conduct affairs or transact business in West Virginia; (3) a name the exclusive right to which is, at the time, reserved in the manner provided by law; or (4) the name of a corporation, limited partnership, limited liability partnership, or limited liability company which has in effect a registration of its business name as provided by law. The foregoing requirements do not apply if the applicant files with the secretary of state either: (1) a written consent to the use and a written undertaking by the present user, registrant or owner of a reserved name submitted in a form satisfactory to the secretary of state to change the name to a name that is distinguishable from the name applied for; or (2) a certified copy of a final order of a court of competent jurisdiction establishing the prior right of the applicant to the use of such name in West Virginia. Any terms or abbreviations required to be included in the business name to identify the type of business entity shall not alone be sufficient to make one name distinguishable from another. A corporation with which another corporation, domestic or foreign, is merged, or which is formed by the reorganization or consolidation of one or more domestic or foreign corporations or upon a sale, lease or other disposition to or exchange with, a domestic corporation of all or substantially all the assets of another corporation, domestic or foreign, including its name, may have the same name as that used in West Virginia by any of such corporations if such other corporation was organized under the laws of, or is authorized to conduct affairs or do or transact business in West Virginia.

- The period of duration, which may be perpetual;

- The purpose or purposes for which the corporation is organized, which may be stated to be, or to include, the transaction of any or all lawful business for which corporations may be incorporated under law;
- The address of its principal office, and the name and address of the person to whom shall be sent notice or process served upon, or service of which is accepted by, the secretary of state, if such person has been appointed by the corporation;
- The number of directors constituting the initial board of directors and the names and addresses of the persons who are to serve as such directors;
- The name and address of each incorporator;
- The aggregate number of shares which the corporation shall have authority to issue; if such shares are to consist of one class only, the par value of each of such shares, or a statement that all of such shares are without par value; or, if such shares are to be divided into classes, the number of shares of each class, and a statement of the par value of the shares of each such class or that such shares are to be without par value.
- If the shares are to be divided into classes, the designation of each class and a statement of the preferences, limitations and relative rights in respect of the shares of each class.
- If the corporation is to issue the shares of any preferred or special class in series, the designation of each series and a statement of the variations in the relative rights and preferences as between series insofar as the same are to be fixed in the articles of incorporation, and a statement of any authority to be vested in the board of directors to establish series and fix and determine the variations in the relative rights and preferences as between series;
- Any provision limiting or denying to shareholders the preemptive right to acquire additional unissued or treasury shares of the corporation;
- Any provision, not inconsistent with law, which the incorporators elect to set forth in the articles of incorporation for the regulation of the internal affairs of the corporation, including any provision

restricting the transfer of shares and any provision which under this article is required or permitted to be set forth in the bylaws.

The existence of the corporation begins upon the issuance of a certificate of incorporation by the secretary of state. Upon creation, the corporation may have a meeting of its incorporators or initial board members to elect directors, officer, adopt bylaws (which may contain any provision consistent with law and the articles of incorporation), and carry on any other business of the corporation. This meeting may be held inside or outside of West Virginia.

Minimum number of Incorporators: Any individual or entity may incorporate or organize a corporation.

Management Requirements: Directors or original incorporators, depending upon the terms of the article of incorporation, may approve bylaws for the corporation. There must be at least one director on the corporation's board of directors, and the corporation must have a president, secretary, and treasurer.

State Tax Classification: The State charges a graduated corporate license tax, a business franchise tax, a corporate net income tax at the rate of 9%, and sales and use taxes at the rate of 6%.

Contact Information:
Corporations Division
Secretary of State
Bldg. 1, Suite 157-K
1900 Kanawha Blvd. East
Charleston, WV25305-0770
Phone: (304) 558-8000
Facsimile: (304) 558-0900
E-mail: wvsos@secretary.state.wv.us
(include the division name in the subject line)
www.state.wv.us/sos/corp/default.htm

Wisconsin

Formation: Before filing its articles of corporation, a domestic for-profit corporation may reserve a name with the secretary of state's office. The articles of incorporation must include the following:

• The name of the corporation, which must contain the word "corporation," "incorporated," "company," or "limited," or the abbreviation "corp.," "inc.," "co.," or "ltd.," or words or abbreviations of like import in another language. The name may not contain language stating or implying that the corporation is organized for a purpose other than that permitted by law and its articles of incorporation. Except as provided below, the corporate name of a domestic corporation must be distinguishable upon the records of the department from all of the following names: (1) the corporate name of a domestic corporation or a foreign corporation authorized to transact business in Wisconsin; (2) a reserved or registered corporate name; (3) the corporate name of a dissolved corporation or a dissolved non-stock corporation that has retained the exclusive use of its name; (4) the fictitious name adopted by a foreign corporation or a foreign non-stock corporation authorized to transact business in Wisconsin; (5) the corporate name of a non-stock corporation incorporated in Wisconsin; (6) the name of a limited partnership formed under the laws of, or registered in, Wisconsin; (7) the name of a cooperative association incorporated or authorized to transact business in Wisconsin; and (8) the name of a limited liability company organized under the laws of, or registered in, Wisconsin; the name of a limited liability partnership formed under the laws of, or registered in, Wisconsin. The corporate name of a corporation is not distinguishable from a name referred to above if the only difference between it and the other name is the inclusion or absence of the words "limited partnership," "limited liability partnership," "cooperative," or "limited liability company," or an abbreviation of these words. A corporation may apply to the department for authorization to use a name that is not distinguishable upon the records of the department from one or more of the names described above. The department shall authorize use of the name applied for if any of the following occurs: (1) the other corporation or the foreign corporation, limited liability company, nonstock corporation, limited partnership, limited liability partnership or cooperative association consents to the use in writing and submits an undertaking in a form satisfactory to the department to change its name to a name that is distinguishable upon the records of the department from the name of the applicant; or (2) the applicant delivers to the department a certified copy of a final judgment of a court of competent jurisdiction establishing the applicant's right to use the name applied for in Wisconsin. A corporation may use the name, including the fictitious name, that is used in Wisconsin by another domestic corporation or a foreign corporation authorized to transact business in Wisconsin if the corporation proposing to use the name has done any of the following: (1) merged with the other domestic corporation or foreign corporation; (2) been formed by reorganization of the other domestic corporation or foreign corporation; (3) acquired all or substantially all of the assets, including the corporate name, of the other domestic corporation or foreign corporation.

- The number of authorized shares, except that an investment company may declare an indefinite number of authorized shares.
- If more than one class of shares is authorized, all of the following: (1) the distinguishing designation of each class; (2) the number of shares of each class that the corporation is authorized to issue, except that an investment company may declare that each class has an indefinite number of authorized shares. Before the issuance of shares of a class, a description of the preferences, limitations and relative rights of that class;
- If one or more series of shares are created within a class of shares, all of the following before the issuance of shares of a series: (1) the distinguishing designation of each series within a class; (2) the number of shares of each series that the corporation is authorized to issue, except that an investment company may declare that each series has an indefinite number of authorized shares; (3) the preferences, limitations and relative rights of that series.
- Any provision authorizing the board of directors to act;
- Any provision granting or limiting preemptive rights.
- The street address of the corporation's initial registered office and the name of its initial registered agent at that office.
- The name and address of each incorporator.

The existence of the corporation begins upon the filing of the articles of incorporation with the secretary of state. Upon creation, the corporation may have a meeting of its incorporators or initial board members to elect directors, officers, adopt bylaws (which may contain any provision consistent with law and the articles of incorporation), and carryon any other business of the corporation. This meeting may be held inside or outside of Wisconsin.

Minimum Number of Incorporators: Any individual or entity may incorporate or organize a corporation.

Management Requirements: Directors or original incorporators, depending upon the terms of the articles of incorporation, may approve bylaws for the corporation. There must be at least one director on the corporation's board of directors.

State Tax Classification: The State charges $25.00 for annual corporate reports, assesses a corporate franchise and income tax at the rate of 7.9%, and sales and use taxes at the rate of 5%.

Contact Information: Corporations Section, 3rd Floor
P.O. Box 7846
Madison, WI 53707-7846
Phone: (608) 261-7577
Facsimile: (608) 267-6813
E-mail:
info@dfi.state.wLus~wdfi.orglcorporations/
www.wdfi.org/corporations/

Wyoming

Formation: Before filing its articles of incorporation, a domestic for-profit corporation may reserve a name with the secretary of state's office. The articles of incorporation must include the following:

• The name of the corporation. A corporate name may not contain language stating or implying that the corporation is organized for a purpose other than that permitted by law and its articles of incorporation. Except as provided below, a corporate name may not be the same as, or deceptively similar to any trademark or service mark registered in Wyoming and shall be distinguishable upon the

records of the secretary of state from the name of any profit or nonprofit corporation, trade name, limited liability company, statutory trust company, limited partnership or other business entity organized, continued or domesticated under the laws of Wyoming or licensed or registered as a foreign profit or nonprofit corporation, foreign limited partnership, foreign joint stock company, foreign statutory trust company, foreign limited liability company or other foreign business entity in Wyoming or any fictitious or reserved name. A corporation may apply to the secretary of state for authorization to use a name that is not distinguishable from one or more of the names described above. The secretary of state shall authorize use of the name applied for if: (1) the other person whose name is not distinguishable from the name which the applicant desires to register or reserve, irrevocably consents to the use in writing and submits an undertaking in a form satisfactory to the secretary of state to change its name to a name that is distinguishable from the name of the applicant; or (2) the applicant delivers to the secretary of state a certified copy of the final judgment of a court of competent jurisdiction establishing the applicant's right to use the name applied for in Wyoming. A corporation may use the name, including the fictitious name, of another domestic or foreign corporation that is used in Wyoming if the other corporation is incorporated or authorized to transact business in Wyoming and the proposed user corporation: (1) has merged with the other corporation; or (2) has been formed by reorganization of the other corporation; or (3) has acquired all or substantially all of the assets, including the corporate name, of the other corporation.
- The number of shares the corporation is authorized to issue, which may be unlimited if so stated;
- The street address of the corporation's initial registered office and the name of its initial registered agent at that office; and
- The name and address of each incorporator.

The existence of the corporation begins upon the filing of the articles of incorporation with the secretary of state. Upon creation, the corporation may have a meeting of its incorporators or initial board members to elect directors, officers, adopt bylaws (which may contain any provision consistent with law and the articles of incorporation), and carryon any other business of the corporation. This meeting may be held inside or outside of Wyoming.

Minimum Number of Incorporators: Any individual or entity may incorporate or organize a corporation.

Management Requirements: Directors or original incorporators, depending upon the terms of the articles of incorporation, may approve bylaws for the corporation. There must be at least one director on the corporation's board of directors.

State Tax Classification: The State assesses a corporate franchise tax at the rate of $50.00 or 2/10 of one mill on the dollar, whichever is greater, based upon the sum of the corporation's capital, property, and assets reported. Wyoming also assesses sales and use taxes at the rate of 4%.

Contact Information: Secretary of State
Corporations Division
200 West 24th Street
The Capitol Building
Cheyenne 82002-0020
Phone: (307) 777-7311
Facsimile: (307) 777-5339
E-mail: corporations@state.wy.us
www.soswy.state.wy.us/corporat/corporat.htm